The Complete Idiot's Reference Card

Your Action Plan

Charts help when pursuing the goals you've set. Here is a simple matrix to help guide you:

Goal	Subgoals	Identified Resources	Timeline
A	A1	1. 2. 3.	
	A2	1. 2.	
B	B1	1. 2. 3.	

Milestone or Gantt Chart

By plotting what you need to do and when on a chart such as the one below, you have a clear, graphic representation of the timelines and sequencing of what you wish to pursue.

	Month 1	Month 2	Month 3	Month 4	Month 5	Month 6
XYZ project						
Article published						
Pilot program						
Hotline program						
Attend key conference						

Goals

A desired outcome. "Desired" says it's something that you're seeking, something that you want, something you're willing to strive for and lend energy to. "Outcome" means a result, a situation you can describe, an achievement to which you can point, or a feeling that is real and unmistakable.

1. A goal needs to be challenging, but reachable.

2. A goal needs to be quantifiable.

3. A goal needs to be associated with some timeline

tear here

alpha
books

W9-CEA-714

The Seven Basic Goal Areas of Life

The seven goal areas that are common to most people include mental, physical, family, social, career, spiritual, and financial goals.

➤ **Mental Goals:** Stop worrying so much about money and success; improve my memory of names; increase my vocabulary proficiency; broaden my knowledge.

➤ **Physical Goals:** Eat less junk food; do stress reduction exercises every night; floss teeth every night; maintain an ideal weight.

➤ **Family Goals:** Call Mom and Dad once a week; spend ten minutes daily with my spouse and each child.

➤ **Social Goals:** Go to weekly Rotary Club meetings; socialize with more sales-people and exchange ideas.

➤ **Spiritual Goals:** Go to church once every two weeks; be more helpful to people every day.

➤ **Career Goals:** Make three more sales per week; earn a Master's degree in marketing.

➤ **Financial Goals:** Own my own home; purchase a sports car; provide for an ample retirement fund by the time I'm 55-years-old.

Self-Initiated Contract

This may be an effective tool for you:

Self-Initiated Contract, Simple Version

I, Jeff Davidson, agree to accomplish the following goal before the 30th, and hereby do formally contract myself to these purposes. This goal is challenging, but reachable, and I willingly accept the challenge:

_____

_____

_____

Signature: _____   Date: _____

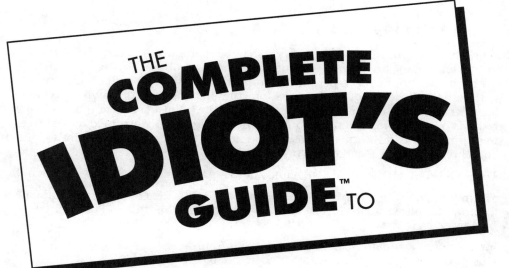

THE COMPLETE IDIOT'S GUIDE™ TO

Reaching Your Goals

by Jeff Davidson

alpha books

A Division of Macmillan Reference USA
A Simon and Schuster Macmillan Company
1633 Broadway, New York, NY 10019-6785

Macmillan Publishing books may be purchased for business or sales promotional use. For information please write: Special Markets Department, Macmillan Publishing USA, 1633 Broadway, New York, NY 10019-6785.

International Standard Book Number: 0-02-862114-X
Library of Congress Catalog Card Number: 97-80961

00   99   98   3   2

Interpretation of the printing code: The rightmost number of the first series of numbers is the year of the book's printing; the rightmost number of the second series of numbers is the number of the book's printing. For example, a printing code of 98-1 shows that the first printing occurred in 1998.

Printed in the United States of America

Contents at a Glance

Contents

Foreword

Welcome to your official guide to setting and reaching your goals!

Given that you've picked up this book, chances are that you're a goal-oriented person—someone who seeks to get more out of life. You are, perhaps, proud of some of your accomplishments, but you're not content to rest on your laurels for long. That's why this book can be so valuable to you.

Jeff Davidson approaches the subject of reaching your goals with the same care and comprehension he applied to his other books in *The Complete Idiot's Guide* series, including *The Complete Idiot's Guide to Managing Your Time*, *The Complete Idiot's Guide to Managing Stress*, and *The Complete Idiot's Guide to Assertiveness*.

If you know Jeff as I do, you know that he tackles his subjects with vigor. As both an author and speaker, Jeff does everything with high energy. Engaging in whatever amount of research it takes to find the answers, Jeff approaches his topic areas with almost encyclopedic command. Then, semi-miraculously, he converts all he has learned into an enjoyable, user-friendly plan that readers can easily understand and apply. In essence, Jeff creates systems for personal accomplishment that work well the first time you put them to use.

So often in my own life and career, I've observed others and wondered why, with so much literature and so many courses available on setting goals, aren't more people actually achieving what they set out to do? It seems that too many people are moving in the opposite direction. At least in America, personal debt in recent years has reached all-time highs. What could be the financial goals of the great masses of individuals who owe more money than ever before in their lives?

The divorce rate is at an all-time high. What could be the social/family goals of so many millions of people? The average weight of adult men and women has steadily increased for more than 30 years. What could be the physical goals of people whose waistlines are expanding?

Do people consciously set out to continually be in debt, have their marriage or primary relationship end in ruin, or become too heavy to fit into any of their clothes? Yet, that is what seems to be occurring for many people today. As such, *The Complete Idiot's Guide to Reaching Your Goals* can be such a valuable guide for you. If you seek to gain or regain control of your life in critical areas, such as advancing in your career, maintaining spiritual balance, or having time for your loved ones and friends, keep reading.

Jeff Davidson charts a course for you that you'll want to follow. He has assembled this book so that you won't get bogged down with unnecessary details or end up attempting to bite off more than you can chew and fail to achieve the success you deserve. Instead, he focuses on one-at-a-time, proven, practical approaches to enable you to attain the rewards of life and career you so richly deserve. Jeff draws on time-honored principles as well as late-breaking developments to tell you what works and what doesn't when setting goals.

In my own business, I speak to groups about the fundamental changes facing us as we enter this age of technoshift. Never before have you faced so many fundamental changes in how you work, play, and live brought about by new communications technology. The onslaught of new information is overwhelming. Losing focus has never been easier.

As Jeff points out in his other books, it would be fair to say that the current generation of career professionals is easily the most distracted in history. In that regard, reaching your goals becomes a challenge of a higher order. Fear not, because you have in your hands the wisdom, the insights, and the plan that will help you get from point A to point B in virtually every area of your life.

Before you begin reading, I suggest that you get a felt-tip pen or highlighter. To derive the most from this book, you'll want to mark passages of importance to you as you encounter them. Chances are if you don't highlight a section of text as you read it, you won't remember to incorporate that point into your overall goal-setting strategy.

Also, choose an area of your life or career in which you are particularly motivated to affect a change for the better. Then, singularly pour your energies into that area as opposed to tackling too much at once. I'd rather see you achieve an early win in a critical area as the first order of business before attempting more.

I'm excited for you and for the journey you're about to undertake. If you're serious about reaching your goals, you're about to embark on a personal new era. May the most for which you strive be the least that you attain!

Dr. William Metcalf, president
Technoshift, Inc.
Oak Park, Illinois

Introduction

When you think about it, everyone in life has goals. Whether your goals are well set, well defined, and within reach, or hazy, nebulous, and oceans away, they exist. Whether you have clearly written down goals that you can point to, or you believe that you have none at all, you still have plenty of goals. Let me explain. For some people (hopefully, not you), a continuing daily goal is to simply make it through the day. Some people come home from work, and the first thing they do is whip off their shoes, go to the fridge, get a six-pack, and sit in front of the TV for the rest of the evening.

Wait a second! That couldn't be anyone's goal. Ah, but it is. It's an unvoiced, unarticulated goal to have as little stress and challenge as possible after having made it through eight hours of work. Couch potatoes anesthetize themselves against what they probably see as the harsh realities of making a better living, having a better relationship, or making a better life.

A friend of mine has a poster on the wall in his office that says, "Not to decide is to decide." This means that although making a choice about something is clearly a form of decision, making no choice at all is also a decision.

Failing to do something is a choice. In essence, not deciding how you want to maintain your life, relationships, career, and finances is a form of goal setting—more specifically, goal setting by default. What would you surmise the couch potato with the six-pack has chosen by not actively setting such goals? How about this: to not maintain physical tone, to not spend more time with loved ones or friends, to not read great books, and to not engage in household improvements.

My Goal of Helping You Reach Your Goals

As a fundamental notion of goal setting and themes repeated throughout this book, I want you to immediately understand that whether or not you actively set goals, you are always pursuing them. It benefits you to actively set goals, because this gives you greater control of your life and career. That, of course, is what you seek; otherwise, you would have never picked up this book. Let the couch potatoes with six-packs do what they do (unless you're married to one and can't stand it any longer!).

Meanwhile, you've got work to do. You want to better your life and have more fulfilling relationships, more enriching experiences, and more peak moments. You're not content to let *The Simpsons* or *Seinfeld* reruns be your primary form of relaxation and relief. You know there's more within your grasp.

For whatever you're seeking, recognize this: You wouldn't even harbor the notion unless there was some capacity for its attainment within you. Given that you maintain worthwhile, positive goals that do not diminish the rights of others, your quest represents a highly worthwhile pursuit for you and, potentially, many others. After all, those who have achieved substantial and outrageous goals often end up benefiting society. Nelson Mandela's personal pursuit for freedom and justice eventually led to a greater level of freedom and justice for the people of an entire nation and many other people throughout the world. The same is true of Lech Walesa in Poland and Vaclav Havel in the Czech Republic.

Michael Jordan's personal pursuit of athletic excellence in basketball simultaneously led to a ton of championships for the Chicago Bulls and provided inspiration and enjoyment for several hundred million people throughout the world. The same can be said for the personal pursuit of excellence of Placido Domingo in operatic singing, Ralph Nader in consumerism, Betty Ford in chemical-dependency recovery, Dr. David Ho in AIDS research, Mother Theresa in helping the poor, and Tom Hanks in motion pictures.

The Quality of Your Life

You're about to explore how to improve the quality of your life by reaching the goals you set for yourself. The wonderful thing about reaching goals, as you'll soon discover if you are not already aware of it, is that as you reach one goal, you mobilize the atmosphere and mechanics for reaching another. One of the most magnificent secrets about effective goal setting and attainment is that the process itself opens the doors wider to further attainment. That's why highly accomplished people rarely limit their achievements to only one aspect of their lives. Sure, occasionally you'll see people who have poured all their eggs into one basket—business entrepreneurs whose pursuit of a certain revenue level supplant their goals regarding family, fitness level, and spirituality. These people, however, often are confronted by a rude awakening: Their one-dimensional success feels hollow. They're often left questioning whether they're successful, lonely, on the verge of a heart attack, or spiritually bankrupt.

This book focuses on reaching your goals with the fundamental notion of maintaining a sense of balance. In essence, you can't ultimately feel good about attaining spectacular goals in a few limited areas if you completely ignore other facets of your life in the process. Most people need to maintain a sense of balance in various aspects of their lives. I suspect that this is the case with you as well.

On your way to reaching the goals you set for yourself, it's vital to understand the importance of pacing and simplicity. Rome was not built in a day, and if it had been, it would have fallen apart just as quickly. Sometimes, reaching your goals too quickly can have disastrous effects. How often do you read about that? In our gung-ho, go-get-it society, too many authors and achievement gurus forget about the importance of balance as they lay out their goal-attaining systems for you.

Yes, there are some goals you'd like to reach by tomorrow or, at least, next week. Would you be prepared for them, though? Most lottery winners, for example, are not prepared for the millions of dollars that suddenly enter their lives. Did you know that most widows or widowers who inherit the fortune of their deceased spouse end up spending most of it within seven years? They are not prepared to handle the sums.

In the pursuit of your goals, you want to proceed as simply as possible. It's all too easy to overcomplicate your life in contemporary society. If your goal is to earn $1 million, of what value is it if you end up complicating your life so much that you don't enjoy yourself? What's the value of achieving any other goal if having it and maintaining it require such complexity that its onerous burdens beset you daily? So, my fine-feathered friend, let's engage in reaching your goals while maintaining balance and relative simplicity. Otherwise, you're likely to engage in a self-defeating loop that has you squirming in your chair replaying the refrain of that haunting Peggy Lee tune, "Is That All There Is?"

One Step at a Time

In addition to balance and simplicity, I want to introduce a third notion on your path to achieving what's important to you. This is the idea that small, incremental changes in pursuing your goals can work as effectively and with greater long-term impact than with other approaches. As I discussed in *The Complete Idiot's Guide to Managing Stress*, if the changes you undergo in pursuit of your goals are too painful, too upsetting, or too radical from what you're already doing, they won't last and they probably won't be effective. Watch out for anything you're doing that represents too great a leap from what you were doing the day before. Whether it's learning a new routine, absorbing technical instructions, or emulating behaviors, anything that represents too much of a stretch might just snap back in your face.

Feel free to take things one step at a time in incremental and bite-size portions. I don't want to steer you away from marvelous leaps if that is part of your nature, though. Some people are simply able to leapfrog ahead, skip several steps, and still do very well. For example, my daughter, Valerie, was able at age four to hit the fastest underhand pitches I could throw. Lest you think this was an easy feat, let me tell you that I pitched in the Babe Ruth League in my town as a youth. Even in my 40s, I can throw an extremely fast underhand pitch.

At age six, without ever having practiced, Valerie suggested that she bat lefty. Not being an overdirecting father, I said, "Sure." She missed the first couple of pitches, and then she miraculously started whacking them back with the same fervor she had while batting righty. Even at age six, Valerie was a natural when it came to hitting a baseball. It might be the same with you. There are times—and you'll feel them without my prompting—when you can skip some steps. That's okay—go ahead and do it. If it feels natural and comfortable, it's probably okay. If you feel stressed or anxious, that's as good a signal as you'll ever get that you probably need to slow down. At all times, let your internal decision-making apparatus be your guide.

How to Use This Book

This book has been laid out so that you easily can proceed through each chapter in chronological order. After Chapter 11, "Now for the Biggie: Your Financial Life," you can tackle chapters out of order with no real harm. That's because each chapter is self-contained and gives you valuable tools and techniques for reaching your goals. It's best to approach the first 11 chapters in order, because there I lay out a seven-point plan for reaching your goals while maintaining balance and relative simplicity.

The seven-point plan focuses on mental, physical, family, social, spiritual, career, and financial goals. Although you might feel like skipping over one or more of these categories, at least browse though each of these chapters so that you'll gain a relatively good understanding of the importance of these seven categories and how they combine to help you achieve a critical balance.

Part 1, "All About Goals," focuses on topics such as the difference between a goal and a wish, New Year's resolutions, opportune times for setting goals, and the basic seven categories of goals: mental, physical, family, social, spiritual, career, and financial.

Part 2, "Assessing Yourself," contains seven chapters—one for each of the seven basic categories highlighted in Chapter 4, "The Seven Basic Goal Categories." In each of these seven basic categories, I ask you to consider your fundamental strengths, your past accomplishments, your current situation, and your desired changes. You'll then focus on your big, broad, expansive goals in life for each of the seven categories. You will find many compelling, enlightening ideas that are well worth considering.

Part 3, "Secrets of Master Goal-Setters," contains five chapters: "Personalizing Your Goals," "It's All in the Wording," "Committing to Paper," "A Question of Time," and "Gotta Have a Challenge." In this part of the book, you will learn the nuances of setting and reaching goals, the methods of effective goal achievers, and ways to keep yourself moving forward.

Part 4, "Bring In the Reinforcements," includes five chapters. Creating simple systems for reinforcing the goals you've set for yourself is as important as setting the goals in the first place. After all, you are not a machine; you are subject to stresses and strains, obstacles and setbacks, and, hey, let's face it, occasional behavior that may be entirely contrary to the goals you've set for yourself.

Part 5, "Going for the Gold: Advanced Strategies for Reaching Your Goals," includes five chapters. Here, you'll examine making your goals realities, proceeding in the most efficient manner, and revising and upgrading your goals. You'll also look at world-class goal setters and how they reached their goals. Finally, you'll see how to enjoy what you've attained while moving on to even higher ground.

Building On What You've Done

Undoubtedly, you've racked up some admirable achievements in your life. Now, added to what you'll learn in this book, think how wonderful life can be as you begin to reach one goal after another. So, just sit back, adjust your seat belt, and prepare to go on a ride that can last you a lifetime!

Extras

I've used some special boxes throughout this book to help you proceed through each chapter. These sidebars are shown here so that you'll be familiar with them as you encounter them in the text.

Go for the Gold!
These are action steps or tips you should practice right away while you're still thinking about them.

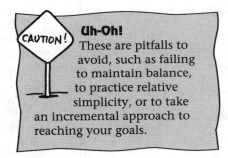

Uh-Oh!
These are pitfalls to avoid, such as failing to maintain balance, to practice relative simplicity, or to take an incremental approach to reaching your goals.

For Sure

These are age-old or new-world realities or substantiated facts on which you can depend.

Word Power
Here, I explain how certain words or terms apply to your goal-setting activities.

Now, it is with great pleasure that I invite you to flip to Chapter 1 and delve right into the fundamental question: What is a goal as opposed to a wish? Of course, you might want to take a minute to read on about the good folks at alpha books and Macmillan General Reference, who richly deserve a lot of credit.

Acknowledgments

If you know any authors personally, you might have heard horror stories about their relationships with their publishers. This is not the case. I have nothing but praise for the professionals at alpha books and Macmillan General Reference. They know how to conceive, design, edit, publish, and promote books like few other people in the business. They also had the wonderful sense to choose me as the author of this book.

There are many people to thank. (Sounds a little like somebody picking up an Oscar, doesn't it?) A big thanks to Gary Krebs and Jennifer Perillo, who were involved from beginning to end in the editing and producing of this book. Thanks also to Nader Mikhail, Phil Kitchel, and Fran Blauw for their careful editing and all-around expertise. A big thanks to Megan Boyle, Erika Meyers and Mittie Jones in Chapel Hill for their precocious editing work and Sandy Knudsen for her word processing excellence and diligence.

Thanks to Jeff Jackson in International Sales for making sure that this book benefits people in nations around the world. Thanks to Julie Sanders in Special Sales for selling this book by the tens of thousands to interested parties with big money.

Thanks to Margaret Durante in Promotions for ensuring that major media outlets could easily find me, and thanks to Gardi Wilkes for scheduling me on radio and TV broadcasts and lining up reporters and journalists eager to interview me.

Finally, a big thanks to Valerie Davidson, age 7, who makes it easy for me to achieve one of my goals: being a good parent. Every day with you, girl, is sweeter than the day before.

This book is dedicated to the people who have inspired me the most in life—those close, those distant, those famous, those relatively unknown, and everyone in between—including Emanuel Davidson, Shirley Davidson, Valerie Davidson, Sandy Koufax, Arthur Ashe, Larry Bird, Michael Jordan, John Stockton, Christopher Reeve, Ron Howard, Dr. Warren Farrell, Dr. Neil Postman, Jeremy Rifkin, Dr. Wayne Dyer, Alvin Toffler, Dr. Thomas Sowell, Dr. Terry Paulson, Dr. Janet Lapp, David Meinz, Freddie Pierce, Scott McKain, Deb Giffen, Karen Stelmach, Mary Lange, Angela Brown, Chris Beiers, Deenie Kenner, and so many others.

Part 1
All About Goals

So, you have a goal or two you'd like to achieve. What will it actually take to make this goal a reality in your life? Heck, you can be setting goals from now until your dying day, but that doesn't mean you're going to reach any of them.

You're a serious type of person, though, and you don't intend to engage in idle fantasy. This time around, you aim to reach your goals.

You know what? You actually can! You have what it takes to make your goals a reality. Otherwise, you would have never had such a notion to begin with. Although people all around you are setting goals in an almost frivolous manner (making a half-baked New Year's resolution that is all but forgotten within three days), you're different. You've got some specific things you want to achieve, a quality of life you want to attain, and even certain ways you want to feel. You're not going to settle for symbolic success—you want the real McCoy. If this describes your situation to a tee, flip the page.

What Is a Goal as Opposed to a Wish?

When you wish upon a star, you're wasting your time. Stars are simply great masses of inflamed gases light years away from Earth. They are visible to the naked eye because of their sheer magnitude and luminescence. They, however, have no effect on your life, the goals you're seeking to reach, or anything else about you. If you think I'm belaboring the point, it's only because so many people engage in wishing instead of effective goal setting. It's enough to make anybody want to head for the stars and stay there.

This chapter lays the groundwork on setting and reaching your goals. After completing it, you'll be able to differentiate between goals and other things that seem like goals.

A Wish versus a Goal

"I wish I could get a big raise."

"I wish I could save some money."

"I wish I could travel around the world."

If you've had any such wishes recently or over the years, is it likely you've made any progress toward them? If you hear others make such wishes, do you suspect for a second they're actually going to attain them? Hardly.

A wish is a daydream—a fleeting fantasy about how things might be. It might be one time or recurring. It might be within or totally beyond the realms of possibility. The common denominator of all wishes is that they are not attached to a plan of action.

Wishes Have Their Place

I'm not knocking wishes, per se; they do have their place. Wishes, fantasies, and day-dreams all serve a purpose, including these:

➤ They temporarily relieve you from a trying situation.

➤ They build up your anticipation for something that might occur in the future.

➤ They help you see new possibilities.

➤ They lay the groundwork for what might become a goal.

This last purpose is particularly worth examining. A wish can be the forerunner to a goal. In other words, by wishing something were so, you might take the steps to make it so. The gap for many people between wishing and taking action, however, is large. Too many people, I fear, are content to wish their lives away.

"I wish I could lose 10 pounds."

"I wish I could get the boss to notice me."

"I wish I had the time to take my kids to the circus."

Wishes Can Lose Power

One of the dangers of continually wishing without taking action toward those wishes is that your wish actually begins to lose power. Have you ever wanted something so badly or for so long, done little to achieve it, and then one day realized that you didn't really want it after all? Sure—we all have.

What happens when you continually want something but make no effort whatsoever to achieve it? In a sense, you're confusing your inner being. On the one hand, part of you is longing for what you don't have. On the other hand, another large part of you intrinsi-cally recognizes that you're

➤ Making no plans

➤ Expending no energy

➤ Taking no action

That part of you concludes that you don't really want this after all. Therefore, you are in a state of perpetual frustration. You apparently want something and, concurrently, are behaviorally locked from taking action.

What Is a Goal?

"Okay," you ask, "what specifically is a goal?" So much has been written about goals over the years that I hardly know where to begin. Because this is a *Complete Idiot's Guide*, and you want hard-core information boiled down to its essence, I'm going to give you the most practical and simple definition of a goal.

Here it is in three words: *a desired outcome*. That says it all:

➤ "Desired" says it's something you're seeking, something you want, and something you're willing to strive for and lend energy to.

➤ "Outcome" means a result. It's a situation you can describe, an achievement to which you can point, and a feeling that is real and unmistakable.

> **Uh-Oh!** **CAUTION!**
> In your own life, if you wish upon a star, or say one thing but do something entirely different, is it likely you're going to achieve any of your goals? Not!

The Sword in the Stone

Certainly, after achieving a desirable outcome, you're not fixed in stone; you can set new goals beyond those you've achieved. It's also very important that you enjoy yourself in the pursuit of your goal.

You've heard the old expression, "Life is a journey, not a destination." So too, pursuit of your goals is as much a journey as a destination. As a classic illustration, what value would your goal have if it was to earn a million dollars, but you chewed up 30 years of your life earning that million, were miserable all that time, and now have nothing to show for it but the money—all other aspects of your life suffered?

On the other hand, people such as

➤ Teachers who want to empower their students,

➤ Spouses who want to have strong and happy marriages, and

➤ Ecologists who want to enjoy interacting with nature every day, all have lifetime goals that can be achieved a little each day and are enjoying the trip as much as they will the destination.

Assumptions About You!

As groundwork for the entire book, I'm going to make some assumptions about the goals you seek to pursue before getting into more specific information about goal setting:

➤ Your goals are of a positive nature. They are designed to propel you forward in your life and career.

➤ Your goals do not interfere with the rights of others. They don't jeopardize anyone's safety or well-being.

➤ Your goals, however outrageous or lofty, are based on reality—for example, your goals are not to return to the year 1820, become immortal, or distort the fundamental atomic structure.

➤ You intend to support your goals through energy and effort.

If your goals don't fit what I've described here, stop reading!

Goal Setting for the New Year

Legions of people commit the all too common mistake of setting goals for the new year. Such New Year's resolutions (the topic of Chapter 2) hardly ever result in the outcome the person making the resolution wanted. Why?

Go for the Gold! The mere fact that you made a resolution often means that there is a larger issue behind it that is valid and worth tackling.

In her book *The Art of the Fresh Start*, Glenna Salsbury says that "Resolutions usually are designed to fix or improve a surface problem or concern or habit in life without looking at the root cause of our dissatisfaction." She believes that if people have too much stress or too many preoccupations, they will not be likely to muster the energy needed to sustain a commitment to that resolution.

If you told me that this year, you're going to take more vacations or lose 10 pounds, I'd be willing to believe that you're probably working long and hard, so the idea of vacations came to you. Perhaps you're a little overweight and the idea of losing weight is appealing.

So, as the new year rolls around, go ahead and make resolutions if it makes you feel better, but recognize that unless you put effort behind them, they'll be useless gestures. You'll examine New Year's resolutions, their origins, the reasons people make them, and ways to put some punch behind them in Chapter 2.

Developing Effective Goal-Setting Techniques

Goal setting is a complex process that takes into account a person's psychological and physiological makeup. Because you bought this book with the express purpose of getting to the root of what it takes to set and reach your goals, though, I'm going to clear away all the excess and boil down goal setting to the absolute fundamentals.

You only need to be aware of three elements. So, drum roll please...

➤ Your goal needs to be challenging but reachable.

➤ Your goal has to be quantifiable.

➤ Your goal needs to be associated with some timeline.

In this section, you'll look at each of these elements in detail.

Challenging but Reachable

Suppose that you're 25 years old, have just graduated with a Ph.D. in political science from an Ivy League school, and are considered brilliant by everyone who knows you. Your goal is to become a U.S. senator within the next three years. You have the academic credentials, family background, connections, good appearance, strong voice, and well-developed views that foster a large constituency in contemporary society.

The only problem is that your goal is unreachable. Why? You forgot one thing about running for the U.S. Senate. You have to be at least 30 years old.

Not totally out of the question, you say? You could lobby members of Congress to bring about change. Perhaps 28 should be the minimum. After all, in many respects, people are more knowledgeable today than their counterparts of generations ago.

Even if you could start working to have this reform enacted, is it likely that it would happen in time for you to run for office and be elected by age 28? If so, it's a long shot.

Suppose that you're a woman in NASA and aspire to be the first woman to walk on the moon. NASA has no plans for having any "manned" probes of the moon scheduled for the next three decades.

So, what's an ambitious female astronaut to do? Get into the policy and planning division of NASA, redirect it toward the moon, and then find a way to be in the next ship headed there?

Boldly Going Where No One Has Gone Before

In these scenarios, the goals set by the individuals are challenging but unreachable.

As a general principle, if your goal involves achieving something that no one in history has achieved, such as redirecting large institutions or a government agency or vastly exceeding your organization's historical norms, it's reasonably safe to conclude that the goal you've chosen is unreachable. Notice that I didn't say unworthy or unmerited.

Work for Change

In the first scenario, the brilliant political science student certainly could work toward enacting change, enabling people who are 28 or perhaps 25 to run for the Senate. I think it's a wonderful idea. There are brilliant minds among us who are less than 30 years old who could do a bang-up job. When you consider the performance of some current Senators, the argument is all the more sound.

Nevertheless, a challenging but reachable goal, in this case, would be to become a senator by age 30, which, on rare occasions, *has been* achieved by a few people.

For Sure

John F. Kennedy became a senator by age 35 as his father paved and paid the way with millions of dollars, as well as business and political influence that many people can't even begin to imagine. Mr. Kennedy then became U.S. president at the tender age of 43—again with the massive aid of his father's money and influence.

Head for a Different Target

The female astronaut certainly could start pushing papers, making speeches, lobbying members of Congress, and working within NASA to redirect the agency's value in resuming moon walks.

Are other options available? Always! Perhaps our astronaut could strive to be the first person to walk on Mars, a pioneer for some element of the U.S. space station, or a person who sets a new type of record for endurance or performance in space.

Don't Get Me Wrong

I want you to understand that when you're bucking up against something as large and relatively intractable as the U.S. Constitution, the prevailing political climate, a government agency, or any other institution or organization with decades of history, it's important to understand the scope of the effort necessary to break the tide.

To tackle highly challenging goals that you deem reachable, I suggest that you do the following:

➤ Understand the turf. Look at the historical record, talk to insiders, and read about where things are headed.

➤ Prepare to commit yourself on a level you might not have considered.

➤ Check your time horizon. Is the goal challenging but reachable within the time limit you've given yourself? (More on this shortly.)

➤ Identify crucial resources. Who else or what else do you need to make this goal a reality? (More on this in later chapters.)

Pursuing Quantifiable Goals

The second major element for effective goal setting is to choose goals that are quantifiable. So often, you hear somebody say, "I want to be the top salesperson in the company." What does that mean?

Let me tell you a little story. While driving a rental car in Kansas to a convention where I was speaking, I heard an advertisement on the radio. The president of some car dealership was saying that he was striving to be "the largest car dealer in the state." Seems like a lofty goal, but what could that mean?

Word Power
If something is *quantifiable*, that means you can measure or count it.

The Largest What?

When I got to the hotel, for the fun of it, I took a piece of paper and started writing all of the possibilities. Here is a *partial* list of the many meanings I derived from the unquantified goal of being the largest car dealer in the state:

➤ To have the greatest amount of cars available for sale

➤ To have the largest annual sales volume

➤ To have the largest lot or largest showroom

➤ To have the highest profits

➤ To have the most dealership branches

➤ To have the most sales representatives

➤ To have the greatest number of car models available for show

➤ To have the greatest number of buyers

➤ To be the heaviest owner (weigh the most!) among car dealerships in the state

Unleashed Ambiguity

I could go on with at least 20 other possible meanings for being the largest car dealer in the state. As you can surmise, because this goal was stated in a non-specific way (to be the largest), it lacks the specificity to provide those who have such a goal with marshaling effort, energy, and attention.

The specific goal of having the highest sales revenue among car dealerships in the state would require a different approach than the specific goal of having the greatest amount of vehicles available for display. Similarly, other potential meanings would require different steps for their realizations.

Uh-Oh!
If your goal is to be the best at something in your organization, on your athletic team, or in your personal life in general, watch out! Being the best doesn't have a quantity attached to it, so it's hard to know when you've reached your goal.

A Specific Timeline

The third essential element of effective goal setting is to have a specific timeline. This involves simply attaching some date or time unit to the end of your goal statement. If your goal is to achieve a 10 percent pay increase, for example, you can add a specific timeline to your goal such as the following:

➤ My goal is to achieve a 10 percent pay increase by December 31st of this year.

➤ My goal is to achieve a 10 percent increase in pay within 12 months from now.

➤ My goal is to achieve a 10 percent pay increase by the end of the next quarter.

➤ My goal is to achieve a 10 percent increase in pay within six months after completing my degree.

All these statements represent valid timelines associated with a specific quantifiable goal—achieving a 10 percent pay increase. You'll examine timelines in detail in Chapter 15, "A Question of Time."

Why Goal Setting Is Misunderstood

So much has been written and said about goals, it's easy to understand why goal setting often is misunderstood. This section looks at some common myths about goal setting and the realities.

Goals Set for You by Others Won't Work

There's a common misperception that a goal you undertake has to be your own, devised by you, set by you, and pursued by you. This is not true. Studies have shown that it's entirely possible for one person to set goals for another and to have the entire process work. In fact, this happens every day in sales organizations where sales managers develop quotas for the sales staff.

The key element here is to have the person for whom the goal is set adopt the goals as his or her own. The fact that goals set by others can be met is welcome news for parents, managers, or anyone who has the inherent or mandated responsibility for the performance of others.

Never Tamper with a Set Goal

This is true much of the time, but there are enough exceptions to merit discussion. Often, when you set an appropriate goal, factors outside your control change. Some of these changes could include

➤ A new regulation levied by government.

➤ Something a competitor has done.

➤ A change in the social environment.

➤ A significant reduction or increase in resources allocated to you.

Any one of a number of factors can change in your environment, so there are times when it makes sense to revise your goals midstream. Now, I'm not saying that this is an open-ended excuse to modify goals on a whim or when the going gets tough. Instead, it's a simple recognition that even the most intelligently and appropriately set goals sometimes cannot withstand the fluctuations of a changing environment.

A Goal Is an End in Itself

Although a goal *can* be an end in itself, it rarely is. If your goal is to achieve an increase in earnings, a reduction in weight, or a better-quality relationship, ask yourself what's behind that.

In the case of increased earnings, it might be to better afford the education of your children, enjoy greater leisure, or donate more to worthy causes. In the case of reducing weight, the ends might involve having a healthier lifestyle, reducing your risk of heart attack, and increasing your longevity so that you'll be around to enjoy your grandchildren. Even having a better relationship might not be an end in itself. Other goals beyond that might be to create such abundance as a couple that the overflow enriches others, to be better role models for your children, or to spur each other to even greater growth and personal development.

Go for the Gold!
Set challenging and reachable goals that are quantifiable and have a specific timeline. Pursue them with vigor. All the while, recognize that they might end up as stepping stones to other goals that emerge as you realize one desirable outcome after another.

It's also vital to recognize that many people are not content with the goals they set and achieve for themselves. That's why people who initially had the goal of graduating from college sometimes find themselves seeking master's degrees and then doctorates.

I know many multimillionaires, and not one of them is content with his or her current net worth. Even in my own career, after establishing myself as a speaker and author on business and career-related topics, I had a hankering for delving more deeply into self-help and personal-development topics. That's why I wrote books on managing time, reducing stress, being more assertive, and setting goals. Not surprisingly, as a professional speaker, my topics also shifted to those areas.

You Have to Go Public with Your Goal

Many goal-setting gurus advocate making your goal public. This could involve sharing your goal with others who act as reinforcers to help you achieve what you set out to do by publishing your goal in a department newsletter or broadcasting it at a meeting.

Uh-Oh!
Announcing your goals can have disastrous effects in some situations. Why? You might be locked into having to achieve your goal at a visible and measurable pace so that *others* feel comfortable about your progress.

I think such measures can be useful and effective, depending on who you are, what your goal is, and how you can best pursue it. It's not essential, however, for all your goals to always be publicized.

Even Progress Is Best

Sometimes the pace isn't even in the pursuit of your goal, even though you take a balanced, incremental approach. Weight loss particularly does not follow such a pattern.

Research has shown that in the first few weeks, your weight is not likely to change at all. Your body is adjusting to new levels of exercise and caloric intake, as well as a new rate of metabolism. Often, the greatest change comes after you might have expected it. This explains why so many people give up on diets too soon. Just when they are about to see progress toward their goal, they conclude that it's not working.

Chip Away at Your Goal a Little at a Time

I mentioned in the book's introduction that incremental progress toward pursuing goals will work as well as anything. That's true, but it's also true that sometimes your perceived progress is anything but incremental. This uneven progression is called *germination*.

Word Power
Germination, which in biology means sprouting, can mean development, growth, or maturation; none of these concepts suggests an even progression.

When learning to play the piano, for example, you might have the darndest time practicing a particular song. Suppose that you try something a bit more complicated. After spending days attempting to learn the more complicated piece, you return to the easier piece.

Guess what? All of a sudden, you can play it with a flourish. Why? You experienced germination while learning to play the piano. As you jumped to the more difficult piece, you were laying the foundation for being able to effectively play the easier piece *even though you weren't practicing it*. This seemingly uneven type of progression happens all the time.

For Sure
In his book *Maximum Success*, Brian Tracy says that your pursuit of success is rarely an even progression. It's more like two steps forward and one step back.

12

Goal Setting versus Useless Gestures

Okay, you've learned that it's best to approach your goals while maintaining balance and proceeding with relative simplicity. You know that an incremental approach to reaching your goals will work as well as anything, although attainment of your goals rarely follows a smooth progression. You also know that you want to set challenging, reachable goals that are quantifiable and have specific timelines.

What's the difference, then, between goal setting and useless gestures?

Merely Discussing or Contemplating Your Goal

If you only talk about your goal, it's a nearly useless gesture. It is possible to mentally maintain a goal without writing it down, but the probabilities are on the side of writing it down.

It's kind of analogous to listening to a brilliant lecture and taking brilliant notes. The notes are your own, in your own hand, and have particular relevance for you. Suppose that the lecturer distributed notes for you, though, and you didn't need to take notes at all. You'd probably be less inclined to apply or act on things contained in the prepared handout than on the page of notes you personally recorded.

Go for the Gold!
By recording your goals on paper or on your computer, you have an increased probability of attaining them, if for no other reason than that you have the opportunity to review what you've written or typed. What's more, the act of logging your goals is a reinforcing process.

I suppose that the best of all worlds is when you get a prepared handout and make notes on top of that. In any case, the fact that you recorded with your own hands information, insights, or suggestions for action increases the probability that you actually will do something with what you've written.

Goals you've set when you're light-headed, tipsy, or outright inebriated aren't worth the barroom napkin they're scribbled on—unless, of course, you later examine it, determine its relevance, and make the effort to pursue those goals.

Setting goals as a boast or challenge also is often a useless gesture. Although competition can induce participants to turn in stronger performances, boasting often produces the wrong kind of energy, particularly if you're talking about goal attainment that requires long-term efforts.

For Sure

If one shot-putter in the Olympics lets fly an Olympic record heave, statistics show that the other participants in the contest often exceed their average as well because they are stirred by the competition. Sprinters in the 100-meter dash come within hundredths of a second of each other and often exceed their personal bests because of intense competition.

Boasting, particularly in the face of your competition, can backfire. If you tell an opposing team "We're going to whip your butts," they're likely to play harder to show you how wrong you are. You might notice that when athletes refer to other teams they're about the face, they often say something respectful. This is an intelligent and psychological ploy to avoid giving the other team something they can be riled by or use for inspiration.

For Sure

The most notable exception to the strategy of not riling the opposition in the annals of sports is Mohammed Ali.

Ali would boast to reporters, onlookers, and his boxing opponent that he would win by a knockout in a certain round. He used rhyming phrases like, "You'll barely be alive at the end of five," or "The world will end before you last 10" as a way to psychologically intimidate his opponent. In Ali's case, using boasts to announce his goal worked. In your case, I'm suggesting that you play it a little safer and not boast.

Not Revisiting Your Goal

Perhaps the all-time useless gesture is to make a goal—even writing it down or saving it to a disk—and then not revisit it often enough for it to be effective. This is somewhat similar to what most people do when making a New Year's resolution. You identify a desirable outcome, but then you remind yourself of your quest to achieve this outcome so infrequently that it loses potency.

The Least You Need to Know

- ➤ When you wish upon a star, you're wasting your time.
- ➤ In the simplest terms, a *goal* is a desirable outcome.
- ➤ In the best of all worlds, you achieve your goals with balance and relative simplicity, a little bit at a time.
- ➤ Effective goal setting involves selecting challenging, reachable, and quantifiable goals that are associated with a timeline.
- ➤ It's entirely possible to achieve the goals set for you by others if you internalize the goals and make them your own.

Chapter 2

New Year's Resolutions

The end of one year, the start of the next—what will be different about it? It seems that since the beginning of recorded history, people have had a strong need to make prognostications about the future, and one of the most opportune times to make them is at the start of a new year.

Let's Raise a Glass

It's not clear when New Year's resolutions became a social custom. One theory holds that holiday toasts in December fostered a climate in which people raised their glasses and made mirthful proclamations about how they would approach the coming year.

For Sure

In *Toasts*, author Paul Dixon tells us that toasts have been a part of social gatherings since people first raised a glass. Because those glasses often were filled with alcohol, it's not surprising that the toasts fostered a spirit of brotherhood or fellowship and prompted people to say positive things about one another, as well as their prospects for the future.

Here's to the Harvest

Of the four great ages of humankind, including the age of hunting and gathering, the age of agriculture, the age of industry, and the emerging age of information, the age of agriculture particularly lent itself to optimistic forecasts.

Farmers hoped for rain, no frost, or a long growing season. They hoped and prayed to God that next year's harvest would be bountiful. They hoped to be better at their craft. They hoped to be better human beings. They resolved to be more effective at what they did, be more charitable, be more forgiving, or be more of whatever it was they felt they were lacking.

To this day, resolutions made around the start of the year haven't varied much. Hardly anyone resolves to gain weight, spend more money, have less fun, be meaner, or live in less healthy ways. Part of being human is the eternal quest to improve oneself. If not in major ways, then in little ways. If not all the time, at least now and then. If not absolutely, then tentatively.

You Say You Want a Resolution

Have you ever noticed that people make resolutions in the company of others? Few people make resolutions on their own with no one around. From that standpoint, resolutions are more of a social convention than an act of goal setting.

Suppose that somebody comes up to you and asks what your New Year's resolutions are. If you don't have any, do you want to stand there flatfooted? No sir. You let loose a few well-chosen platitudes to satisfy the ears of your inquirer.

Perhaps you're one of the few who actually does establish resolutions before being asked. How long can you go before you let somebody else know about them? A day? Two days? Sooner or later, you have to give in to the reality that most people devise resolutions so that they can tell others about them.

For Sure

At the start of 1842, Lord Tennyson "dipt into the future" and "saw the heavens fill with commerce." Tennyson was making a forecast as opposed to a personal resolution, but the gesture had the same characteristics as a personal resolution.

Speak into the Mic, Please

In the United States, the practice of making New Year's resolutions is kept alive by the media. On any local TV station, starting around December 28th or 29th, building up by the 30th and the 31st, and blatantly in force on January 1st, some roving reporter trots around with a microphone and besieges innocent people on the street with this question:

"Pardon me, do you have any New Year's resolutions, and would you share them with us?"

During this time, your local newspaper undoubtedly will have an article about New Year's resolutions. Major weekly news magazines always have an article ready on this topic. Even monthly magazines that have to prepare articles three to four months in advance are likely to have some feature on resolutions. Hence, the gesture has become institutionalized.

Woe be the person on the street who is asked by a reporter if he has any resolutions. If he happens to answer "No" or "I never make them" or "I think they're silly," he might make the newscast as the last person featured, but he certainly will not be favored by the reporter. Why? The reporter is filling air time, and the quaint though useless gesture of making New Year's resolutions is just what the station producer choreographed for that day's show.

Why People Make Resolutions

People make resolutions to shore up a shortcoming in their life, personality, or day-to-day activities. Resolutions are not nearly as powerful as goals, because goals ideally represent movement toward some positive, desirable outcome.

For Sure

In *The Psychology of Winning*, Denis Waitely says that you gain much more power and accelerate your progress when striving for something positive instead of avoiding what you don't want.

Concentrating on your current weight and how you barely fit into your clothes does not generate as much power as dwelling on the desired outcome of actually losing the weight. Think about how you'll look and feel when you finally shed those 10 pounds. (See Chapter 13, "It's All in the Wording.") So, you don't want to tape a picture of yourself at your heaviest to the fridge. Post a picture of yourself at your lightest as an adult.

Whether people proceed with positive direction toward a desired outcome or use the less effective approach of attempting to avoid what they don't want, it's clear that people make resolutions because they want to improve their lives, careers, or businesses.

Executives Caught in the Act

Because of the media's propensity for asking people to say a few words to a reporter who is doing a story on resolutions, even top executives in multinational corporations who otherwise use highly effective goal-setting techniques are likely to make New Year's resolutions.

Many top business magazines routinely poll corporate presidents and CEOs as part of their January issues. *Forbes* magazine, for example, annually polls several top executives who report that they have, indeed, made resolutions for coming years. (I suspect that they simply relented to the reporters' urgings to state their goals in the form of New Year's resolutions.)

Here's a sampling of what some of the most successful people in America have to offer on the topic of business- and personal-related resolutions:

➤ Chairman and Chief Executive of Liz Clairborne, Inc.:

"To assure consistent and sparkling products is my resolution."

"My personal resolution is that I'm going to take a cooking course in Italy with a couple of friends…"

➤ Chairman and Chief Executive of the Dial Corporation:

"Last year was filled with change and uncertainty. I would like to promise our employees that this year will be a comparatively dull year. Now we simply get to do our jobs."

"My personal resolution is to catch more fish…"

➤ Chief Executive of Frontier Corporation:

"My resolution is to develop at least three new services that will benefit our customers in ways that they have never imagined. What these services are… I don't know yet…"

"Personally, I want to find more hours each month to give to charities. I also want to do something different every month, to find time to learn a new language, to lose 30 pounds, and to be more direct and assertive."

➤ Chief Executive of Clear Channel Communications:

"My resolution is to make sure that my two sons take on more and more responsibility. Because they are young and bright, my sons give us an advantage for succession and continuation."

"Then, I can spend more time driving around my longhorn ranch in my Jeep."

Pollsters Get into the Act

As you might have guessed, some of the top polling organizations also keep the process of making New Year's resolutions alive by asking corporate leaders what they've chosen for the coming year. The Gallup Poll surveyed more than 400 chief executives of organizations and found that pressing issues for the coming year included organizational profitability, long-term strategic planning, customer loyalty, employee morale and attitudes, and information in computer technology, among several other issues cited.

Gallup found that although these issues were deemed pressing by respondents, it was unclear what the actual level of commitment was to resolving them. Gallup estimates that not even half the people who make New Year's resolutions manage to keep them. I say such an estimate is somewhat generous. If you consider how many people probably achieve the promises they set out to achieve, it probably would be far less than half. Resolutions are far less potent and probably aren't achieved even 10 percent of the time.

Who Says You Can't Have Fun?

As with the wishes, dreams, and fantasies discussed in Chapter 1, resolutions are not totally useless gestures. Indeed, if wishes, dreams, fantasies, resolutions, and proclamations serve as forerunners for you in your quest to identify, establish, and reach your goals, wonderful. Also, if you make resolutions just for fun, go ahead and keep doing it. Who says you're not supposed to have fun in this life?

Here's how Americans rank their dreams based on a survey in *Prevention* magazine:

Dream Element	Percent Ranking Very Important
Having a happy home life	97.8
Giving children a good education	95.7
Competent, affordable healthcare	91.6
Having a job you like	90.4
Having enough savings	88.7
Owning a home	82.3
Sending children to a good college	78.7
Living well in retirement	72.4

continues

Dream Element	Percent Ranking Very Important
Being free of debt	71.3
Having enough free time	69.7
Having a job that pays well	69.3
Having children	68.0
Getting ahead on your job	64.4
Being able to work as many years as you want	64.0
Having your home appreciate in value	62.3
Being married	62.3
Living in a nice community	60.3
Being able to travel when you want to	43.3
Having money for occasional luxuries	43.3
Being able to leave an inheritance for the children	30.0
Retiring early	26.7
Owning your own business	23.0
Owning a late-model car	10.7
Owning a vacation home	7.0

Out of the Mouths of Everyday People

Curiosity killed the cat, but satisfaction brought him back. Intrigued by the magazine interviews and articles I had encountered, I was curious to know what kind of New Year's resolutions everyday people make. I never make them myself! Here are several groups in case you're curious, too.

The local channels in my corner of the world—Raleigh, Durham, Chapel Hill (commonly known as *The Triangle* or *The Research Triangle*)—probably operate similarly to your local stations. Here are some of the resolutions people made on local broadcasts:

➤ To spend more time with my children

➤ To be a better Wolfpack fan, whether or not the team is successful (*Wolfpack* refers to North Carolina State University)

➤ To stick to my jogging schedule

➤ To watch less television

➤ To live up to the resolutions I made last year

➤ To be more charitable to others

➤ To stay more focused more often

Although I don't make New Year's resolutions, there are compelling reasons why identifying what you want to achieve at the start of the year or at other notable intervals makes sense. As I'll discuss at length in the next chapter, there are opportune times in the course of a year, decade, or your entire life when it's appropriate to carve a path for attaining desired outcomes.

Resolutions Off the Web

I visited the archives of some newsgroups and some chat rooms on the Internet and saw these resolutions:

"To upgrade my whole system"

"To spend less time online"

"To get an unlisted phone number"

"To get off of mailing lists"

"To not flame anybody"

"To read some great novels this year"

"To complete all of my needed dental work"

"To see all the episodes of the *X Files* I've missed"

Jeff Takes a Poll

To round out my search, I asked people I already know whether they made resolutions. Here is what they told me:

➤ College student (age 21): "To graduate on time"

➤ My daughter (age 7): "To be a ballerina and a teacher, and to go to Ben and Jerry's every week, and to go to Amaze'n Castles"

➤ Computer software instructor (age 51): "Just to enjoy life"

➤ Bookkeeper and accountant (age 39): "To leave the office at a reasonable hour"

➤ Entrepreneur (age 51): "To be on the road less and be with my family more"

➤ Insurance agent (age 54): "To find my soulmate"

➤ Psychotherapist (age 37): "To expand my business horizon and get into something that's more extroverted"

➤ Stockbroker (age 36): "I really haven't given it much thought."

➤ Management trainer (age 60): "I don't have any—I think they're a complete waste of time."

➤ Author (yours truly, age 47): "I never make them."

Putting Teeth into Your Resolutions

If you never get any farther in this book than this chapter, and you're content to simply make New Year's resolutions, at least use some of the guiding principles you've already learned so that your resolutions will have a decent chance of helping you bring about change in your life.

How can you specifically make challenging yet reachable and quantifiable resolutions with a specific timeline? Suppose that you resolve to be more charitable toward others. How can you use the fundamental elements of effective goal setting so that you actually begin to see the results of your resolution?

1. *Your goal needs to be challenging but reachable.* To be charitable toward others, especially if you're not currently, is challenging in itself. To be more charitable assumes that you already exhibit some level of charitableness. It's therefore likely that this resolution is reachable.

2. *Your goal has to be quantifiable.* How might you quantify this resolution? Let us count the ways!

   ➤ You could target an amount of money you would give to charitable organizations or homeless people within a given year, quarter, or month. Measure your charity by the amount of donations you make.

   ➤ You could chart the number of times you said something nice to other people or went out of your way to help them. Perhaps your goal is to do this once a day. The act of logging how many times you're charitable to others is as good a measure as any if you intend to live up to your resolution.

   ➤ You could log the number of hours you spend serving in charitable organizations. Perhaps you can set a quota of one hour per week working in charitable organizations, making five phone calls per weekday evening on behalf of some worthwhile group, or devoting one weekend a month to some group's planned activity.

3. *Your goal needs to have a timeline.* Even a resolution as nebulous as being more charitable to others can have a timeline attached to it, such as six times per week for the next 12 months.

Booked Up

If you want to gauge whether or not making New Year's resolutions proves to be an effective gesture for you, try this: The next time a new year rolls around, make some resolutions, write them down on a piece of paper, and file them. Don't look at the paper for several months or, better yet, a whole year.

When the end of the year rolls around, take out your file, look at your piece of paper with your resolutions, and see for yourself. You've probably made little progress on any of them. If you have made progress, you're among the rare few. Even if the items you listed represent burning issues for you, it's still unlikely that you made any significant progress. Why? Today, in this society, we are bombarded on all sides by more things competing for our time and attention than we can keep up with.

> **Go for the Gold!**
> Take action in a couple of key areas that are important to you instead of being passive by theorizing about problems. You will not only help others, but you'll also help yourself. Taking action is invigorating!

It Could Happen to You

Anyone can be easily and quickly diverted these days; it's possible to come into work and by 10 o'clock in the morning have no active connection with what you've identified as being important in your life.

Even if you are among the lucky few who make some significant progress toward some of your resolutions, you probably could have achieved those and many more if you had turned them into formal goals. Without using specific goal-setting procedures, any success you achieve satisfies your resolution conditions. Look at these scenarios, for example:

> ➤ You say you'd like to lose more weight. If you lose half a pound, that satisfies the condition. Would this amount of weight loss be significant over a year?

> ➤ You resolve to spend more time with your children. On 44 out of 52 weekends last year, you had no time for your children. This year, miraculously, you were tied up or away on only 43 weekends. You're back for one weekend more than the year before. That satisfies the condition, but are your children happy about it?

Qualifying But Unsatisfying

OK, so you want to be more charitable toward others. Last year, you were one mean son-of-a-gun, fly-off-the-handle, cussing, rogue of a person. This year, you've managed to smile at people a couple of times every couple of months. You also buy $5 worth of Girl Scout cookies.

Does that qualify as being more charitable than you were the year before? In the strict sense, it does. Yet, would anyone suppose for a moment that you're a charitable person?

If You Insist

Okay, you're among those who annually make New Year's resolutions, or you'd like to try it based on what you've read. Here are some guidelines for making your next set of New Year's resolutions more rewarding than those you've made so far:

Go for the Gold!
I know a woman who chooses a theme for each year. One year, she'll focus on getting better at using computers. Another year, she'll focus on learning more about nutrition. She has even directed her efforts toward watching many of the movie classics on video. In this regard, she's using the year itself as her timeline. Such a technique might work well for you, too!

➤ Only make a handful of resolutions. Something between four and seven seems manageable and reachable. If you have too many resolutions, just as if you have too many goals, you might end up draining your energy and slowing your progress.

➤ When you can identify the few key things you'd like to accomplish or experience, your progress in that direction generally will be more significant.

➤ Keep in mind that if you approach each resolution with a balanced perspective, maintain relative simplicity as often as possible, and recognize that progress made one step at a time can result in spectacular achievement, you'll probably do just fine.

The Least You Need to Know

➤ New Year's resolutions have been around since people raised a glass to toast one another during December holidays.

➤ People make resolutions because they're fun, they seem worthwhile, and the media keeps the tradition going.

➤ People from all walks of life make resolutions. The most successful, however, make resolutions while using effective goal-setting techniques.

➤ When it comes to making resolutions or goals, no one says you can't have fun!

Chapter 3

The Times of Your Life

> **In This Chapter**
>
> ➤ Assessing your life cycle
>
> ➤ Setting goals before and after moving
>
> ➤ Setting goals before and after changing jobs
>
> ➤ Setting goals before and after a mate change
>
> ➤ Let your age or the seasons tell you when

One of the alluring things about making resolutions or goals around New Year's day is that it's such a distinctive interval: A time between one year and the next—a marker, a place setting. In this chapter, you'll explore setting goals at opportune times. You'll begin with your life cycle and pinpoint when it's particularly fitting to set certain types of goals.

Go for the Gold! Do you realize that the younger you are when you set goals, the more you increase your chance of achieving short-term and lifetime success? Nearly all the people I know who set goals at an early age had the wonderful experience of not only realizing their goals at a still relatively early age, but moving way beyond those goals.

Following Your Life Cycle

Let's begin with the presumption that you're still in college. Goals related to your collegiate years may involve learning, graduating, getting a job, finding a mate, finding an apartment, and earning a certain income level.

My best friend had a goal to be a multimillionaire by a certain age. Earlier than that, his goal was to be an attorney. He achieved both of these goals and has since expanded his horizons so broadly that it's almost impossible to describe.

For Sure

Bill Clinton, the 42nd president of the United States, proved to be a champion goal setter. Early in his teens, he fixed his focus on becoming the president of the United States. He achieved that goal by age 46. This made him the second-youngest person elected to that office. Clinton also had a goal to be a two-term president, which was not an easy feat. He achieved two incredibly lofty goals.

After College

After you get out of college and, perhaps, graduate school, it's understandable that career-oriented goals begin to predominate. Will you get a job? Will it be a good job? Will it be at a decent salary? Will you have to relocate? You've probably embarked on a course of study that prepares you for the line of work you're seeking. Many people, however, haven't done this.

For Sure

Adams Media Inc., in Holbrook, Massachusetts, has published a series of career guides for students who are strategic job seekers. Topics include job opportunities for history majors, job opportunities for English majors, and so on. The books are a neat idea, because they match academic majors chosen for personal interest to practical, postcollegiate jobs.

The best time to set goals for your career is before you graduate from college. The more time you give yourself to plan broad-based careers or lifetime goals, the better your chances of success.

Similarly, you want to establish goals in advance of passing other predictable milestones in life. After your first job, you might find it entirely practical to begin making goals about the following:

➤ Your next job

➤ Relationships or marriage

➤ Moving out

➤ Relocating

➤ Having children

➤ Postgraduate education

➤ Saving so much per month

➤ Maintaining your relationship

➤ Caring for your parents

➤ Starting your retirement fund

➤ Travel and leisure

➤ Health

Uh-Oh!
If you start making decisions the day after you graduate about where you want to work and what you want to do, you might find yourself underemployed, underpaid, and undervalued. You might even find yourself unemployed.

Other situations you might not be anticipating could arise later in life:

➤ Starting your own venture

➤ Dealing with divorce

➤ Overcoming chemical dependency

➤ Receiving a large inheritance

➤ Coping with loss

➤ Running into career plateaus

➤ Having a significant problem with your children

➤ Becoming physically immobile

➤ Living much longer than anticipated

Be Forewarned

If you're only in your 20s or 30s, it might be difficult for you to imagine how life will be in your 60s, 70s, or 80s. Most people don't make plans in the early days of their careers to ensure that their later days are covered financially. The U.S. Social Security

Administration indicates that more than 85 percent of the U.S. population cannot live without their Social Security payments and other entitlements as they proceed past 65.

Polls show that among those in their 20s and 30s, only a small percentage will not have trouble meeting financial challenges when they are older. Something has to give. Not everyone can be among the smaller percentage of people who are well-off in old age. Chapter 11, "Now for the Biggie: Your Financial Life," examines making your financial goals.

For now, recognize that following the predictable pattern of a person's life, today is one of the most opportune times for you to establish goals—particularly financial goals. When it comes to accumulating sums and benefiting from long-term compound interest, there is simply no turning back the clock. Investing for 30 or 40 years yields substantially greater sums than investing under shorter time horizons.

Before and After Moving

You'd think that with all of humankind's technological breakthroughs, someone would do something about the onerous task of relocating. After all these years, there doesn't seem to be any way around loading and unloading every single thing you own. You can hire people to do it, but the process of moving is probably no less upsetting. There are address cards to fill out, phone numbers to change, utility companies to call, and a ton of other activities to manage.

When you get to the new location, you've got to make decisions about where to put furniture and dozens of little artifacts. You might not be able to unpack everything for weeks. Many people, therefore, find moving to be upsetting and downright frustrating despite their good intentions that the move will be for their ultimate betterment.

Then there's finding new friends or good schools for your kids. These things can be more stressful than packing and unpacking.

Seize the Move

Setting goals before and after moving is ideal, because you have to make a decision about everything you own. You have to decide whether something will go with you or be left behind.

More than the physical move itself, there's something about the moving process that is akin to setting goals. A move, like the start of a new year, is a place marker. It's an interval between one era and the next—the time between when you live in your former residence and when you move to your new one.

Some things immediately become clearer. Perhaps you're ready to give up the beat-up old couch because it simply won't be good enough in your new location. Maybe it was hard for you to give up the couch in the past because it had so many memories. Now, in the light of day, you can see that your memories will always linger, but there's no need to take the couch.

Yet, day after day, while you lived in your old residence and saw that rickety old couch, you had no inkling of changing it because there was no particular reason to upset the status quo.

In the new location, perhaps you not only want a new couch, but matching chairs and light fixtures to go with it. Perhaps your whole attitude changes. Maybe you decide it's time to upgrade your lifestyle and do more entertaining.

You might be moving because you got a raise. In either case, you have a new vantage point from which to view your life. From that vantage point springs a new set of goals that may be unlike goals you've chosen before.

New Goals for New Times

If you're married or living with a significant other, a move can be a wonderful time to set mutually established goals. Perhaps your partner will have more space in the new location, or you both agree to set up a home gym and buy some of those exercise machines advertised on television.

I had a friend in college, John McCaffrey, who now works for Amtrak in Washington, D.C. During his youth, John told me that his father worked for Nabisco and frequently relocated to assume new positions. Because the family moved every couple of years, they made decisions about what to retain and what to toss. In the new location, they frequently lived in a clutter-free, streamlined home. Long before I became a conference and convention speaker on the topic of having more breathing space and less clutter in your life, this notion appealed to me.

When John's family settled down in Orange, Connecticut, they still maintained a relatively clutter-free household. It was a pleasure to visit, unlike other friend's houses, which were strewn with stuff in every room.

I'm not saying that you have to move frequently to maintain a clutter-free home. It certainly helps, however. The next time you move, you should realize that a whole new series of ideas about how you want to handle your life, career, or relationships may emerge.

Word Power
The *status quo* refers to things as they are— the existing condition or state of affairs. If things stay the same or nothing changes, one is said to be *maintaining the status quo*.

Go for the Gold!
One of the wonderful things about goal setting is that you can set goals that are inconsistent with your history. You can set goals unlike anything you've attempted before. Your mother, your father, your peers, and those who you think still have influence over you need not have any effect on you as you embark on your own life's journey.

Go for the Gold!
Whether it's a move or any other element of your existence, exploit—in the positive sense of the word—the opportunity to set new goals consistent with where you want to be in life.

Before and After a Job Change

One of the reasons why the book *What Color is Your Parachute?*, by Richard Bolles, continues to be a perennial best-seller is that the author levels with his readers. He paints an accurate picture of what the job-searching process is actually like. He jokes, commiserates, and pulls no punches. Looking for a job when you don't have one is a bear. Looking for a job when you do have one is still not an easy task. Starting a new job, whether or not you were employed, represents a wide variety of challenges. Let's look at the goal-setting opportunities inherent in each of these conditions.

Unemployed and Looking

As nerve wracking as looking for a job can be, it is one of the clearest opportunities you'll have in life to establish effective goals. After all, when else do you get clear, uninterrupted stretches for determining exactly what's important in your life and career?

Still, it's easy enough to get caught up in the notion "I've got to find a job, and find one now!" as your job search wears on. The feeling of desperation can haunt you if you're not careful. Early in my career, I had a couple of bouts with unemployment and, by the fourth and fifth month, I started to feel as though I would never be employed again. I was young and didn't know better, and I let it affect my sense of self-worth. After all, wherever I went and whatever I did, I was among the unemployed. Couldn't people tell? It was as if I was somehow glaringly deficient.

If you're currently unemployed, realize that this is simply a transition period in your long-term career. Perhaps you got fired or left your previous job under less than pleasant circumstances. Maybe you're new in the workplace and have never had a career position. You might be reentering the career world after many years. In any case, you're where you are for a reason, and you have before you the marvelous opportunity to set your sights on what is most appropriate, challenging, and enjoyable for you.

From Job A to Job B

If you already have a job, congratulations. Psychologically and financially, you'll have an easier task of looking for a new job, because you have some sense of security where you currently are. You also have some funds coming in on a regular basis and can pay for the cost of resumes, mail postage, long-distance phone calls, travel, and other expenses associated with your job search.

At all times, it's your professional responsibility to continue to do your best until you officially complete your last day on the job. Doing less would dishonor your professional integrity.

Much like the unemployed person seeking a position, you have before you the opportunity to get very clear about your career goals. How would you like your new job to be? Ask yourself some of these questions:

➤ Where would my job be?

➤ What's the size of the organization?

➤ What type of boss would I report to?

➤ What would my job description be?

➤ What would my salary be?

➤ What kinds of amenities would I enjoy?

➤ What kinds of resources would support me?

➤ What would the benefits package include?

➤ How would this position fit into my overall career progression?

➤ What kinds of professional relationships would I establish?

➤ What types of skills would I want to acquire?

➤ What professional associations would I join?

➤ What compensation increase would I look forward to and when?

➤ What would my next job title be, and the one after that?

➤ Where would I live, and how long would my commute be?

➤ What are innovative ways in which I could accelerate my career growth?

> **Uh-Oh!**
> Far too many people have hazy goals for what their next job will be and how much they'll get paid. Not surprisingly, these are the same people who often find themselves a year or two down the road scrambling to hang on where they are or trying to land something else. They're simply keeping their heads above water.
>
> CAUTION!

If you can answer these types of questions, you're plotting out your career progression with the best of career professionals in any industry.

Making the Leap

When you begin a new job, whether you came from the ranks of the unemployed or employed, a host of other opportunities arises. With the time you have before you begin your new position, you can contemplate the earlier questions as well as the following:

➤ What kinds of relationships do I want to establish with my new co-workers?

➤ What kind of relationship do I want to establish with my boss?

➤ Do I need to upgrade my wardrobe?

➤ Do I need to take additional courses?

➤ Are there articles or books that support my understanding of the new position or new organization?

➤ Do I need new equipment?

If the position involves an increase in compensation, you also have potential goals regarding what you'll do with the additional income:

➤ What investment vehicles will I consider?

➤ Should I consult a certified financial planner?

➤ Does the organization have a pension or profit-sharing plan?

➤ Should I invest the added income back into my career in the form of courses, equipment purchases, new subscriptions, and so on?

First-Day Considerations

After you begin a new position, on that first day and in the first few weeks that follow, more goal-setting opportunities emerge. Consider the following issues:

➤ Are there individuals who can serve as mentors?

➤ What new journals and periodicals would be best for me to read and to which should I subscribe?

➤ How can I strengthen or solidify my relationship with my boss?

➤ How can I strengthen or solidify my relationship with co-workers?

➤ Are there professional organizations, clubs, cliques, or informal groups worth joining?

➤ Are there opportunities to expand my responsibilities?

Because starting any new position will involve some adjustments, realities probably will change after you start. These actualities represent more issues and opportunities for goal setting:

➤ How can I bridge the gap between what I thought this position would be and what it actually is?

➤ How can I assemble the resources I need to do this job effectively?

➤ What kind of changes do I need to make in my commuting routine to arrive and depart more easily?

➤ What routines do I need to establish in my domestic life to keep things running smoothly?

➤ How can I best affiliate with key individuals within the organization?

Milestones for the Taking

Other opportunities may rise in the form of milestones. Did you recently give your first speech to your organization? That's a milestone. Did you get your first article published (even in a newsletter or small publication)? Here's a brief list of other potential career and non-career milestones around which you might find yourself naturally inclined to establish some new goals:

➤ You receive the largest pay increase in your career history.

➤ You are elected to be an officer in your professional association or group.

➤ You are interviewed by a national publication.

➤ People start seeking you out and are willing to pay for your professional expertise.

➤ You are awarded an honorary degree.

➤ You are asked to sit on the board of directors of a prestigious organization.

➤ You are asked to be on a special committee supporting your town council.

➤ Your child earns a four-year scholarship to college.

➤ A literary magazine decides to publish your poem.

Accent the Positive

Whenever any of these types of events occur, given the new situation, you might find it fitting and appropriate to establish new goals. Your daughter getting a four-year scholarship might mean that, instead of her working all summer before entering college, the whole family can go on an extended vacation.

What has happened in your life lately that represents a milestone? What's on the immediate horizon that represents a potential milestone? And, here's one to put down the book and ponder: What milestones have passed without you making any goals surrounding them that you now can use to form goals?

Relationship Changes

If you're in a relationship and it ends, whether your heart is slightly broken or seemingly crushed beyond repair, life moves on. Having your significant other leave you is heavy-duty. Divorce is heavy-duty. Even if you were the initiator of the breakup, the loss of a significant other can have a profound impact on you.

For Sure

Not much information exists on the impact of death on relationships. At any given time in the United States alone, there are some 15 million widowed persons, according to Jarrett Bennett, a certified financial planner in Fairfax, Virginia and author of *Making the Money Last*.

Before a Mate Change

If you know that your relationship is not going to make it, you have the opportunity to establish goals. Chapters 7, "Goals for Family Life," and 8, "Your Social Life and How to Have One," examine where you are regarding family and social contacts.

Many psychologists believe that there are lessons we need to learn, so we attract partners that will help us learn such lessons. Some people believe we are attracted to others who seemingly have what we lack. So, in our quest to be complete, we want a relationship with this person to complete us.

In either case, until we learn the importance of being relatively whole and complete individuals ourselves, we're bound to repeat the same type of relationship mistakes with subsequent partners. Therefore, if you're breaking up with or divorcing your significant other and haven't learned more about yourself and your needs as a result of your relationship, you run a significant risk of replicating your previous relationships.

After a Mate Change

Whether you've just found someone new or you're in a long-term relationship, you have the opportunity to view your mate in a new light. Perhaps it's time to talk about your goals for the coming week, month, year, or five years. There's a scene in the movie *Don Juan de Marco* where the character portrayed by Marlon Brando tells his wife (Faye Dunaway), "I want to know what your dreams and aspirations are." Dunaway replies, "I thought you'd never ask."

If you're in that in-between time, looking for somebody and not sure when and where he or she will appear, then get clear about your relationship goals. Ask yourself these questions:

➤ What kind of person do I want to meet?

➤ What level of commitment am I willing to offer?

➤ What level of sacrifice am I prepared to make?

➤ What kinds of activities do I want to engage in with this person?

➤ How much energy will I devote to the relationship?

CAUTION! **Uh-Oh!**
Changes under duress have a nasty habit of lasting only as long as the pressure is present. What's more, as I discussed in Chapter 1, "What Is a Goal as a Opposed to a Wish?," although goals can be imposed on you by someone else, they have to be internalized (made your own) if they are to be effective.

Don't Wait Until You're Desperate

People often wait for significant pain (a topic discussed in Part 3, "Secrets of Master Goal-Setters") before they make significant changes in their relationships. When one partner or the other threatens to leave, then, and sometimes only then, will the other partner agree to make changes.

Let the Seasons Tell You

Here is a simple list of dates and events throughout the year. Each of these represents an opportunity for you to get clearer and more focused about what you want.

Seasonal Opportunities for Setting Goals

January	New Year's, end of tax year
February	Valentine's Day
March	Spring begins
April	Daylight savings time begins, taxes due
May	Spring cleaning, Memorial Day
June	Graduations, Summer begins
July	Independence Day
August	Vacations
September	Labor Day, Back to school, Autumn begins
October	Government fiscal year, Daylight savings time ends
November	Harvest, Thanksgiving, Election Day
December	Hanukkah and Christmas holidays, Winter begins

The climate where you live, the temperature on a daily basis, and today's weather can all be contributing factors to the goals you set. The very term *spring cleaning* arises from the fact that after you raise windows that have been closed all winter and your spirits begin to rise with the temperature, it's much easier to engage in a thorough cleaning of your home. You can keep windows open and fans on as you transport debris. You can more easily change vacuum cleaner bags when it's warm outside. You can more easily clean windows. It's less treacherous to get up on your roof than it was when ice and wet conditions prevailed.

So, too, at various other times around the year, you may find great incentives to tackle projects that you wouldn't touch at other times with the proverbial 10-foot pole.

Let Your Age Tell You

Age can be a useful factor in establishing goals. The mere fact that you turned 30 or 40 might be enough of an incentive for you to buckle down and establish some new goals. A birthday ending in zero is a huge event. When you turn 30, 40, 50, or 60, you've passed a stage in life you'll never pass again. What a wonderful time to clear out the old and bring in the new. It's used much like people use New Year's or the change of a decade to spur themselves on.

If it has been a long-term notion of yours to clear the cellar of all its clutter and convert it into an office, and you're going to be 40 in three weeks, guess what? If you establish a goal of converting the cellar into an office in the next two weeks, you're likely to proceed with more energy and focus than you would at some other time. After all, you've chosen to finish this before you turn 40.

Easy Marks

Traditional age markers exist that are independent of any personal ones you choose to act on. The age of 16 is, of course, when many people get their automobile license. Others age markers include the right to vote at age 18 and the right to consume alcohol at age 21. Finally, at age 30, you are supposedly no longer to be trusted!

Age 40 traditionally has been a milestone, as in the expression "Life begins at 40." Age 65 is a traditional retirement age. Age 72 is a milestone for the predictable life span for the average American man, and age 77 is the predictable life span for the average American woman.

Age 80, becoming an octogenarian, is, in recent decades, held as a rite of passage. Age 90 is even more exclusive. Age 100 will garner you a postcard from the President.

Happy Anniversary!

Your first anniversary is a milestone. Each anniversary represents the opportunity to establish new goals. A 25th anniversary is certainly notable, and every five-year interval after that is admirable. Fiftieth anniversaries are rare, but you might be among the lucky few.

A 60th, 70th, or 75th anniversary (they do happen) will land you a mention in a national publication and on your local news, if not on NBC's weekend report. Use all these times and more to keep evaluating what you want in life.

Moving On

Now you're ready to move on to the seven basic goal areas or arenas of life. You'll look at these in detail in the next chapter.

The Least You Need to Know

➤ Take the opportunity to set goals based on passages through your own life cycle.

➤ Consider the opportunities for setting goals before and after moving, changing a job, or changing a mate.

➤ Look out for career and personal milestones around which you can establish new goals.

➤ The seasons go 'round and 'round. Take advantage of the opportunities to set goals based on the time of the year.

➤ As you reach age 30, 40, 50, and so on, you can generate great energy in pursuing the goals you set at these times.

The Seven Basic Goal Categories

Too often, when you pick up a book or article on setting and reaching your goals, you encounter a variety of terms; some of these terms are helpful, but many can cloud the issue. What's the difference between an objective and a goal, a goal and a strategy, a priority and a strategy, a tactic and a maneuver, a mission and a mission statement, and so on? There are good books that define these terms in ways that make sense, but I'm going to cut through the clutter and keep the terminology as simple as possible. I simply define a *goal* as something you want to reach or a desired outcome.

While pursuing your goals, you might rely on action steps, strategies, tactics, maneuvers, or other procedures. The terms you use are largely irrelevant. You set a goal, you do things to reach that goal, and you reach the goal. Then, you set another. Does this sound good to you?

The Key Areas of Life

In looking for a goal-setting model, I turned to an expert on the topic—a champion goal setter and goal reacher in his own right, Dr. Tony Alessandra. Dr. Alessandra has written 12 books, including *The Platinum Rule* and *Charisma*, both published by Warner Books. He also has created dozens of award-winning video and cassette programs.

His popular Web site, **http://www.platinumrule.com**, receives up to 4,000 visitors a month. At the site, Dr. Alessandra offers a self-scoring quiz you can take to quickly and easily determine which of four basic personality types you fit into and how you can best interrelate with others. You can even take the quiz for a friend or spouse. In other words, you answer the questions based on what you know about that person, and you get information back telling you how to best relate with him or her.

Dr. Alessandra's basic strategy (on which the rest of this chapter is based) is simple yet profound. He contends that your life is a system. You can't view what you do at work as separate from what you do at home, and vice versa.

In this chapter, I discuss the seven goal areas Dr. Alessandra cites as common to most people—key elements of life, including mental, physical, family, social, career, spiritual, and financial goals.

The Big Seven

Dr. Alessandra says that for many years, people lived with the mistaken belief that their home life and work life could be totally separate. Many people gave their families and personal lives a back seat to their careers, chasing only the carrot of success while other facets of their lives suffered. Yet, you have many needs and wants you seek to fulfill. Basically, human needs fall into seven broad categories:

➤ Mental: The functions of your mind—memory, concentration, learning, creativity, reasoning, and mathematical abilities

➤ Physical: The many functions of your body—overall fitness, percent of body fat, skills and abilities, agility, and endurance

➤ Family: Your relationships with the special people you consider to be part of your family

➤ Social: Your relationships with others outside your family and outside your business—in a word, *friends*

➤ Spiritual: Your relationship between you and your Creator—also defined as the philosophical and humanitarian areas of your life

➤ Career: Your involvement in your chosen field, both on and off the job

➤ Financial: The management of your financial resources and obligations

Oh, So Delicate a Balance

In many ways, you are like a fragile ecosystem. The elements of your life are interdependent. One need affects the others, especially when it is grossly neglected.

Everyone knows that financial problems affect your outlook, health, social life, and family life, for example. That's why practitioners of holistic medicine examine all facets of a person's life when they search for the cause of a physical illness.

You are a complex being with complex needs. Moreover, your needs are dynamic rather than static—they are always changing. At one point in your life, your career pursuits may require more time than your spiritual or family needs. At some other time, another need may be emphasized more than the others.

Goals as Targets

Striving for and attaining a balance of goals makes life meaningful. Yet, for all that has ever been written about goals, the great masses of people haven't much to show for it.

> *Most people aim at nothing in life...and hit it with amazing accuracy.*
> —Anonymous

Go for the Gold!
Creating balance among the seven need categories in your life is particularly important. Each category can positively or negatively affect the others, depending on the attention or lack of attention it receives.

Uh-Oh!
Having one need that is more urgent than others doesn't mean that the others disappear. They, too, must receive at least a minimal amount of your attention. You rarely can neglect a need completely without suffering unpleasant consequences.

Such a statement is a sad commentary about people, but it is true. Lewis Carroll eloquently stated this point in *Alice's Adventures in Wonderland*:

Alice: Mr. Cat, which of these paths shall I take?

Cheshire Cat: Well, my dear, where do you want to go?

Alice: I don't suppose it really matters.

Cheshire Cat: Then, my dear, any path will do!

If you have no goals, or more likely, vague or hazy notions about goals, don't be surprised if you find yourself feeling emotionally, socially, spiritually, physically, or professionally unbalanced. It's a sign of strength when you make decisions that positively affect the direction of your life.

Stumbling into Great Achievement

Does anyone ever stumble into great achievement? Even when a lab researcher discovers something extraordinary by accident, the discovery usually follows years of hard work.

Can you imagine the following exchange taking place after Sir Edmund Hillary returned from Mount Everest?

Reporter: Congratulations, Sir Hillary! Tell me, why did you become the first man to conquer Mount Everest?

Sir Hillary: I was wandering around trying to become inspired when I ended up on the top of this mountain.

Reporter: Really! Did it work?

Sir Hillary: Yes, but by the time I got back, I forgot why I went up to begin with.

Of course, this scenario is absurd, because such a monumental feat as climbing Mount Everest requires serious goal setting and attainment. Sir Hillary had to work hard to gain the knowledge and physical skills necessary for the climb. He also had to acquire the help of a team of experts and procure all the equipment. His preparation took an enormous amount of time—longer than the climb itself.

A Road Map as Good as Any

When you earnestly pursue your goals, reasons to do some things and to avoid others appear in your life. A young man from a tough neighborhood has never been involved with drugs or in trouble with the law. Do you marvel at his good fortune and strength of character?

When he was 10 years old, he set the goal of becoming an astronaut. At last report, he had graduated from the U.S. Air Force Academy with a degree in astronautical engineering. He is so focused on his goal that he avoids doing anything to hurt his chances of success.

An Easy Mark

It is easy to spot a person who has a clear set of goals. That person exudes a sense of purpose and determination. He or she has abundant energy and is willing to put more time and effort into any given task.

People who continually set, pursue, and monitor their career goals are more productive than people who simply work at a job. The uninspired worker goes home at the end of the day having gained nothing more than a few dollars and a lot of aggravation.

When you clearly set goals in all major areas of your life, the right roads appear in front of you like mirages in the desert. Of course, unlike mirages, these roads are real! Choices become infinitely easier to make, and you'll realize that you have taken a giant step toward living a balanced life.

The Right Outlook

In the past two decades, much criticism has been levied at positive thinking—probably because it has been exploited and overcommercialized. However, if you are serious about succeeding in your chosen field, you'll need to cultivate positive thinking as an every-day habit.

> **Go for the Gold!**
> Being goal oriented can even help you to become more positive, optimistic, and assertive.

> **Go for the Gold!**
> People who have a clear set of goals in life exude a sense of purpose and determination, are taken seriously by others, and are respected by their peers. In contrast, those who have no goals feel emotion-ally, socially, spiritually, physically, and professionally unbalanced, which only causes further anxiety.

Negative assumptions, which set up internal obstacles that can defeat you, usually become *self-fulfilling prophecies*. You assume that you cannot do something, so you then act in ways that guarantee your failure; this, in turn, reinforces your original assumption. Therefore, you must replace your negative assumptions with positive assumptions or positive thinking, which generates positive results.

Self-confidence goes hand-in-hand with positive thinking. It is the food that feeds your personal growth. It is an absolutely indispensable part of achievement. Self-confidence works best when based on your own knowledge and self-respect instead of comparisons between yourself and others. Don't compare yourself to other people, because you're likely to feel pompous or bitter, and neither of these feelings is desirable. So, your self-confidence needs to exist in a vacuum, which it can.

A Skewed Self-Concept

Even when you are armed with positive thinking and self-confidence, something called a *self-concept* may yet be a stumbling block for you. Your self-concept is the image you have of yourself. It is the evaluation you justly or unjustly make based on everything you know (or think you know) about yourself.

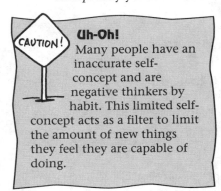

Uh-Oh!
Many people have an inaccurate self-concept and are negative thinkers by habit. This limited self-concept acts as a filter to limit the amount of new things they feel they are capable of doing.

When a new thought or feeling comes into your awareness, if it is consistent with your self-concept, you accept the new idea as valid. If the idea is not consistent with your self-concept, however, you tend to reject it.

Maintaining a positive self-concept is one of the most valuable things you can do for yourself, especially when it comes to considering and establishing new types of goals that may be somewhat outside the bounds of what you've considered or attempted in the past.

Getting Started Through Brainstorming

In the seven chapters that follow in Part 2, I walk you through many ideas for establishing goals that might be right for you. Right now, consider the concept of *brainstorming*. This a mental technique that offers a valuable way of exploring potential goals to select in any of the seven goal categories or supporting goals you establish.

Don't Judge Your Ideas

With brainstorming, you give free flight to your ideas. Let ideas flow without judging them, and you will generate many times the ideas produced through the normal reasoning process. After you generate these ideas, you can begin to evaluate their usefulness.

Here are some guidelines for brainstorming:

Go for the Gold!
Brainstorming is a valuable way of exploring your goals. When ideas flow freely, many more ideas, as well as more novel ideas, are generated.

➤ *Suspend all judgment.* This is a time to remove your internal censor. Nothing is unimportant, too silly, or too wild to include when brainstorming.

➤ *Think quantity, not quality.* The more ideas you generate, the better your chances are of hitting on something new and useful.

➤ *Extrapolate and experiment.* No matter how nonsensical it might seem, take your ideas to the highest level. Combine ideas in unusual ways to stimulate new ideas.

➤ *Evaluate later.* Do not close your mind to any suggestions. An idea that seemed ridiculous yesterday might be ingenious tomorrow.

Brainstorming Mechanics

To brainstorm, find a time when you will not be distracted. Sit comfortably with a pencil and paper or a pocket dictator. Then form a question of a problem to be handled. Make your question specific, such as "How can I increase my level of fitness and achieve my target weight?" After you ask the question, immediately begin jotting down or recording your ideas.

If you're writing, make notes in brief phrases to save time. If you're dictating (my preferred method), use full sentences, but then quickly go back to your brainstorming mode so that other ideas may follow.

When you finish, review your notes. Examine all the possibilities. Discard unusable ideas only at the end. Continue to suspend all judgment during this exercise. Often, wild and crazy ideas, when put together or altered slightly, turn out to be your most novel, effective solutions. So let yourself go.

You might feel a little silly writing down some of the ideas. That's normal.

Uh-Oh!
Record the first thing that comes to your mind. Do not judge your responses, or you'll short-change the process. You can fill in the details of your notes later.

Applied to Your Goals

When considering your life's goals, brainstorm each category using these brainstorming guidelines. Allow about two minutes per category, using one page per category—seven pages in all. Again, shoot for quantity and let your imagination take over!

When you finish, review what you've written (or dictated) and add anything you might have forgotten or that now seems appropriate.

And the Three Winners Are...

When you're satisfied with your responses, look them over and circle the one idea under each category that stands out as being the most important. Don't worry about what others might think of your choice.

Whether there is repetition among your seven circled "semi-finalists" from the seven groups is unimportant. Now, drum roll, please…. Examine the seven goals, and disregarding which group they came from, choose the three that are the most pressing to you.

Write those three goals on a separate sheet of paper with the title "My Three Most Important Goals." These represent the most important goals in your life at this time and undoubtedly merit time and attention. But hold on! A balanced approach to life works best.

Go for the Gold!
Circling one idea per page enables you to see your goals in black and white, on paper, where they show up best.

And the Important Runners-Up Include...

As valuable as it is to isolate your most precious goals, it is equally important to remain *cognizant* of your other goals.

Review your sheet for each of your seven categories and list all the secondary goals that are worthy of action. You now have a good indication of where you are in life and where you would like to be in every facet.

As an example, here is a list that one sales representative compiled:

- ➤ Mental goals: Stop worrying so much about money and success, improve my memory of names, increase my vocabulary proficiency, broaden my knowledge

- ➤ Physical goals: Eat less junk food, do stress-reduction exercises every night, floss teeth every night, maintain an ideal weight

- ➤ Family goals: Call Mom and Dad once a week, spend at least 10 minutes daily listening to my spouse and each child

- ➤ Social goals: Go to weekly Rotary Club meetings, socialize with more salespeople, and exchange ideas

- ➤ Spiritual goals: Go to church once every two weeks, be more helpful to people every day

- ➤ Career goals: Make three more sales per week, earn a master's degree in marketing

- ➤ Financial goals: Own my own home, purchase a sports car, provide for an ample retirement fund by the time I'm 55 years old

A Framework for Reaching Your Goals

You've already looked at the importance of internalizing or personalizing your goals (especially when the goal originates from some external source). Your goal needs to be something you *want* to do rather than something you *have* to do. Even if a sales quota is imposed on you, there are many valid reasons why you may personally want to achieve that goal—among them, pride, competitive spirit, a desire to increase your income, and a quest to improve your job status.

Your Goal Needs to Be Positive

When you hang onto a thought such as *I will not smoke today,* you end up thinking more about smoking! Instead, if you think *I will maintain clear, clean lungs today,* your aim is more direct and you're bound to be more effective in your pursuit.

Chapter 13, "It's All in the Wording," contains a section called "Positive Words for Positive People," which elaborates on this theme.

Write It Down, Jack

Written goals take a jump in status from being nebulous thoughts to bona-fide entities on paper or on your computer! This gives you a visual reminder and confirmation of the importance of your goals. Your goals gain credibility simply from being written.

Ready for Prime Time

How will you actually apply the goals you've set for yourself? For your three primary goals and each of your secondary goals, I suggest that you do the following:

1. Determine whether each goal is challenging yet still reachable, is quantifiable, and contains specific timelines—both personal and positive. If so, continue. If not, rewrite or reword your goal as clearly as possible so that it meets this criteria.

2. Examine obstacles that stand in your way. Do you maintain any negative assumptions or self-defeating thoughts? An obstacle blocks you only if you let it. Write down your innovative ways of overcoming obstacles.

3. Ask yourself why you want to achieve the goal. What kind of payoff is motivating you? It's useful and enlightening to know. Perhaps your underlying reason is not so noble or grandiose—that's okay, as long as you're clear on why you want to proceed.

4. List the steps you will take to achieve your goal. The smaller the increments, the easier they will be to accomplish.

When recording these ideas and observations on your worksheet, fill up the page completely if it helps, and keep it visible! Put your goals in a place you will see them every day. Check off items as you complete them. Use your worksheet to chart your progress, and take pride in your accomplishments.

Go for the Gold!
In the movie *The Ten Commandments*, there is an oft-repeated phrase: "So let it be written, so let it be done." People are trained from childhood to give credibility to written statements. Putting it in writing gives your words more importance. Chapters 14, "Committing to Paper," and 17, "Contracting with Yourself," focus on this idea in more detail.

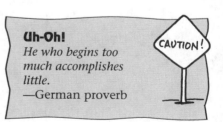

Uh-Oh!
He who begins too much accomplishes little.
—German proverb

```
GOALS WORKSHEET

PRIMARY GOAL #1

BUY NEW HOME WITHIN 24 MONTHS

POTENTIAL STEPS:

  ➤ BEGIN SAVINGS PLAN
  ➤ ASK PARENTS ABOUT ONE-TIME GIFT
  ➤ INVEST MORTGAGE OPTIONS
  ➤ BEGIN VISITING SITES
  ➤ PREPARE FINANCIAL STATEMENTS
  ➤ CHECK CREDIT REPORT
  ➤ ATTEND HOME-BUYING SEMINAR
```

The Thought-Diet Card

Here's a goal-achieving aid that might be right for you. The *thought diet* is a tool you can use daily to become the person who will achieve your goals. It helps you stay focused on daily action in support of your goals—actions that are bite-sized and easy to accomplish.

Thought–Diet Card

Front Side:	Back Side:
My Current Primary Goal: _____ _____ _____	**Minimum Daily Behaviors in each of seven areas to take me to my goal:**
Five Traits I'm developing related to the goal:	Mental_____ _____ Physical_____ _____
1.	Social_____
2.	Family_____ _____
3.	Spiritual_____ _____
4.	Career_____
5.	Financial_____ _____

Reprinted with Permission © Jim Cathcart, 1997
Cathcart Institute ▪ http://www.cathcart. com

Section by Section

In the first section of the Thought-Diet Card, write your primary goal. Write out as explicitly as possible the goal that most strongly affects your motivation right now.

In the second section of the card, write the characteristics you're developing, including five key characteristics you need to develop to achieve your goal.

In the third section of the card, write the minimum daily standards you will meet every day to move closer to your goal. Again, be specific. Here are some examples of minimum daily standards:

➤ Mental: I will spend 15 minutes every evening doing visualization exercises.

➤ Physical: I will do a minimum of 5 push-ups and 10 sit-ups every morning.

➤ Family: I will relax over dinner and enjoy a meaningful conversation with my family.

➤ Social: I will take time to call one of my new friends.

➤ Spiritual: Each day I will do one good deed to help someone less fortunate than I.

➤ Career: I will read something related to my career for at least 15 minutes every day.

➤ Financial: I will keep a complete record of every expense.

'Til Habits Take Hold

Read the Thought-Diet Card twice daily until every-thing on it becomes a habit. After you develop constructive habits, you can move on to new behaviors. Then, fill out a new card and practice the new challenges every day until they become habits.

Go for the Gold!
The secret of success is constancy of purpose.
—Benjamin Disraeli

You will surely (and rather painlessly!) move closer and closer to your goals.

By leading you a little at a time, the thought diet will keep you from being overwhelmed by your more lofty goals.

Optimum Mileage

Here are some suggestions for getting optimal mileage out of the thought diet:

➤ Read the Thought-Diet Card twice daily—in the morning when you rise and in the evening before you retire. Repetition is an integral part of learning and will help you stay on target.

➤ Avoid associating with people who drag you down emotionally. Associate with people who are positive and who can increase your optimism. (See Chapters 20,

"Affiliating with Others: Capitalizing on Those Around You," and 22, "The Tom Sawyer Effect: Formally Enlisting Others to Help You.")

➤ Sincerely read and complete the card. Do not go through the motions! You will be kidding no one but yourself.

The Least You Need to Know

➤ You don't need to complicate the pursuit of your goals with all kinds of terminology; there are goals, subgoals, and steps or actions to reach them.

➤ Don't believe that your home life and your work life are totally separate. If you give your family and personal lives a back seat to your career, other facets of your life will suffer.

➤ You have many needs and wants to fulfill, in basically seven broad categories: mental, physical, family, social, spiritual, professional, and financial.

➤ People with a clear set of goals exude a sense of purpose and determination, positive thinking, and abundant energy.

➤ Brainstorming can lead you to fresh ideas about what you want and how to accomplish it. The Thought-Diet Card can make it easier to reach your goals.

Part 2
Assessing Yourself

Now get ready for a fun-filled ride through seven rollicking chapters. In Part 2, I discuss the whys and hows of setting challenging and reachable goals in the seven arenas of life: mental, physical, family, social, spiritual, career, and financial. Each chapter will stimulate your thinking and, on occasion, will even provoke you.

As you read through each of the seven chapters, think about your strengths, your accomplishments, and your current situation. Part 2 will help you focus on what you'd like to change.

You might want to set goals to be accomplished immediately, within the year, or over the course of several years. Some goals may be continuous (what I call maintenance *goals), whereas others may be unique and nonrecurring.*

So turn the page if you're ready for Chapter 5, "Mind Over Matter."

ANY QUESTIONS

Mind Over Matter

In This Chapter

➤ Inside your head is where the action is

➤ Getting clear about what you want

➤ Beyond pain on the way to gain

➤ Forget about overreaching

Mental development—the first of the seven major goal areas, as identified by Dr. Tony Alessandra—is the most important. The goals you set for your mental development dramatically impact your ability to reach goals in other areas of life. In this chapter, I face the intriguing task of getting inside your head. That's not easy. Others have tried and failed. Besides, each of us is so different. Nevertheless, if you so choose, this chapter will generate some thought-provoking ideas about your mental goals.

More Nature Than Nurture

Studies are busting out all over indicating that nature may play a more dominate role in influencing your success in life than was previously thought.

Some 15 years earlier, researchers from around the world concluded that the left side of the brain controls logic and rational thinking, whereas the right side of the brain controls creative thinking. (Note: *Left brain, right brain* is a metaphor. The brain's construction is actually more complex than a simple division into a left and a right side.) Theorists say that to function most effectively, you need to use both halves of your brain.

More recently, the work of Dr. Hans Eysenck, professor emeritus at the Institute of Psychiatry at the University of London, has gained attention. Dr. Eysenck found that brain scans of introverted people indicate "a high degree of arousal in the frontal lobes of the cortex."

The brains of extroverts, in comparison, are in a consistently low-arousal state. This may explain why introverts tend to shy away from excitement and why extroverts often are characterized as "sensation seekers." Hmmm… so that explains why I often go off into a corner at parties. Know thyself and how thee operates!

For Sure

In the mid-1990s, Daniel Goleman, in his ground-breaking book, *Emotional Intelligence*, elaborated on how some people are able to sail through situations that send others into a tizzy. This behavior is related to how one's brain is wired. Fortunately for the less than emotionally intelligent, one's "EQ" can be raised through awareness and training.

Because you're reading a *Complete Idiot's Guide*, however, I'm going to dispense with all that heavy neuron-and-synapse stuff and in very plain English get right to the heart of how to make your gray matter work for you.

First Up: The Burning Issue

Can you use your mind to improve your lot in life? Can you move from where you are to where you want to be, all starting with the power of a thought? The answer, although not entirely clear, is yes. The fact that you picked up and are reading this book is one of the strongest indicators that you have the ability to set and achieve goals. Let me explain why this is true for you and many others, but might not be true for everyone.

Think and Grow What?

In 1908, a motivational magazine assigned a 25-year-old reporter named Napoleon Hill the task of interviewing the great steel magnate, Andrew Carnegie. Carnegie generally was regarded as one of the most prominent examples of "rags to riches" success in America at the time.

The two apparently hit it off, and Carnegie invited Hill to develop what Carnegie called a personal, practical philosophy that any man or woman could use to improve his or her lot in life. Instead of paying Hill for the project, Carnegie offered him something he couldn't resist—access to business tycoons, government leaders, and some of the leading creative minds of the time.

Five hundred interviews and 29 years later, Hill published the book *Think and Grow Rich*, which went on to become a worldwide best-seller, and still sells to this day. Hill interviewed auto magnate Henry Ford (that's Henry Ford I), former U.S. President and Supreme Court Chief Justice William Howard Taft, inventor Thomas Edison, and virtually everybody who was anybody in the first quarter of the 20th century.

What's Your Plan?

According to Hill, success in life depends on developing a plan. He believed that if you want to be successful, you need to have a definite major purpose, write down that purpose, and study it. By scrutinizing your purpose in life, the strength of your plan as well as its weaknesses becomes apparent. Then, according to Hill, it is simply a matter of exploiting the strengths and shoring up the weaknesses so that you have the best chance of succeeding.

Hill advised his readers to remind themselves of their plan every day and to keep it in "sharp focus." Hence, the choices you make on that day and subsequent days enhance and support your plan. Moreover, you will have an easier time ignoring those choices that are simply diversions.

Check Your Attitude at the Door

Another important facet of success according to Hill was that you *have to believe that what you want is possible.* If you don't, you have little chance of succeeding. With a positive mental attitude, even in the face of countless setbacks, eventually you will succeed.

Hill also was a staunch advocate of self-discipline—the discipline of mind and body that leads to a mastery of money and time. He believed that developing a strong character enables you to get into the habit of doing the most important work first each day.

This sounds good so far, but keep in mind that Hill's inquiry was largely anecdotal and testimonial. In other words, he acquired no hard evidence; he produced no experimental design, research, or testing; no follow-up and analysis were ever performed.

Success Formula Revealed!

During the time of Hill's research, other authors came forward with books that purportedly contained nuggets of wisdom that could propel you from mediocrity to stardom. *A Message to Garcia*, by Elbert Hubbard, was highly popular when it was published and still sells today.

Relying on observations of heroism during the Spanish-American War, Hubbard wrote,

> It is not book-learning young men need, nor instruction about this and that, but a stiffening of the vertebrae which will cause them to be loyal to a trust, to act promptly, concentrate their energies: do the thing.

For Sure

Acres of Diamonds, by Russell Conwell, was equally popular in the first half of the 20th century. Conwell, a pastor in Philadelphia, asserted that men of humble origins (it was always men, never women) could rise to prominence if they had high aspirations and were diligent in their efforts. The story line of *Acres of Diamonds* tells of a man who searched the world for diamonds only to find that diamonds were discovered in the backyard of the property he had owned and had sold to finance his quest.

A Strange Secret

Following World War II, noted radio personality, motivational speaker, and author Earl Nightingale recorded an inspirational message, *The Strangest Secret*. Nightingale, who never highlighted the fact that he was one of the few survivors from the U.S.S. Arizona, which was sunk by the Japanese during the attack on Pearl Harbor, told his listeners, "We become what we think about."

In essence, Nightingale was saying that your lot in life is a direct result of your mental conditioning. If you focus on success long and hard enough, soon enough, you will be successful.

The Rise of the Success Industry

In the American boom times of the 1950s, and throughout the '60s and '70s, such companies as the Success Motivational Institute; Nightingale's own Nightingale-Conant, Inc.; and a host of others appeared, offering cassette tapes to help listeners achieve more.

By the '80s, dozens and dozens of companies had sprung up that offered cassettes, videos, books, training guides, and other materials on virtually all aspects of career and life that ostensibly could help you get from point A to point B most efficiently. By the '90s, such programs were offered via CD-ROM, over the Internet, and through a host of other digital and electronic formats.

In many respects, this book, *The Complete Idiot's Guide to Reaching Your Goals*, is but one if not *the* flat-out most brilliant tool in a long line of success-related resources.

Is It All Hocus-Pocus?

Lack of scientific research in the field of human achievement led many scholars to scoff at what the American public was being told. The most prominent researcher to explore the potential connection between mental functioning and career or personal success is Dr. David McClelland. Although he is currently a professor at Boston University, McClelland earned much of his fame while at Harvard University. For several decades, McClelland studied the potential links between what you think about and what you achieve.

Ultimately, McClelland became convinced that even men and women of humble origins could break ranks and redesign their lives.

The Fortunate Ones

Certainly, this was wonderful news for anyone who ever had a hankering to be all that they could be, and this is where you come in. If you had any kind of decent upbringing, if you were nurtured along the way, if you went to reasonably good schools, and certainly if you went to college, chances are this book and other resources like it can indeed be of great value to you.

You are among the half or so of the population who can use their minds to better themselves, perhaps in all seven areas—mental, physical, family, social, spiritual, career, and financial. You have the ability to summon the requisite motivation to overcome the challenges and road blocks in your path on the road to attaining much of what you want.

As Nicholas Lemann points out in *Atlantic Monthly* (February, 1994), however,

> If motivation to succeed really was both measurable and teachable, it could help people for whom both high educational performance and bare-knuckles money making are unattainable—people with different values, or inconvenient backgrounds, or unruly life trajectories. The benefits in individual happiness, social peace, and economic productivity would be worthy of serious national discussion...

Lemann goes on to say that the only national form in which such discussion seems to occur is in infomercials.

This We Know

What can safely be surmised so far is this:

➤ Simply by picking up this book, the odds are overwhelming that you're in the top half of the pack—among those individuals who can use his or her mind to achieve what you conceive.

➤ A measurable and teachable motivational system has yet to be implemented and demonstrated on a wide basis.

Mentally Related Goal Ideas

How does it feel to be one of the fortunate people? Because you have the power to set and achieve mental goals as well as other goals, you might appreciate this list of goal ideas:

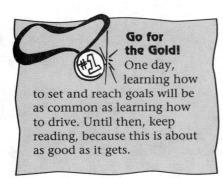

Go for the Gold!
One day, learning how to set and reach goals will be as common as learning how to drive. Until then, keep reading, because this is about as good as it gets.

Uh-Oh!
A classic—something that everybody wants to have read and nobody wants to read.
—Mark Twain

➤ To improve my mind by reading great literature
➤ To tap the powers of my innate intelligence
➤ To be a confident decision maker
➤ To learn from today's great thinkers
➤ To learn from the great thinkers of history
➤ To apply clear thinking in tough business situations
➤ To easily draw from my analytical thought processes
➤ To be self-directed
➤ To channel my creativity in positive ways
➤ To draw on ideas and innovations from other fields
➤ To use my creativity to handle challenging situations
➤ To enroll in a course on…
➤ To tap the full powers of my imagination
➤ To be more creative each day
➤ To be totally focused on the present
➤ To be more understanding of those less fortunate

Making Your Mind Work For You

Have you ever wondered why you chose previous goals? Psychology holds that there are three elements to any behavioral change: antecedents, an action or behavior itself, and the consequences of that action or behavior.

You have a question (an antecedent) that you think a friend can answer. You send an e-mail to the friend (a behavior), and you receive a reply (a consequence).

A Continuing Chain

Your behavior, in its most simple description, is a continuing chain of antecedents that lead to behaviors that lead to consequences. You're driving along on the road, and you see a stop sign (an antecedent), so you stop (behavior). As a consequence, you don't get into an accident, you don't get arrested for rolling through the stop sign, and you contribute in a small part to a smooth, functioning traffic plan.

Take the same situation and alter your behavior. You come to a stop sign, and instead of stopping, you roll through it. What are the consequences? Possibly, there will be no consequences. Maybe no one was around, so you save a couple of seconds and continue on your way. Or, you get into a serious accident. Or, a police officer across the street sees you, stops you, gives you a ticket, and you lose your license.

Identifiable Patterns

When you think back through everything major you've accomplished in your life (making the decision to go to college, getting your first job, getting married, and picking up this book), you will find that everything you've done essentially follows the pattern of antecedent, behavior, and consequence.

When the consequences turn out to be good, your experience can be an antecedent for other people. The date of the final exam is announced, for example. So, you begin studying one week in advance, take the test, and as a consequence, ace it. Your roommate sees what happened, and the next time he has a test, he emulates your behavior and does well.

For Sure

Virtually all best-selling how-to books attain that lofty status because, on some level, great masses of buyers believe the author has been down the path of success and can share critical knowledge that will enable them to achieve success as well.

When books such as *The Seven Habits of Highly Successful People*, *The Road Less Traveled*, and *What Color Is Your Parachute?* keep selling for more than a decade, chances are they'll continue to sell far into the next decade, if not longer—the A→B→C is well established.

So, now you know that virtually every goal you've ever set and every goal you will set is based on some antecedent.

What's Your Antecedent?

Traditionally, authors and goal-setting gurus have pontificated that you engage in goal-setting behavior based on opportunities you envision or pain you want to avoid. Opportunity and fear of pain are the two fundamental antecedents to engaging in behavior that leads to goal achievement. To understand these antecedents more fully, however, you need to look at the nuances—something that most books routinely fail to do.

Intertwined Motivation

The notion of gain is multifaceted, for example. Meanwhile, the avoidance of pain can show up in so many forms that it would take an entire book to elaborate on all of them. Gain and pain often are intertwined as well in ways you don't even realize. If one of your mental goals is to earn a doctorate or Ph.D., for example, it might be for any one of these reasons:

➤ To improve your mind

➤ To be recognized as an expert

➤ To enhance your employment opportunities

➤ To get an increase in pay

➤ To work with some of the top minds in the field

➤ To gain a teaching position

➤ To rise to prominence in your field

At the same time, however, a variety of avoidance-of-pain type goals might be part of the mix. These could include the following reasons:

➤ To avoid missing out on income opportunities

➤ To keep your spouse from being the only one in the family with a Ph.D.

➤ To not disappoint your parents who always wanted this for you and would be crushed if you didn't get it

➤ To gain respect because the only people in your field taken seriously have a doctorate

➤ To proceed now, because if you don't, you are concerned that you never will

➤ To feel adequate, because you feel lacking without one

Perhaps your motivation stems from your perception that everyone expects you to get a Ph.D. Maybe you want people to call you "Doctor." Or, perhaps you want a Ph.D. simply because you know there is someone out there who is convinced you can't do it.

Choosing the Positive Reasons

For any goal you set, in any arena, it's to your *extreme advantage* to understand from a pain or avoidance-of-pain standpoint why you choose what you choose. I know a woman who decided to get a master's degree because her husband had one. She didn't necessarily need it—she was already doing quite well. Indeed, after she earned the degree, her annual salary didn't change much.

Her husband didn't regard her as any less intelligent than himself; in many respects, he thought her to be much more brilliant. During the time she was studying for the degree, she was generally miserable. She was always tired and frequently doubted the course she had chosen.

As it turned out, getting the degree didn't resolve any of the concerns she was trying to address—primarily because she had never precisely identified the positive reasons for pursuing her goal.

All Too True

You've undoubtedly seen this scenario played out time and time again. People set goals and actually achieve them, but because they didn't mentally identify the positive aspects of why they sought to achieve those goals, the achievement seemed hollow.

Hereafter, for whatever goals you choose to pursue, engage in the mental exercise of identifying the highly positive aspects of achieving it. This will keep you on target and give you a more enjoyable experience along the way and after you reach your goal. Chapter 13, "It's All in the Wording," explores this concept in depth.

Don't Play Games with Your Mind

People often pursue a goal they know they won't be able to attain. Therefore, they settle for achieving a small part of their goal instead of the entire original goal. Such advice has found its way into many books and articles on goal setting. The underlying premise is that if you reach for the stars, even if you miss them, you still may reach the moon.

There are so many problems with this approach that I don't know where to begin. First, if you set a goal that is too challenging, you run a much greater risk of abandoning the goal because you instinctively realize that any energy or effort you expend will be futile.

Uh-Oh!
Is that all there is? Is that all there is? If that's all there is, then let's keep dancing. Let's break out the booze and have a ball, if that's all there is.
—from the 1960 hit song *Is That All There Is?* by Peggy Lee

A Less Than Satisfactory Conclusion

What's worse is that in your attempt to reach the stars, even if you end up beyond where you were before, it may be undesirable or less satisfactory than ending up where an attained goal would have placed you.

Feet on the Ground, Eyes on the Stars

I suspect that authors who recommend making reach-for-the-stars types of goals have never actually set and reached such goals for themselves. I have the privilege of knowing scores of highly successful people around the world. None of them has any particular reach-for-the-stars goals. Their goals are challenging but are reachable, are quantifiable, and have timelines.

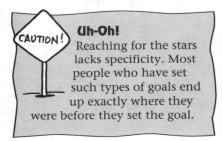

Uh-Oh!
Reaching for the stars lacks specificity. Most people who have set such types of goals end up exactly where they were before they set the goal.

Paradoxically, in their pursuit of these appropriately set goals, many of them have reached the stars. In other words, as you proceed in the direction in which your goal takes you, sometimes you end up with the pleasant experience of achieving far more and at a far greater pace than you had anticipated.

Learn from your experiences, and as you set new goals, factor in what you've learned. Don't fall prey to the trap of so overreaching your grasp that the predictable outcome is no progress at all.

Attending College in Your Car

One of the most brilliant ideas I have encountered for attaining mental-related goals involves making great use of your drive time or commute time. If you drive to work, there are many things you can do to support mental goals you have chosen.

Go for the Gold!
Of course, you have the option of wearing headphones if you take the bus or subway. Or, if you carpool, you can hold mini-discussion groups on the way to and from work.

Install a CD or cassette player in your car to control your environment to and from work. When it comes to cassettes, you have five broad-based areas from which to choose:

➤ You can listen to books on tape via subscription or by visiting your local bookstore. Or, you can check out your local library, which also may offer lectures and plays as well.

➤ You can listen to cassettes on a variety of topics, such as self-improvement, leadership, sales, and career advancement. SkillPath, Nightingale-Conant, and Dartnell are the leading producers in this category.

➤ You can learn a foreign language by listening to tapes such as those by SyberVision and Berlitz.

➤ You can keep up with the latest business books and articles summarized by such groups as ExecuTrak and Audio-Tech Business Book Summaries.

➤ Of course, you can simply listen to music—any music that relaxes you or puts you in a desirable mental and emotional state.

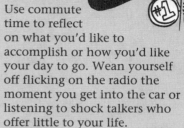

Go for the Gold!
Use commute time to reflect on what you'd like to accomplish or how you'd like your day to go. Wean yourself off flicking on the radio the moment you get into the car or listening to shock talkers who offer little to your life.

In a little more than a year, you could achieve the equivalent of having audited five college courses or an entire semester. The beauty of such an experience is that you get to pick what you want to hear; you make an otherwise meaningless commute worthwhile; and there are no quizzes, term papers, or final exams.

Obviously, when the mood suits you, you also have the option of driving in silence.

The Least You Need to Know

➤ Nature may play a larger role in influencing your future success in life than was previously thought.

➤ The fact that you picked up and are reading this book actually is one of the strongest indicators that you have the ability to set and achieve worthwhile goals.

➤ Opportunity and fear of pain are the two fundamental motivators for choosing goals. These two factors often are intertwined in ways you don't even realize.

➤ Learn from your experiences, and as you set new goals, factor in what you've learned. Don't fall prey to so overreaching your grasp that the predictable outcome is no progress at all.

➤ If you commute 25 minutes daily, in 11 weeks, you could listen to the equivalent of a college course via cassette.

Chapter 6

Let's Get Physical

In This Chapter

➤ Checking up and checking out

➤ Get your motor running

➤ A lean, mean, fighting machine

➤ Fitness on the run

Where are you physically? What are your goals for your physical well-being? Do you have a trim, toned body that serves you well, or are you huffing and puffing after one flight of stairs? Do you get home at the end of the workday feeling like you've got a lot more day to go, or do you park yourself in front of the TV at around 7 p.m. for an extended couch-potato session? In this chapter, I get to the heart of some nagging, pervasive issues when it comes to fitness and how you can more easily build a better you!

Checking Up on Yourself

Regardless of your age and level of fitness, the first order of business for you when it comes to setting and reaching physical goals is to get a comprehensive health checkup.

For Sure

If you're between 20 and 35, and you haven't had a complete physical exam recently, it's probably no big deal. Don't delay, however: Get a checkup within the next month. If you're 40 or over, and you haven't had a checkup for a while, put down the book right now, and schedule one for the next week or as soon as possible. Why? You need a baseline at which to begin, and the information generated is so basic and so vital, it is unwise to go much longer without it.

Under or Over 40?

For those under 40, many experts advise that a checkup every five years or so should be adequate. For those over 40 and certainly over 45, a biannual checkup is just about mandatory, and an annual checkup is not a bad idea. For women, obvious concerns regarding breast and ovarian cancer and for men, concerns about prostate cancer all but necessitate that you get yourself to your doctor's office as soon as possible.

A blood test certainly is standard procedure for such a checkup. Miraculously, blood tests reveal much, and all you did was suffer a pin prick for a couple of seconds. Also, make sure that the exam you get is comprehensive. You'll want to get on the treadmill so that your doctor or healthcare provider has a more well-rounded view of the state of your physical being.

An Operating Plan

Based on the results of your test, you'll have an operating game plan that includes the most appropriate goals to set regarding your physical well being. If you have a high cholesterol count, for example, a change of diet is in order. If your breathing capacity is poor because you are a smoker, a serious dialogue with yourself about quitting smoking is in order.

Do It Yourself

In addition to having a comprehensive physical checkup, at any time along your life's trail, and at least on a monthly basis, check yourself out as well. This is more mental than physical, but it aids in your physical well being enormously. Sit in a comfortable area where it's quiet and you won't be disturbed. Then, starting at the top of your head, working all the way down to your toes, think about each area of your body and how it is functioning. Starting with your head, ask yourself questions such as these:

➤ Am I experiencing any pressures or pains at the top of my head right now?

➤ Do I have frequent headaches at work or after work?

➤ Do I experience dizziness?

Take Notes

Keep a pen and paper nearby so that you can mark down anything you notice during this mental inventory of your physical well being. Although some aspects of this mental checkup might seem obvious, too often, in this rush, rush world, you can forget about or—worse—ignore minor ailments or physical irregularities and later find that the situation has escalated into something of greater concern. As you move down your body, continue to ask yourself questions such as these:

➤ Do I feel pressure in my forehead, such as sinus pressure?

➤ Are my eyes clear and white or tired and red?

➤ Am I breathing easy or am I congested?

➤ Do I feel any tension in my jaw or mouth area?

➤ Is my neck area tight? If you work at a desk with a PC, chances are the back of your neck is as taut as piano wire. The same may be likely for the inverted Y that starts at the back of your neck and extends out to each shoulder.

➤ Do I feel any tension in my upper back?

➤ Do I feel any pain in my lower back?

Moving down to the lower half of your body, are there any unusual feelings or sensations? Any pains or issues over which you are concerned?

Think about your thighs, knees, calves, shins, and ankles. Are you experiencing any soreness, aches, or pains? Move farther down to your feet, including your heels, your arch, and the tips of your toes. Once again, mark down anything that seems even a tad out of the ordinary. Now, do one more sweep based on observable characteristics. Do you see any rashes, discolorations, apparent bruises, red or purple blotches, or sores that haven't healed?

A Mini-Inventory

Essentially, you've completed a mini-inventory that will have great value when you bring it in to see your doctor at checkups or other times. After all, it's so easy to be focused on some acute physical pain, while letting longer-term, more insidious conditions fall by the wayside.

Rounding Out Your Activities

While you're in this physical-inspection mode, make an appointment with your eye doctor if you haven't done so recently, and then do the same with your dentist. Pay the extra amount to have the complete checkups done so that when you leave, you know all you can about your physical condition. With your eye doctor, get the glaucoma test. With your dentist, get the oral cancer test. Spend a few extra minutes this time talking with these professionals about what you should be doing between visits, given your age and overall health.

The Best Get Rest

Whether you're still in college, on your first job, the veteran in your organization, or running your own business, chances are you've been physically taxing yourself and not getting the proper rest and relaxation. What are your goals in relation to getting the sleep you need?

Suppose that you average eight hours of sleep per night. If you were born 100 years earlier, chances are you'd get 10 hours of sleep. People used to go to bed soon after dark. Then they would get up at dawn. Electric lights, radio alarm clocks, television, and crazy work schedules have irrevocably changed that way of life.

For Sure

Around the turn of the century, the typical American man and woman got 20 percent more sleep than the typical adult in the late 1990s. This is a remarkable and potentially devastating change in the span of 100 years. The National Commission on Sleep Disorders Research reveals that approximately 60 million Americans have some form of chronic sleep deprivation and that too little sleep is the primary cause of health problems in America.

To Sleep, Per Chance to Function

The connection between an adequate amount of sleep and your proper physical and mental functioning is so strong that you simply cannot ignore it.

While you're sleeping, your body distributes 70 percent of the human growth hormone that you need each day. This hormone helps build muscles and bones, repairs your skin, and better prepares you to fire on all cylinders. Lack of sleep contributes to a decrease in your physical abilities. You won't be able to move as quickly, lift as much, or have the endurance you would otherwise. In one university study, otherwise healthy men who missed a significant portion of their nightly sleep produced fewer disease-fighting immune cells. In another study, people who slept less than four hours per night had a higher blood pressure reading than normal the next day.

Although the effects of sleep deprivation on blood pressure are still hotly debated, why would you want to take chances? I say err on the side of caution—get sufficient sleep each night.

For Sure

In *Sleep Thieves*, Stanley Coren, Ph.D., theorizes that chronic fatigue may have contributed to the space shuttle *Challenger* disaster on January 28, 1986. The severely sleep-deprived staff was unable to focus on crucial details, such as not to launch in very cold weather, which may have led to the tragic mid-air explosion. Coren also found that two managers in essential positions who were part of a prelaunch meeting the night before had slept less than three hours the night before the meeting and at the time of the meeting had been awake for more than 18 hours straight.

Macho Man, Iron Woman

For whatever reason, too many people seek to prove that they can get by on less sleep. In the 1960s and '70s, the Soviet Union attempted a variety of experiments to reduce the typical eight-hour requirement for sleep down to two or three hours. Test subjects were wired so that researchers could monitor brain waves and brain activity. The experiments failed miserably.

Among some high achievers, it is at least a dubious distinction to claim to get by on less sleep. Thomas Edison was one of the pioneers when it came to making these claims. Edison frequently told reporters that he got by on very little sleep each night. Later, this was proven to be untrue.

Uh-Oh!
When you attempt to alter the basic functioning of your body, you're playing a fool's game. If you try to talk faster, walk faster, eat faster, sleep less, or engage in any other basic activity at a frequency or duration that is not comfortable or suitable for you, you'll run into problems.

I can't speak for Eastern societies, but in Western societies, having to get sufficient sleep each night is almost seen as a sign of weakness—as if only wimps need to bed down at a reasonable hour.

Weekends in the Sack

If you are a parent of a young child or are in a demanding job, you might try to catch up on sleep on the weekends. Granted, if you're chronically sleep deprived, any immediate sleep you can get will be a benefit. However, sleeping late on Saturdays or Sundays, holidays, or sick days in general is no more beneficial than, say, having more heart beats on those days or breathing more.

What is the best way to give your body the sleep you need so that you can function at peak physical capacity and increase your long-term mental alertness and stamina? You guessed it: Getting good sleep on a regular basis.

Sleep-Related Goals

If you haven't set goals in this area before, here are some suggestions:

➤ Assuming that eight hours plus or minus an hour is the right amount of sleep for you each night, how about choosing to get a sufficient night's sleep at least five nights out of seven starting this week?

➤ If you've been cheating yourself of sleep for days, weeks, or months on end, why not choose to devote an entire Saturday or Sunday to staying in bed all day? Give your body's systems a chance to engage in some form of repair. You can't "catch up" all in one day or in one weekend, but you can do yourself a world of good.

➤ In as little as one month of practicing a desirable and appropriate sleep pattern, you can emerge feeling like an entirely new person.

A New Lease on Your Physical Life

A minor miracle may occur in your life at the end of one month after you've given yourself the sleep you need and certainly deserve. Your motivation to accomplish the goals you set in terms of your physical being, as well as in all the other major goal areas, may take on a new intensity.

Uh-Oh!
As you deprive yourself of adequate sleep on a long-term basis, the magnitude and quality of your goals may inexorably begin to diminish. And, in your sleep-deprived haze, you might not even notice.

What are some activities you might want to engage in to support your newly made goals regarding sleep? I suggest the following as possibilities:

➤ Go down to the bedding store and buy a new mattress with the latest innovations designed to ensure the highest probability of a complete, restful night of sleep.

➤ Safeguard your room from outside and surrounding noises. Close the window and turn on the air conditioner to benefit from the white-noise hum.

➤ Let others in your household know that you're retiring for the evening and do not want to be disturbed.

➤ One evening each week, go to bed as early as 8:30 p.m.

➤ Turn off the ringer on your phone and let your answering machine handle calls after you've gone to bed.

Is There More of You?

Over the last several decades, more and more Americans have become obese. In addition, many more people are simply overweight and not fit. As the population in general grows ever heavier, height and weight charts that show norms among populations have become more or less useless.

Weight Watchers International, a company with a vested interest in having people lose weight, reports that one-third of the American population today is obese—more than, say, 15 percent to 20 percent overweight. Linda Webb Carilli, General Manager, Corporate Affairs, Weight Watchers International says,

> "Research shows that obesity increases the risk for disabling and life-threatening chronic diseases, including diabetes, hypertension, heart disease, and some cancers. There is overwhelming scientific consensus that achieving and maintaining a healthy weight, or at a minimum preventing further weight gain, should be a national public-health priority."

For Sure

Weight Watchers reports that obesity costs the nation more than $100 billion annually and causes the premature death of approximately 300,000 people each year. "There's indisputable evidence that being obese is unhealthy," says Linda Carilli. She observes that the public often is confused about this serious health issue. A very small percentage of people may be both fat and fit, but most people who are fat are out of shape and unhealthy, says Carilli. Obesity is one of the most rapidly growing health problems in this country.

Losing Weight By Having Fun

If it has been a continuing wish or desire of yours to get back into shape (notice that I didn't say *goal*, because you probably have not approached it yet by using the goal-setting procedures discussed earlier in this book), perhaps the most important element to your future success is to look for ways to make achieving the goal fun. If you regard working out as drudgery, don't do it. There are other ways to get to your chosen weight. Here are some ideas for achieving your targeted weight in a manner you can sustain:

➤ Look for little ways all day long to engage in a few moments of exercise. Park your car a block or two away from a store you're going to, for example. If you're in a mall parking lot, park at the far end of the lot and walk the two to three blocks.

➤ If you use public transportation, get off the bus or subway one stop or a few blocks before you normally would, and walk the rest of the way.

➤ If you're in a high-rise building, take the stairs whenever you're heading down to the bottom. Also, take the stairs if you're only going up one floor or two.

➤ Get in the habit of taking a walk before and after each meal, even if it's just for a couple of minutes. You'll feel the difference, and after a while, you'll begin to notice the difference.

➤ Enroll in an exercise course with a friend. That way, you'll reinforce each other, attend more regularly, and stay the whole time. Don't start off with something rigorous—even simple stretches will do for openers.

➤ Investigate courses you might not have considered previously, such as yoga, tai chi, belly dancing, power walking, or water calisthenics.

➤ If you watch television regularly, get in the habit of doing some kind of exercise while you watch. With all those exercise machines being advertised on infomercials, perhaps you'll find something that will be fun and enjoyable for you.

For Sure

In many communities throughout the U.S., there are stores called *Play It Again Sports* where used equipment is offered for sale. The advantage of shopping in such stores is that you can survey and sample a variety of exercise devices, purchase equipment in excellent working condition at half or less than the original price, and start using it that evening. If it turns out the equipment isn't right for you, you can go back to the same store, which almost always will buy it back from you (obviously, at a lower price so that they can make a profit when they resell it). You then have the opportunity to try something else.

Come-Ons You Should Ignore

Consistently losing one pound a week is no easy feat. That would mean four pounds in a month and perhaps as many as eight pounds in two months. Don't be fooled by the infomercials, advertisements, and just plain come-ons. When you see a parade of people come up to a microphone and say how they lost eight pounds in the first four days or six pounds in the first week, switch the channel. Most of this loss is water.

You don't need to be conned like the masses. Annually, just in America, as many as 120 diets are published. If the diet books were effective, only three or four would need to be published, and then everyone could simply buy those, follow what's said, and achieve their goals. Then, every few years, this handful of books could be updated as new breakthroughs in research are achieved.

> **Uh-Oh!**
> It is not healthy or desirable to lose weight too fast. Those who engage in crash course weight loss are most susceptible to putting that weight back on just as quickly, and then some. People who have lost 40 or 50 pounds often turn around months later and add 60 or 70 pounds.

Honoring the Basic Equation

No, my friend, you don't need to watch infomercials or even buy a book about dieting. Just keep in mind the basic equation that governs the weight of each and every creature on Earth: To maintain your weight, simply eat an amount of calories equal to the number of calories you burn.

To reduce your weight or, in goal-setting terminology, to achieve your target weight, you need to burn more calories each day than you ingest.

Remember that an incremental approach is desirable even if your results are anything but incremental.

When it comes to weight loss, your results probably will not be incremental. As your metabolism changes and your body receives less calories than it's burning on any given day, at first, your attempts to lose weight will be stymied. For a week or two, you might realize no weight loss. Yet, as you're throwing your hands up in despair (not a bad gesture, because it's a form of exercise), take heart. Your body is readjusting to the new you, and soon enough, you'll see progress.

> **For Sure**
> Physiologically, what happens when you initiate a weight-loss campaign is almost beyond belief. Your body—the product of millions of years of human physiology—retains calories when it senses that there might be a food shortage or drought. As time passes and you consistently burn more calories than you consume, your body is forced to surrender part of its stored fat.

71

Slow and Sure Weight Loss

Suppose that you start consuming less calories. Your body goes into conservation mode saying, "Hmmm, Jeff isn't eating as much as usual; I'd better hang on to what we have, because there could be some tough times ahead." Each day, week after week, as Jeff burns more calories than he eats, his body gradually draws on the fat reserves available to maintain proper functioning.

If you sustain the pace for one or two months, eating healthy, taking vitamins, and burning more calories than you ingest, you'll find that reducing is not the ominous, near-impossible task everyone makes it out to be.

Indeed, you can get to the point where it even becomes fun.

Fun? Good God, are you nuts, man? Yes! Fun! It all depends on what your goals are.

Let the Fun Begin!

If your goal is to reach your target weight in six months, and you're making tremendous progress by the third, I assure you that many aspects of your pursuit will seem like fun:

➤ It's fun to have your clothes start to fit again, or, when you've reached your goal, to go shopping for entirely new clothes.

➤ It's fun to get admiring glances from people who didn't previously offer them.

➤ It's fun to have more energy, to feel more fit, and to feel more in control of your life.

➤ It's fun to gather up an armload of diet books and drop them all into the recycling bin.

Looking Forward to Hunger Pangs

Any goal for your physical well being is achieved through both physical and mental means. For the few times each year when I gain five to seven unwanted pounds, beyond doing all the things I described in this chapter so far, I look forward to hunger pangs. Don't start making rash judgments here—I'm not masochistic.

A hunger pang signifies that your body is burning fat and relying on stored glycogen for fuel. It's taking from your fat reserve, which is overstocked anyway, to supply your needs of the moment. If I'm on a several-week campaign to get back down to fighting weight, I look forward to a hunger pang at least once every two days. No, I don't formally list this as one of my goals, but it's certainly a reinforcer (more on goal reinforcement in Chapter 21, "Steering Clear of Barriers").

I also use visualization, which is covered in detail in Chapter 19, "Visualization Techniques." If I'm tipping the scale a little too high, I envision myself as a slim, trim whippet dashing up to the stage as I'm about to give a speech. Visualization, as you will see, is powerful and can accelerate your goal progress.

Note: After finishing this chapter, if you want to skip to the chapter on visualization, be my guest. (Just be sure to go back later and read the other chapters!)

Physical Goals Worth Attaining

Near the end of my speaking presentations, I often urge my audiences to set physical goals. Anyone is likely set a goal for income or savings. How many people actually form comprehensive physical goals to be achieved one year or maybe two years from now?

What would you like your blood pressure to be six months from now? This assumes that you know what it is now, of course. There are steps you can take over the course of six months to lower your blood pressure. This includes making changes to your diet, taking vitamin supplements, and getting regular exercise.

Another possible goal is to become pill free if you currently take various medications. (Don't forsake anything currently essential for your well being!) Obviously, you're going to have to consult your doctor or health professional. Nevertheless, wouldn't it be wonderful if you no longer had to take such and such tablet every day? Sure it would.

Guess what? In many cases, a natural food supplement can supply many of the same things you're getting from prescribed medications.

I find that, for me, the lady who manages the vitamin section of the Wellspring Grocery in Chapel Hill (I call her the Vitamin Lady) has the answers I need in regard to vitamins and food supplements.

Whatever you do, get sound advice from someone who knows what he or she is talking about. If you're seeking to get off a certain medication, consult with a doctor who understands the ramifications.

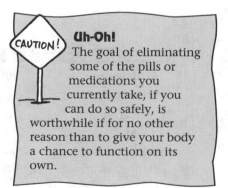

Go for the Gold!
You can set all kinds of physical goals that are challenging and reachable, definitely quantifiable, and most assuredly subject to some timeline.

Uh-Oh!
Men's Health magazine (August, 1997) reports that 78 percent of the nation's medical schools don't require students to study nutrition. Shocking, just shocking.

Uh-Oh!
The goal of eliminating some of the pills or medications you currently take, if you can do so safely, is worthwhile if for no other reason than to give your body a chance to function on its own.

Human nutrition is as complicated a subject as rocket science. Every day, a new study is conducted or a breakthrough happens that supersedes and in some cases directly contradicts what was concluded earlier.

Too often, the common remedy for curing what ails you is to take a pill. One hundred years ago, if people ate something that disagreed with them, do you know what they did?

I'll give you a couple of seconds to formulate your answer. Ready? They didn't eat that item again. Today, not only do people eat the item again, but they also take some antacid to try to diminish the effects of their dietary sin. They don't realize the logic of avoiding what does not agree with them.

Go for the Gold! It's time to choose new goals about your physical well being, what you consume, and why.

Commercials routinely suggest that you can have whatever you want for lunch, just as long as you make sure that you take their product afterward. How utterly and amazingly absurd. Why would you do that to yourself? Why would you fall prey to such advertising?

Miles to Go Before the End

Society has come a long way in the last 200 years. The U.S. Constitution was written by men, for example—young men. Life expectancy in the 1760s, '70s, and '80s was barely 40. Yeah, there were some old-timers around, such as Ben Franklin and a few others, but on average, the founding fathers were very young by today's standards.

Whether you're in your 20s or your 60s, chances are you're going to live far longer on average than you currently think. Breakthroughs in medical science already are in the pipeline that all but guarantee it. Heck, at 40, you're probably not even halfway through your life.

The following chart shows the ages of some professional athletes who are still valuable to their respective teams at 40 or beyond.

Professional Athletes at Advancing Ages (as of January 1997)

Athlete	Sport	Team	Age
Clay Matthews	Football	Atlanta Falcons	40
Warren Moon	Football	Seattle Seahawks	40
Joe Mullen	Hockey	Pittsburgh Penguins	40
Paul Molitor	Baseball	Minnesota Twins	40
Dennis Martinez	Baseball	Cleveland Indians	41
Dennis Eckersley	Baseball	St. Louis Cardinals	42
Rick Honeycutt	Baseball	St. Louis Cardinals	42
Rob Parish	Basketball	Chicago Bulls	43

Even if you're heavier than you care to be, you're depriving yourself of sleep, and you're failing to set appropriate physical goals, chances are you've got many more years to go. Why not have them be highly productive, vibrant years, almost all the way through to the end? It's within your capability, and I'm hoping that after finishing this chapter, it will be one of your goals.

The Least You Need to Know

➤ You probably need to get a checkup, and if you're over age 40, get one right away.

➤ Taking a personal inventory of how you feel from head to toe is helpful before getting a checkup.

➤ You're not getting enough sleep and you need to rectify this starting tonight.

➤ It's possible but unlikely to be both fit and fat. To reach a target weight, start an exercise program that is fun for you.

➤ You have the opportunity to set physical goals such as the blood pressure, waistline, or hours of sleep you want to achieve.

Chapter 7

Goals for Family Life

In This Chapter

➤ Children need parents

➤ An institution in transition

➤ Strengthening the family unit

In her book *The Art of the Fresh Start*, Glenna Salisbury begins her acknowledgment with a memorable phrase. She says, "Love fires my life and I have been surrounded by an abundance of supply of this precious commodity." She is referring largely to her family. Unfortunately, many people don't have that experience. Moreover, unless you've been working in the far reaches of Antarctica for the last several decades, you might have noticed fundamental changes in families all around you. The once-traditional single bread winner in the family and the mother who stays home and raises two children is all but a memory. Today, this structure represents less than seven percent of all households.

Whether your family fits the traditional pattern or represents something new, in this chapter, you'll get a lot of goal-related ideas to improve the quality and overall health and well-being of your family and family relationships.

The Data Is In

Studies commissioned by the U.S. Department of Health, Education, and Welfare—as well as studies by a host of other organizations—indicate that boys and girls grow up with the best chance of succeeding in life when they have two loving, caring parents. Certainly, a single parent raising children can do a wonderful job. Many single parents perform everyday acts of heroism when you consider all they do.

Suppose that you are married and have children, are married and will have children, were married and have children, or will be married and contemplate having children sometime in the future. With that in mind, what kind of family goals do you have and what type of goals might be appropriate for the whole family—where every member gets to have some input?

An Interrelationship

Go for the Gold! Any financial goals you choose to pursue for you and your family should be initiated as early as possible. All benefits, including compound interest, accumulating principal, and even the discipline to start saving and investing in this manner are all facilitated when you begin at as young an age as possible.

Let's take the first issue first. Many of the goals you have for your family life are likely interrelated with the other major goal areas of your life. One of your goals might be to provide for your children's education, for example, to buy a new home, and to be able to retire with grace and ease when the time comes (these financial considerations are covered in abundance in Chapter 11, "Now for the Biggie: Your Financial Life").

If your child is in grade school now, and you want to be able to send him or her to college, it will be much easier if you start early. If your child is 13 years old and you have five years to save, in order to accumulate a given sum, you'll have to put away three times or more the amount you would if you started when your child was 3 years old. Hey, it's just the way time and money work.

A More Active Interest

Suppose that your goal is to take a more active interest in your family's activities. This means spending more time with them, actually conveying your interest, being a good listener, and so on. Many people say they want to be more involved with their family—they want to spend more time with their son or their daughter.

The reality for some parents, however, is much different. On some days, if they're lucky, they catch the last 10 minutes of their daughter's recital, spend a scant three minutes per day actually listening to their spouse, barely know their son, and so on. Is any of this slightly familiar to you? I'm guessing that it is.

As you learned in Chapter 4, "The Seven Basic Goal Categories," the key to pursuing goals in a variety of areas is balance. Nowhere is this more clear than when in pursuit of family goals, because your family members are more likely than others to let you know when you're not keeping your word.

The Family That Plays Together

Another common goal area is family vacations. How often would you like to go away with your family? Once a year, twice a year, quarterly, monthly, perhaps even biweekly? Suppose that your goal is to take an extended vacation of between three and six days quarterly. Perhaps during each of the eight other months in which this time away is not taken, you also want to go on at least one weekend venture.

Reaching this goal involves a good deal of planning—making reservations, coordinating schedules, allocating funds, ensuring that projects and tasks at work are taken care of well in advance of departure dates, and coordinating your children's academic schedules and other responsibilities accordingly.

Family Dynamics

In many respects, how your family operates is representative of how your life operates. Do you want your children to greet you enthusiastically when they come back from visiting friends or participating in some after-school activity? If they don't regularly do this, you might want to set a goal of greeting them daily or at some other interval with open arms when you return from work or time away.

Assuming that you've married the right person, if he or she hasn't been responsive lately, perhaps it's because you haven't been communicative. In essence, when you draw up a list of the things that aren't necessarily working in your family, and hence those areas for which you choose to establish goals, often what you find is that *your own behavior and mindset* are what needs changing first.

Before a person can be motivated or changed, that person must contain the seeds of change or the desire to move. Without this, it's tough to get anybody to revise his or her approach to life.

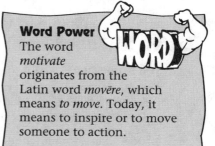

Uh-Oh!
Modern psychology holds that you can't really change someone else's behavior. As much as you think you can motivate and inspire somebody to do something, all you can do is plant the seed and hope that it grows.

Word Power
The word *motivate* originates from the Latin word *movēre*, which means *to move*. Today, it means to inspire or to move someone to action.

Changes Within

You have nearly unlimited leeway when it comes to making changes within. As you've already learned, you have the opportunity at any time to set goals unlike those you've ever set before. You have the chance to set goals that enable you to head in an entirely new direction.

Denis Waitely, in *The Psychology of Winning*, says that although you never outgrow certain types of behaviors you learn when very young, you can uncover new directions in which to move. Think of yourself in a vise that leaves you very little room for maneuvering. Trying to move left or right is futile, but you might be able to move up and down quite freely due to the fashion in which the vise is constructed.

Maybe you'll never be the type of parent who comes home at the end of the day with boundless energy, all smiles and hugs and ready to play with your children until their bedtime. However, even if you've been a stick in the mud to this point, there is certainly some room for you to expand your range of behaviors with your children. Perhaps you can play some of their favorite video games with them. Perhaps you can engage in riddles, shared storytelling, or something they enjoy and that will spark laughter and mirth.

> **CAUTION!** **Uh-Oh!**
> *I can govern the United States or I can govern my daughter Alice, but I can't do both.*
> —Theodore Roosevelt

If your goal is to be more responsive to each member of your family, there are a variety of activities you can engage in that will help make this so. The following sections present just a few suggestions among thousands of possibilities. Although all the suggestions and ideas for goal-setting are in relation to your children, with a twist and a turn, they could be applied to your spouse as well.

Applaud Accomplishments

If your child comes home from school with an A on a spelling test or a piece of artwork he or she is particularly proud of, seize the moment. Pick up the item, look it over carefully, ask questions about it, and show interest.

It's not that difficult to show interest in something your son or daughter brings you. In fact, it's a most worthwhile goal for many reasons. It tells your children that you're interested in them and that what they do is important. Most importantly, it tells your child that the next time they're taking a test or drawing a picture, they'll want to do their best because after all, Mom and Dad will see it.

Listen to Songs from Their Favorite CD

You might like classical music or rock 'n roll. Your kids might like heavy metal, hip hop, or God knows what. Is it too much to simply sit down with them for a few minutes and listen to two of their favorite songs, even if you're secretly thinking, "How can anybody buy that, let alone record it in the first place?"

Have you even wondered why teenagers in those jazzed-up cars play their music above the 100-decibel level? They really want others to hear what they're hearing. Music, and specifically lyrics, can reach deep into the human psyche. Why not establish a goal of listening to two of your children's songs at least once per week? Listening to music together, much like eating together, is a form of bonding. People seem to want others to hear what they hear and to enjoy what they enjoy.

Bring Them into Your Discussions

Suppose that you're talking with your spouse and your children are nearby. How often have you excluded them from the conversation as if they don't have a worthwhile opinion? As little as once a week, what if you were to say, "Mark, don't you feel that we…?" or "Allison, do you think if we were to…?"

After the initial shock wears off, you'll find that your children are quite pleased to be called on. In essence, what you're really doing is respecting them on the interpersonal level. You're saying that they're full-fledged human beings, even if they are smaller than you, and that they have opinions and observations that count.

I sometimes forget to bring my daughter (age 7) into conversations, but she often simply includes herself. At the perfect time, she'll ask, "Can I say something?" We'll pause, take a look at her, and in that split-second opening, she will just dive right in and speak her mind. I always let her proceed at this juncture, because she usually has something worthwhile to offer and has a right to be part of the conversation, at least occasionally.

The few times I have to say to her, "Valerie, I'm talking with so-and-so," she understands I mean that it's not a good time for her to chip in. Fortunately, these instances are few and far between.

Drop in on After-School Activities

I don't care how busy you are, how demanding your job is, or what a slave driver your boss is. At least once a month, you can drop in on your child for 10 minutes at some activity that he or she would love to have you see.

Visiting your child unannounced minimizes your child's need to have you around every minute you're at home and enables him or her to be more understanding when you're traveling. After all, if Dad or Mom drops in on me unexpectedly every now and then, they certainly love and care about me.

Maybe you'll be the only parent who does this, but so what? It's your family. Let others buy this book and come across the suggestion themselves. Why not set a goal to visit your child once each calendar month at a school or after-school activity and hey, if the spirit moves you, bring a camera along.

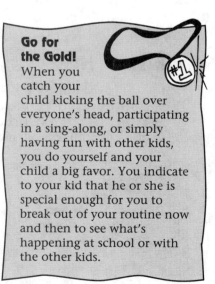

Go for the Gold!
When you catch your child kicking the ball over everyone's head, participating in a sing-along, or simply having fun with other kids, you do yourself and your child a big favor. You indicate to your kid that he or she is special enough for you to break out of your routine now and then to see what's happening at school or with the other kids.

Say Yes a Little More Often

Kids ask to do so many things that for many parents it almost becomes automatic to say no.

Can I stay up later? No.

Can I get some ice cream? No.

Can I go across the street with my friends? No.

Go for the Gold!
Why not set a goal of saying yes one more time per week than you would otherwise? This is not so hard to monitor, because you'll have to ponder the situation for at least a few seconds and realize that you're about to say yes when your instinct was to say no.

What's the real reason behind some of these refusals? Is it fear for their safety or well being? Do you think they'll be corrupted if some family rule is bent on one particular evening? Or are you just exercising authority the same way your parents did?

Often, we forget that although our rules are conceived with good intentions, some of them may be rather arbitrary. We don't have hard evidence that each of the rules in and of themselves creates a desired outcome—a goal we established for our family and specifically for our children. Hence, saying yes a little more often has its place.

If it helps, keep a running log of the times you surprised your child with a yes. At the least, you'll have ammunition for later when your child says you never say yes.

Seek Their Help

Do you have business and financial problems, and you don't think your children can be of much assistance? Think again—out of the mouths of babes sometimes come great ideas. In his book *A Whack on the Side of the Head*, Dr. Roger von Oeck contends that the solution to problems often comes by looking at a situation with creativity—taking a different view than you did before. Who better to help you than someone small who doesn't know all the givens of a situation?

Uh-Oh!
Of course, you don't want to cause your children anxiety or freak them out by making them think something terrible will happen if they can't help you solve a problem.

When it comes to using technology, one of my pet sayings is, "Always give a technical problem to a younger person." Perhaps your son or daughter has an insight or two you might never have considered. Perhaps what they say leads you to think about something else that leads to a solution. How often have you asked your children for some type of support? Could you ask this of them as least once a week?

Communicating Effectively

When you boil down the elements of a successful family, besides love, the most crucial element is effective communication. Without it, you and your family could be in for years of misunderstandings, hurt feelings, and even alienation from one another.

When it comes to dealing with your spouse, a growing body of evidence suggests that to be effective, you need to connect with your spouse so that he or she believes you're on his or her side. In other words, achieving the outcome you want often involves helping your spouse achieve the outcome he or she wants.

Go for the Gold! Regardless of whether you believe your children can help you with a particular issue, go ahead and ask them. You may be pleasantly surprised by what you discover. Kids often have more imagination and creativity than adults, so they could offer a new perspective.

Uncover Expectations

In his book *Relationship Strategies*, author Jim Cathcart says that most family conflicts revolve around misunderstandings regarding expectations:

> "I didn't know you expected me to..."

> "I didn't expect you to treat me..."

> and so on

When speaking of the Cold War, John F. Kennedy once said, "If we cannot now end our differences, at least we can help make the world safe for diversity." If you cannot end your family differences, at least you can help make your family a place that's safe for diversity.

Go for the Gold! It's all too easy to be the beacon of knowledge and understanding when you're on your own. Try it with members of your family if you really want to see how good you are. We all want to think that what we have to say is important, and we all need to have a forum in which we can air our views.

Cathcart observes that every relationship—whether or not within the family—has roles, responsibilities, and expectations, whether they are open and agreed on or lurking unstated on the outer edges of the relationship.

To avoid the conflicts that result from unequal expectations, write down the specific expectations of each person. If those expectations are agreed on, conflict resolution becomes fairly simple compared to continuing in the same old way and falling into the same old arguments.

Uplift Each Other

Dr. Leo Buscaglia gave a series of lectures on the general topic of love that were aired over the Public Broadcasting System in the 1980s. Many of his lectures offered poignant, family-oriented stories.

He told one story of his father coming home around the holidays and reporting to his family that he had lost his job. Papa was devastated. As it was, the family was barely making ends meet. Now they faced the prospect of no gifts to exchange, no money coming in for perhaps months, and potentially a miserable, cold winter. Each member of the family seemed to buck up, though, as if this was their chance to chip in and show Papa that feeding and clothing the family wasn't his responsibility alone. They had been through hard times before, and they would make it through this latest round of hard times.

That night, Mama returned from shopping with an array of food and cooked one of the biggest feasts of young Buscaglia's life. "Mama knew a secret," he said. "When it appears that life has otherwise got you down, that's the time to get up." That night, the Buscaglias had one of the most joyous dinners ever.

Sometimes, when things don't seem to be going so well, why not choose to celebrate what you do have, be it good health, a good home, or simply each other?

A More Satisfying Sex Life

Perhaps you need to have a more satisfying sex life with your spouse. Hey, lots of couples do. Here are some quick ideas that have worked for many couples and are bound to work for you.

Alternate Who's in Command

Choose a goal of alternating who gets to be in command perhaps for one evening of lovemaking every other week. In other words, one of you has to serve the other, fulfilling every wish. The other has to be very gracious as he or she accepts such devoted attention.

Get Kinky

If you haven't done anything kinky lately, or anything kinky at all, try it. May I suggest experimenting with bondage, something in the bathtub, or something in a closet? You figure out the details.

Bad Acting, No Plot. Who Cares!

Several soft-core adult videos are available at your local video store designed to arouse both men and women. You might start watching them while naked on a sheet on the floor or on a couch with the remote nearby, so that you can flick off the TV as the live action takes precedence over what's on the screen.

Auto Sex

Head out to the car one evening. I know, you haven't done this in years, there's hardly any room, and what if somebody passes by? Still, it's exciting to recapture those early days of your relationship or sexual escapades when you had no legitimate place to go, and the back seat of your car was the hottest spot in town.

If you set a goal to do this even once a month between, say, May and September, you could be in for a whole lot of fun. You probably won't be able to use the missionary position, but you won't miss it.

Every Room in the House

Get started in a different room than the bedroom. The kitchen works well, and dens, living rooms, dining rooms, and even bathrooms have been put to great use by couples looking for excitement.

If you have lots of kids or older children, perhaps you'll have to rent a hotel room. More power to you. You can have a lot of fun once you pull the blinds and retreat from the world. Many major hotel chains offer highly affordable weekend packages designed specifically for couples who live nearby. What about setting a goal to do this twice a year? It will spice up your relationship, or your money back.

Birds of a Feather Flock Together

I used to scoff when I'd see that one actor had married another. I used to think, "How incestuous—they're too good for the rest of the world, so they just stay among themselves." So Warren Beatty marries Annette Benning. Sean Penn marries Robin Wright. John Travolta marries Kelly Preston.

Now I understand why such individuals may have married people "in the business." It's a fast-paced and hectic world, and couples sometimes get few chances during the day to converse with each other at length.

If you're going to be a family with someone for 15, 30, or 45+ years, it makes sense for that person to be someone who understands your occupation, predisposition, and passion. During my courting years, I continually met women who were teachers, nurses, social workers, and other helping professionals. They were altruistic people with good jobs. You know what? They didn't match up with me in any way.

It would have been helpful to meet someone who was also a speaker or an author. The darned thing was, at the time, I figured it didn't make any difference. My mate would have her career, I would have mine, and we could learn from each other, even if we didn't have that much in common career-wise. Not!

How about you? What are your choices for your next significant other?

Go for the Gold!
If you seek to attract someone with certain characteristics, it makes a heck of a lot of sense to be that kind of person yourself. If you want someone who's warm, generous, and caring, first consider whether you are the same. So it is with every set of traits you can imagine.

I marvel at how some couples find each other, stay together for years, and seem to have an all-consuming passion about the same things. Whether it's renowned philanthropists, authors, or simply a husband and wife who run a bookstore together, have you thought about how well these people match up in terms of partner-related, career, and life goals? It would be interesting to see whether a before-and-after study has been conducted questioning couples about their goals while they were engaged and after they were married for a few years. My strong hunch is that they matched up well before getting married.

Marriage Partner Goal Review

Whether you're about to have a new spouse or have been married for years, you have the ever-present opportunity to get more in sync with your partner by better understanding his or her goals.

Never Too Late

One of my friends got married for the first time in his mid-40s. Why did he match up so well with his wife who, by the way, is in her 40s? Both wanted to have a child. Both wanted to engage in worldwide travel. Both had ambitious plans about how much they wanted to earn, save, and invest.

As it turns out, they've had a baby, have taken many trips to distant points around the globe, and already have made great progress in terms of their earnings, savings, and investing goals. As reticent as my friend was to getting married, and as fearful as he was to do it in his mid-40s, I can safely predict that they'll be together for a long time. Why? Common goals!

Go for the Gold!
Your goals don't need to be a one-to-one match—the mirror image of each other. You might word your goals one way, and your partner might word something in a somewhat different manner. The important thing is to identify the goals you share.

Conversely, you might have oodles of chemistry with your significant other. You might enjoy every facet of being with him or her. However, if you don't have common goals, I'd be skeptical about your long-term chances for success as a couple. Not that I don't want you to have long-term success. When you boil down everything, as author Robert Ringer said in *Looking Out for Number One*, the relationships that remain intact are value-for-value relationships, wherein one person receives great value, and the other receives great value in kind.

The Least You Need to Know

➤ Young boys and girls grow up with the best chance of succeeding in life when they have two loving, caring parents.

➤ Many of the goals you have for your family life are likely interrelated with the other major goal areas of your life.

➤ It's axiomatic but true: The family that plays together stays together.

➤ Every relationship has roles, responsibilities, and expectations—whether they are discussed and agreed on or unstated.

➤ Long-term relationships happen when both parties have common goals.

Your Social Life and How to Have One

The fourth broad area of life in which someone traditionally sets goals is one's social life. By the term *social life*, I mean your relationships with others outside your family and outside your business. Who does that leave? Mainly, the rest of the world. Outside of your immediate family or business circles, there's another 6 billion people in the world. How many do you know and spend time with? How many do you enjoy being with? In this chapter, you'll explore some social goals you might find worth setting and pursuing.

When Like Attracts Like: Celebrated Friendships

Some friendships are celebrated, life-long relationships. Charlie Chaplin and Douglas Fairbanks, Sr. had many reasons to be life-long friends (although Fairbanks died relatively young, while Chaplin lived to a ripe old age). Both were acrobatic individuals with well-developed acting abilities. Both had strong appeal to women. Along with Mary Pickford, they formed the movie-producing company United Artists, which still exists today.

Friends in Peace

U.S. President Jimmy Carter helped engineer a lasting peace in the Middle East between Israel and Egypt. These were two countries with a long history of warfare with one another. When Carter got Israeli Prime Minister Menachem Begin and Egyptian President Anwar Sadat together at Camp David, history was made. In 1979, these two great leaders signed the Camp David accords and, for bringing peace to that area, they were awarded the Nobel Peace Prize.

Even after Carter lost to Ronald Reagan in the 1981 presidential election, President Sadat followed up a visit to Washington with a special side trip down to Plains, Georgia to visit his friend, former President Carter.

Instant Matches

Speaking of Reagan, he hit it off so well with Great Britain's prime minister at the time, Margaret Thatcher, that the two seemed like they had known each other for ages. Thatcher shared many of Reagan's conservative philosophical viewpoints. Reagan greatly admired Thatcher's diplomatic skills, breadth of knowledge, and strong-willed leadership. Years after both were no longer in office, they maintained strong ties.

Likewise, Bob Hope and Bing Crobsy enjoyed a lifelong friendship. Director Martin Scorcese and actor Robert DeNiro have had a personal and professional relationship that has spanned more than 20 years.

For Sure

Michael Jordan, who could have been a golfer in another life, if not a superstar basketball player and mediocre minor-league baseball player, hooked up with golfing phenomenon Tiger Woods. The two played a round of golf and shared insights of the joys and burdens of being a worldwide sports superstar and media icon. Although Jordan is some 13 years older than Woods, it's likely that the bond the two share will last years into the future.

You, the Social Animal

Everyone could stand to have some good friends in this life. Most people would like to have a few more friends than they presently have, although sometimes they get so busy with work and their family life that they don't have enough time for the friends they do have. I'm going to make the not-so-bold assumption that if you were able to easily attract into your life a handful of new, true friends, you'd certainly do it.

Why Do People Befriend You?

Whether you're extroverted or introverted, chances are you have some friends and you enjoy seeing them and doing things with them. Have you ever stopped to consider why these people are your friends? You know what you see in them, but what do they see in you?

Right now might be a good time to consider why people have chosen you as a friend. This might be the key as to how you can improve the friendship factor in your life and have more people befriend you more easily.

Are you, for example,

Loyal	Generous
Trustworthy	Energetic
Fun-loving	Witty
Intelligent	Resourceful
Empathetic	Encouraging

Take a moment right now to write down at least six of your personal traits that you suspect might draw others to you:

1. _____   4. _____

2. _____   5. _____

3. _____   6. _____

To further explore the friendship factor, consider other elements at play that might have resulted in a friendship between you and another person. For example, are you

Close by	Ready at a moment's notice
Available	Willing to pay
Willing to drive	Willing to wait
Visible	Easily convinced

It might not be flattering to consider these last qualifications, but in many ways, they are as important as anything in prompting friendships. Perhaps you're some people's friend simply because you've been around forever. Right now, why don't you take a moment to jot down five or six factors, such as proximity, that contribute to your friendship with another person? And, while you're compiling this list, don't forget such factors as reachability, such as by phone, fax, or e-mail.

1. _____ 4. _____

2. _____ 5. _____

3. _____ 6. _____

Now for a little personal history. When or where did you meet your friends? In high school or college, on your first job, or on some local team you both play for? Are your friends confined solely to those with whom you work? Or among your relatives?

Chances are you've got a friend or two in the neighborhood, someone from across town, and a long-distance friend, if not several. By identifying where and when you met friends, you might be prompted to consider yet other opportunities to attract friends into your life, if that is of interest to you:

1. _____ 4. _____

2. _____ 5. _____

3. _____ 6. _____

Finally, consider a host of factors that also might enable you to bond with another person. Are you roughly the same age? Are you the same gender? Do you have the same role, such as father, mother, single parent, and so on? Are you passing some of life's milestones at roughly the same time (see Chapter 3, "The Times of Your Life")? As you did before, take a minute or two to jot down as many as six characteristics you might have in common with some of your current friends:

1. _____ 4. _____

2. _____ 5. _____

3. _____ 6. _____

Name That Pattern

Is a pattern emerging? Most people will be able to detect some sort of pattern. *You tend to attract people who are like yourself.* If this is news to you, you have marvelous insight. Perhaps, for the first time in your life, you'll set goals to begin seeking friends who are not nearly so like yourself. In that regard, you'll expand your range of experiences and your ability to engage in relationships with a wider variety of people. How exciting!

If you already have friends from a wide variety of backgrounds, including many who are not like you, congratulations. Still, even among the diverse group of friends you might have, you could and perhaps someday will have other types of friends.

Counting on Your Spouse Too Much

Like the Bette Midler song, "You Gotta Have Friends," many married couples—particularly young couples—make the mistake of counting on their spouse to be their lover, domestic servant, financial partner, and best friend. This is okay if it works. There are stories of marriage partners who were best friends for life. If only it could be that way for everyone. Often, it's not.

Even if you truly are good friends with your spouse, do you want to count on only one other person in this life for all your social needs? I suspect that the high divorce rate in Western societies may be due in part to spouses counting on each other far too much. The level of expectation gets so high that no one can fulfill it.

So, your wife doesn't want to go to the football game on Sunday. What are you going to do? Try to get her interested in I-formations, play-option passes, and field-goal kicking? You can find a lot of buddies who already are interested in those things.

So, your husband doesn't want to go to the opera. Maybe he thinks seeing people in costumes jumping around the stage for two hours and randomly breaking out in song is more than he can take. There will be plenty of other friends who would love to go to the theater with you.

Why do we get wrapped up so often in having our spouse as the be-all and end-all? I don't know—it could be insecurity, or it could be because our lives are so hectic that we might as well befriend the person we live with. It certainly can be convenient in terms of scheduling events.

Getting to Know You

Because becoming friends with someone is nearly synonymous with getting to know them, perhaps the following strategies for getting to know someone quickly will appeal to you.

Just Start Talking

Uh-Oh! Another way of counting too much on your spouse friend-wise is having only your spouse's friends as your friends. It's important that each spouse has at least a few of his or her "own friends."

It takes two to converse, and if *you* don't start, maybe there won't be a conversation. When Michael Jordan rejoined the Chicago Bulls in March 1995 after a year and a half away from the game, one of his new teammates (someone who hadn't been there during the championship seasons of '91, '92, and '93) found it hard to strike up a conversation.

Bulls teammate Jud Buechler tells of how he was alone in the locker room with Michael for 10 minutes, yet couldn't bring himself to say anything. The gap between teammates—one a superstar and the other a role player—seemed too great. Later, the Bulls didn't play well as a team in the playoffs, perhaps because Michael was not in sync with the rest of the team. He needed to have made friends sooner with his "new team" following the reunion, and perhaps they needed to make friends with him.

Enlist Someone in What You're Doing

If you want to get to know someone quickly, get him or her to join you. I once met a man who ran a hardware store. He told me how he met his wife many, many years before. She was very attractive, he said, and he was afraid to try to win her over. A lot of other guys were also interested in her.

He had a bowling team and asked whether she would join. She liked to bowl, joined his team, and they've been rolling strikes and spares together ever since.

Go for the Gold!
If you want to get to know someone quickly, go to the same events. Meet and converse early on the first day or during the first hour of the event. Give yourself time to build up a relationship.

Uh-Oh!
CAUTION!
Remember not to spill your guts and scare others away by being *too* disarming right off the bat.

Be Earnest From the Outset

There's something disarming about speaking from the heart even when you're speaking with someone who is less than intimate with you. We each have some kind of receptive zone that allows another person to penetrate our defenses more naturally when they've conveyed to us, through their words and expressions, that they're speaking to us on a deeper level than is usual. Maybe it's because they create in us some level of trust that we want to be receptive to but so frequently are not.

If you can appeal to something that has meaning for them, perhaps a cause, or even a fond memory, your words and gestures will have impact. Touch them emotionally.

Show Immediate Interest

Convey more interest in the other party than in yourself. You've heard of the old acronym WIIFM, an overused but useful way of remembering that whenever you have any type of message for another person, the primary thing they're concerned about is *What's In It For Me?*

Solidifying Friendships

After you get to know someone, if your goal is to befriend that person, these ideas may help:

➤ *Visit the person at his or her home.* If you have to drop off a report, pick up something, attend a holiday party, or do anything else that brings up a friendly, professional reason for visiting a co-worker at his or her home, go ahead.

➤ *Exchange letters, e-mail, and so on.* After people have saved your e-mail address, they have a higher probability of corresponding with you. Frequently dispense short, nice notes to office co-workers and brief, positive, informative e-mail messages to co-workers—perhaps via your office intranet.

➤ *Show happiness at hearing from them.* Relationships last when at least one of the parties continues to say, "Hey, I'm glad to hear from you." If both convey this message, the relationship is solid.

➤ *Work through a crisis together.* When you're on the same team against the same obstacles and you overcome them, you've laid the groundwork for an amicable relationship.

Go for the Gold!
Seeing the other person in a change of setting will tell you a lot more about him or her.

Looking for Mr. or Ms. Good

In general, follow the Will Rogers philosophy of looking for the good in others. Find something about a co-worker you admire and let it be known.

With the widespread use of database software, recounting the details about another person's life isn't hard to do anymore. When you learn something about someone, such as a birthday or spouse's name, you can simply log it into the note section of your record on that person in your database. Superstar salespeople do this all the time to track the needs and interests of customers. It works just as well with the people you see on the job every day.

Extend Yourself for a Friend

Some of these strategies may require that you extend yourself a bit, but to gain a new friend, why not?

With a gesture such as visiting where they live, for whatever reason (to simply pick up a recipe, magazine article, or what have you), you make friendship possible. Once you step into somebody's home, you enter a whole other world. You see the art or paintings they have on the wall. Perhaps they have a bookcase displaying some of their books.

Go for the Gold!
Do you have a common interest away from the office, or do you share a common need? Do you remember the names of the important people in a co-worker's life, such as his or her spouse, children, and so on? Do you remember birthdays? If so, surprise your co-worker with a card or a gift.

Likewise, inviting potential friends to your home for whatever reason—to pick up something, to play cards, to discuss an upcoming event of some club or association to which you both belong—increases the probability that a new friend may be in the offing. If you're well off, you might go so far as to prepare a guest room in your home, or if you're buying a new house, you might want to keep such a room in mind.

Open Your Home

If your children are off at college or have left the nest, it might be easier for you to accommodate guests than it is for those who are just getting started with a family. The ability to easily entertain guests prompts you to engage in such behavior.

For Sure

When President Reagan was visiting the Palm Springs area in California, he stayed in the home of Walter Annenberg, multimillionaire and philanthropist. More precisely, Reagan stayed at Annenberg's estate—for indeed, the guest facilities are more spacious and more lavish than most people's homes, and the grounds are just as secure as the White House.

My friend Peter in Boston has a 20-room house that includes not one but two guest bedrooms. Peter doesn't go out of his way to invite people to stay over. Still, knowing that I can stay over simply by calling and saying "I'm coming" makes the trip that much easier and enjoyable.

If you can clear out *some* space in your home that indicates to guests that they are welcome, you may be on the road to a more vibrant social life.

Long-Term Friends

Based on solely my own observations, women seem to instinctively understand the need to have good friends in life and display the skills necessary to initiate and maintain such relationships. I've concluded that often, a woman will seek out one good lifelong friend while having many others. Men may or may not have a lifelong best friend but often have several other pals with whom they are friendly for stretches of time.

Friendships between men and women vary based on the status of each person in the friendship. If both parties are happily married to others, the friendship can be long-lasting and usually seems harmless and non-threatening to both marriages. This type of friendship may well be entirely rewarding.

If one party is not married, the spouse of the other party could see the friendship as a threat, although I wish this were less true. If both parties are not married, depending on the age and circumstances of each partner in the friendship, the nature of the relationship can vary widely.

A Man and a Woman

A man and a woman can be a great source of strength and comfort to one another as they proceed through the travails of life and career—whether they have dated but have now decided to be friends, have never dated one another, or have simply initiated a relationship as friends and intend to keep it that way. Such a friendship can be rewarding—particularly during one's twenties, which often can be a time of tumult.

Find a Friend

Because of the growing number of divorced adults and single parents, groups such as Parents without Partners and other men's and women's support organizations have popped up in many communities. People find friends through such groups as a prelude to getting remarried, as a means of giving the advice and empathy they can offer as a fellow single parent, or simply for fellowship or companionship.

If you find yourself at this point in life, perhaps you'd like to make a goal of exploring one new group per month over the next four months. After you identify the most appealing group, you can join it. In any event, it's hard for you to begin creating a vibrant, mutually rewarding, long-lasting friendship by sitting in your armchair. The world is out there—as in outside your door.

Uh-Oh!
Even with all the high-tech gadgets you can surround yourself with, you'd be hard pressed to find something that takes the place of going on an adventure, taking a hike, or seeing a movie with a friend.

Making Friends Easily

As you learned in Chapter 5, "Mind Over Matter," by changing the quality and direction of your thoughts, you can change the quality and direction of your life. Here are some high-quality thoughts to assist you in a more rewarding and balanced social life.

Sometimes you discover someone who has been in your life all along but for whatever reason hasn't crossed the friendship threshold. A great friend of mine in the D.C. area didn't start out that way. In fact, the first time I met him, I got into an argument with him.

Go for the Gold!
If you maintain a mindset that you attract and make new friends easily, at least one or two more friends will start to show up in your life.

Not Your Typical Start

I was attending a professional association function. I had called in days earlier to say that I might have to leave late in the morning and would not be attending the lunch or afternoon sessions because of the schedule conflict. Therefore, I wanted to know if I could pay only for that session I would be able to attend. I was told it probably would be okay.

My friend-to-be was serving as the host for that session, greeting people as they arrived, dispensing tickets, and so on. As I left the meeting room late in the morning, I stopped at the table where he was sitting and explained my situation. He said he didn't know of any such rebate procedure and that he didn't have the authority to refund a portion of my payment. I explained to him that I had called and indicated that there could be a schedule conflict (which I confirmed during a break earlier that morning).

He was adamant about not returning a portion of the money, and I became upset with both his behavior and the potential loss of funds, however small. The conflict did not escalate, because I had to be on my way. As you can guess, in the following months, when I thought about that fellow, it wasn't with pleasant feelings.

Not the First Impression, the Lasting Impression

I encountered this man again at other association functions; I don't even remember how we got past the initial squabble, but we ended up becoming lifelong friends! (Well, it's been 16 years and counting.) We have been good friends for so long that today it is difficult for either of us to accurately and entirely reassemble the events leading to our ignominious beginnings.

I tell you this story because, on some level, each of us had to have chosen to make friends easily. Such an affirmation transcends immediate circumstances—even circumstances in which you would presume there's no way you'd be friends with this person.

Being with Your Friends Often

Although many of my friends are scattered across the United States, whenever I'm traveling for work, I see whether it's possible to create circular routes so that perhaps on my way back, I can stop off and see a good friend. I've done this with Paul in Cleveland on my way back from Chicago, with Bob in Nashville on my way back from Dallas, with Jeff in Marina del Ray anytime I'm headed toward Los Angeles, and with Peter in Boston anytime I'm headed toward the Northeast.

> **CAUTION! Uh-Oh!**
> What's the point of having good friends if you don't see them often enough to keep the friendship going? It's far too easy today to take a friend for granted.

Because I lived in the Washington, D.C., area for many years and still have many friends there, I see each of them on a rotating basis on subsequent trips back to D.C. It's simply too difficult to see everybody on one trip.

Likewise, in your own life, how easily can you keep up with your friends to ensure that they're in your path? Here are a few ideas:

➤ Look for events at which you can include your friends, even if you normally wouldn't think of doing this.

➤ Plan vacations at the same time and destination.

➤ Be a member of the same local group, cause, or activity.

➤ Have a designated encounter each month, such as the last Friday, the first Saturday, or what have you.

➤ Introduce your spouses so that they will get to know each other better, which will increase the probability of you seeing your friend more often.

Broadening Your Friendships

How sweet it is when someone who is your friend on one level for so many years moves up to the next level, and vice versa. Often, this is prompted by some change in life. One or the other of you moves closer to each other geographically. Perhaps your children share some activity.

Friendship Upgrades

Right now, think about the people who are your friends and which of those relationships could be enhanced. I'll bet there's at least one, if not several. As it often works out in the cosmos, that friend may be thinking of you in the same terms at the same moment.

Those old AT&T commercials that urge you to "reach out and touch someone" contain more wisdom than the advertising agency that crafted the term ever envisioned. For the price of a phone call, you can get together with someone in ways that reward or empower both of you. Perhaps you don't even know who that special friend is going to be. In that case, why not call all your friends?

Go for the Gold!
Independent of the initiating event, having a friendship deepen and broaden and hence move to a higher level is one of the great mysteries and beautiful aspects of life.

Telephone Night

Michael O'Hara made millions as the owner of Tramps Discotheque in the 1970s. Then he made multimillions by developing the concept for the Champion Sports Bar in the Georgetown section of Washington, D.C., which has since been franchised all across America. O'Hara once told me that one of his secrets to success is getting on the phone.

Some evenings, he'll sit by the phone with his list of numbers and call everyone he knows—everyone who happens to be home at the time he calls—and just talks. He has no particular agenda. He's not trying to sell them something or even arrange to get together. He just wants to stay in touch.

O'Hara says that as a result of this lifelong ritual, he has deepened many friendships and not so accidentally stumbled into a variety of lucrative business deals. He feels that he is a richer person for doing so.

Contrast what O'Hara does with how most people typically spend their evenings. Many people sit in front of the television and feed their face. The typical person in America today spends eight solid years of his or her life watching how other people supposedly live (on television) while not getting to know the flesh-and-blood person down the block.

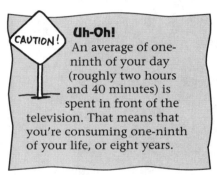

Uh-Oh!
An average of one-ninth of your day (roughly two hours and 40 minutes) is spent in front of the television. That means that you're consuming one-ninth of your life, or eight years.

May I suggest that, as a goal, you spend one evening a month—say from 7:00 p.m. to 10:00 p.m.—on the phone calling everyone you know. If the notion particularly appeals to you, perhaps you'll make this a more frequent activity.

What will happen as a result of such calls? You'll feel closer to some people, learn about issues and events, be invited to activities, and heck, maybe even enjoy yourself. You'll rediscover elements of yourself and your friends that you might have forgotten.

Being a More Supportive Friend

This section is perhaps the most important of the chapter. Long-term and rewarding friendships require maintenance and nurturing. Whether it's calling, writing, visiting, or engaging in activities together, if you're interested in an active friendship, you need to be active.

We all have friendships in which we talk to somebody every so many years. But because there are things within both ourselves and our friend that keep the relationship going even in the absence of regular contact, it's easy to catch up in a matter of minutes.

Instant Recall

I received a call from someone I knew in college. I hadn't heard from her for at least 15 years. When she called, she started off with a ploy. Instead of saying who she was, she asked, "Who was that girl you knew in college named Mary something?" I immediately caught on that it was Mary Kovacik and was glad to hear from her. As is the case with you and some of your friends, Mary and I hit it off and were back in high gear in a matter of seconds.

Still, it would be so much nicer to maintain an active and ongoing friendship as opposed to an intermittent and inactive one.

On the Front Burner

In addition to the suggestions already presented in this chapter, here are some other ideas for you if one of your goals is to keep your good friendships on the front burner of your life:

➤ Call them, call them, call them.

➤ Remember their birthdays and send a card or gift.

➤ Remember their spouse's and children's birthdays.

➤ Be on the lookout for items of interest to them, and alert them when you come across these items.

➤ As you consider leisure-time activities for yourself and your family, think of ways to bring your friends into the loop.

➤ Meet for lunch.

➤ Exchange photos.

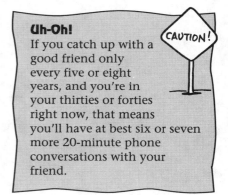

Uh-Oh!
If you catch up with a good friend only every five or eight years, and you're in your thirties or forties right now, that means you'll have at best six or seven more 20-minute phone conversations with your friend.

Finally, engage in whatever the phrase "being a good friend" prompts within you.

The Least You Need to Know

➤ Everyone could stand to have a few more good friends in this life.

➤ Because you tend to attract people who are like yourself, perhaps you are ready to seek out friends who are not nearly so like yourself to expand your range of experiences.

➤ It's far too easy today to take a friend for granted. Don't make this mistake.

➤ If your goal is to keep your good friendships on the front burner of your life, call them, call them, call them.

Chapter 9

The Spirit in You

In This Chapter

➤ Where's the spirit?

➤ Where would you like to go?

➤ How would you like to be?

➤ Spirit in everyday life

The fifth of the seven major goal areas is spirituality. Of all the goal areas you might have, this one is potentially the most difficult to quantify. You can set a goal that is challenging but reachable and assign a timeline to it, but how do you place a number on spirituality? I'm glad you asked...

Defining Spirituality

If you've decided to read this chapter, increasing your spiritual awareness is probably important to you. In this chapter, whenever the words *spirit*, *spiritual*, or *spirituality* are used, they relate to a sense of inner peace; this sense may have many possible derivations, such as faith in some higher power, love of humankind, or the ability to enjoy each moment and live without fear.

Religion and Spirituality

Where are you when it comes to being spiritual? Is it a way of being for you, something you aspire to, or something you never think about at all? Traditionally, society has tended to regard those who attend some type of religious service on a regular basis as spiritual. If you're among them, more power to you. If you're not, that doesn't preclude your ability to be spiritual.

Actually, you can achieve such spirituality independent of regular attendance at religious services. Conversely, you can be a devoted member of a church and have little spirituality in your life. How can this be so? To get to the heart of the issue, first let me say that I believe organized religion to be a wonderful thing and that most people who are members of an organized religion benefit greatly from their participation. I wouldn't want to see any of the world's great religions fall by the wayside, and I am inspired by the numbers of people who feel uplifted or gain a great sense of community when participating.

Being steeped in religious observance does not necessarily equate with being spiritual for many reasons. If you're inspired by the Sunday sermon but never take the message to heart (it goes no further with you than the exit), where is your spirituality?

If charity and kindness are important to you, and your principal means of upholding these values is to write a handful of checks to a couple of charities a few times a year, are you living up to your ideals?

No, my friend, your attendance every Saturday, Sunday, or other day of the week at a place of worship does not necessarily equate with being spiritual. As so many people do, you could merely be going through the motions.

Do you confess your sins or atone for your wrongdoing once a week, once a month, or once a year but take no action to right your wrongs? Do you think that merely *saying* you're sorry and promising that you'll be better equates with being spiritual?

Dr. Stephen Covey, founder of the Covey Leadership Center in Utah, says, "You can't talk your way out of what you behaved your way into."

A Clear Path

Aside from following the rules of organized religion, how and where might you be more spiritual in your life?

You can practice being more spiritual in little ways that add up quickly to being a more spiritual person. The next several pages tell you about some relatively minor things you can do to start the process, although nothing is minor when it comes to acting spiritually. After all, *each little action sets in motion the potential for greater good.* So, as you proceed through this list, don't discount the value of engaging in any of these. They all have the potential to add up to more.

Spirituality Behind the Wheel

Sociologists tell us that when people get in their cars, they think they're in some type of invisible vehicle. No one sees them as they motor down the road. If you curse or scream, who's to know? Obviously, you're not invisible, and the way you conduct yourself as a motorist potentially impacts other motorists as well as pedestrians.

The next time someone cuts you off in traffic, fails to use a turn signal properly, or otherwise engages in improper driving, practice maintaining your composure. Don't curse, don't scream, don't honk your horn, and don't engage in one-upmanship. If the other person is in view, look at him or her blankly, but not with disgust, anger, or a mocking smile.

Often, people know what they did was wrong. If they don't, venting your spleen is not likely to change that behavior.

If you travel frequently—as part of your job, for example—and often traverse high-traffic arteries, chances are you'll have an opportunity at least several times a week to practice engaging in small displays of spirituality. As a goal, why not establish for yourself one composed response per week?

> **Go for the Gold!**
> Each time you can remain composed, you increase the probability that you will be more composed in other aspects of your life. Perhaps you'll even be kinder to people in face-to-face encounters when they commit a transgression.

Aid the Less Fortunate

It's one thing to write a check to charity, but it's another to encounter someone who is in need and to aid that person on the spot. As a small gesture of spirituality, what can you do for someone you see right on the street?

I'm not a paragon of virtue, but I learned a technique years ago that I think you might enjoy. When you have shoes that you no longer wear but that are not necessarily in pieces, keep them in your trunk as you motor around town.

Then, if you see a homeless person with less than sufficient footwear and it looks like you might be roughly the same size, pull over. Without equivocation, get the shoes from your trunk, walk up to the person, and offer your shoes. If he or she accepts, fine—say good day and be on your way. If he or she chooses not to take the shoes, that's okay, too.

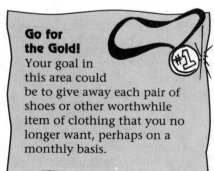

> **Go for the Gold!**
> Your goal in this area could be to give away each pair of shoes or other worthwhile item of clothing that you no longer want, perhaps on a monthly basis.

Serve in Volunteer Groups

You might want to volunteer once a month to serve a meal at a local shelter for the homeless. If you're a busy career type, perhaps serving dinner will work best for you. I can tell you from firsthand experience that whatever your preconceived notions about this may be, once you actually serve dinner to real-life people, you'll see that reality is different than you thought.

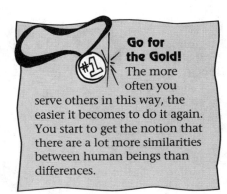

Go for the Gold!
The more often you serve others in this way, the easier it becomes to do it again. You start to get the notion that there are a lot more similarities between human beings than differences.

At first, I thought that people would be reluctant to speak up for what they wanted. Or worse, they'd be endlessly thanking me, and I would have to do my best to remain humble. I also feared that I'd come on as some kind of "goodie-two-shoes," dispensing dinners with an overly pleasant, "And how are you this evening? Here's a nice dinner for you."

Actually, none of these things happens. Person to person, you simply serve another, as if you were in partnership. More peas? Less carrots? It's much more matter-of-fact than you might imagine. They're appreciative but not fawning. Some of the people who show up at a shelter are well-dressed. Perhaps they're temporarily unemployed. Perhaps they had a financial emergency they were not prepared to handle.

Look for the Good in Others

Will Rogers, a political satirist, entertainer, and beloved figure in the first half of the 20th century *allegedly* said, "I never met a man I didn't like." Many people have interpreted this comment as meaning that Rogers could find something admirable in everyone he met. So, too, can we all.

Uh-Oh!
You're going to be on this planet for a finite amount of time. Do you want to go through your life trading hostilities with people, never having the wherewithal to restore some semblance of civility to the relationship?

Is there a coworker with whom you've had a strained relationship? Is there something good about this coworker you can draw on so that you can get yourself to actually say something nice at your next encounter?

Is there a neighbor with whom you have had a continuing squabble? What would it do to your relationship if you sent your neighbor a card or a brief note that said something along the lines of, "I noticed how lovely your garden was the other day and wanted to let you know that I appreciate the work you've done in maintaining it." Too syrupy, or pardon the expression, too flowery? Guess again.

Now list five people at work or elsewhere in your life with whom you might not have a good relationship but now can acknowledge:

1. _____
2. _____
3. _____
4. _____
5. _____

Next to each person's name, write what you think is good about that person. Do they maintain a clean work area? Here are some ideas for you in case you're drawing a blank. This person…

➤ Is kind to the receptionist at work.

➤ Turns assignments in on time and supports the team.

➤ Walks softly past your office so as not to disturb you.

➤ Greets you in the morning when you arrive.

➤ Maintains his or her office well.

Away from work, here are some ideas for finding the good in others. This person…

➤ Keeps the street in front of the yard free of debris.

➤ Is respectful of others' need for quiet.

➤ Dresses well.

➤ Has well-behaved children.

➤ Drives safely in the neighborhood.

Become a Better Listener

Listening is one of the most underrated skills. Your ability to listen to another person, giving your full and undivided attention, can be an act of spirituality. In this rush-rush world, too often we want people to summarize everything they say.

Human beings have a profound need to be heard. I cover this extensively in my book *The Complete Idiot's Guide to Assertiveness*. When you give others your full and complete attention, in essence, you're telling them that you value them as people. All activities and concerns in your life stop as the words and emotions of another person take on paramount importance.

Uh-Oh!
There's a running joke that if Moses came down from the mountain with the 10 Commandments this afternoon, the evening news, instead of citing all the commandments, would report *only* the top three.

Consider the people in your life who have mattered the most to you; chances are they were the people who listened to you best. Whether it is your parents, a brother or sister, a good friend, a relative, a teacher, a coach, a coworker, a mentor, or just somebody down the street, you tend to value those who value you by listening.

For Sure

In *Siddhartha*, by Hermann Hesse, the young Siddhartha speaks about his most well-developed skills. He can *listen*, he can *fast*, and he can *wait*. These talents don't seem like much to the Western mind, but they come in handy if you want to increase the spirituality of your life. As a goal, why not decide to listen in earnest to one person per week in the workplace to whom you would not have otherwise given such time and attention?

At home, give your significant other one good listening to per day, and I promise things will go better. Do the same with each child.

The Challenge of Not Judging Others

It's likely that you judge things, including others, all day long. Judgment *is* a necessary and practical skill. After all, if you want to choose the colleges appropriate for you; friends who share similar values; and the professional, social, and civic groups you will enjoy being a part of, you need to make some judgments.

We all judge one another at some point—and sometimes harshly. I have a particular problem with people who speak too loudly in restaurants or on planes (especially on those 7:00 a.m. flights to Chicago, when no one in their right mind ought to be talking anyway).

Go for the Gold!

We can all learn from each other. It is so easy to fall into that game, as psychologist Carl Rogers articulated, of "mine is better than yours." It is too convenient to conclude that people who walk, talk, or look differently than we do must be vastly different, and by extension, inferior.

People who cover their bodies with tattoos or earrings in weird places also throw me for a loop. Many people are suffering serious infection as a result of the tattoos they have in various places. Figures indicate that as many as 40 percent or more of the people who get tattoos want to have them removed. The *tattoo removal* business is thriving.

You get one body in this life, so why would you go out of your way to disparage it, let alone reduce your chances for getting any type of high-income job!?

At more noble moments, I recall that it would be more spiritual of me to be *less* judgmental about certain types of people. They know things that I don't. I can learn from them.

Conversely, we make judgments about others attributing superior or noble traits to them when it is not appropriate. We base our assessment on the scant information we have of them as individuals. You see someone well-dressed or well-coifed and assume that they have superior intellect, are morally upright, or are financially sound.

For Sure

Lookism is rampant in the world. Those people who have an appearance that is more aesthetically pleasing are accorded privileges unlike others. Studies have shown that attractive people have a distinct advantage when it comes to job interviews and asking for assistance. Defendants in jury trials routinely receive more favorable verdicts from juries than do their less physically blessed counterparts. If convicted, they receive a less harsh punishment.

Even newborn babies will spend more time looking at pictures of highly attractive models than they will looking at pictures of ordinary people.

An appreciation for aesthetics seems to be a built-in characteristic of human beings. Do you prejudge a speaker based on his or her appearance and not based on the content of that person's character? Can you even listen to a person who does not fit your relative description of how he or she ought to appear?

Finding the Good All Around You

If you believe that the world is going to hell in a handbasket, then handbaskets marked for hell will show up all around you. If you believe that civilization is at the dawn of a new era in which everyone treats everyone else with respect, evidence to that effect will start showing up wherever you go.

For Sure

A woman once approached the spiritual leader Ram Dass after a lecture he gave. She told him that she was having a terrible time finding spirituality in her city. She happened to live in New York City.

Ram Dass thought about her predicament and then told her, "I want you to spend the next two years finding spirituality every place you go…in New York City." It's not necessarily a question of *where* you live, but *how* you live.

An old fable has it that a man was passing through a small town and asked the shop-keeper what the townspeople were like. The shopkeeper thought about the question and asked what the people were like where the traveler lived. The traveler explained all that was good and bad about the people who lived in his town. Most of his explanation was about what he didn't like in his neighbors and fellow citizens.

When he was through, the shopkeeper said, "Well, I guess the people around here are pretty much like that."

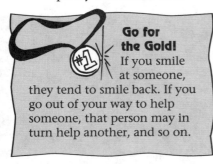

Go for the Gold!
If you smile at someone, they tend to smile back. If you go out of your way to help someone, that person may in turn help another, and so on.

Go for the Gold!
Always do right—this will gratify some and astonish the rest.
—Mark Twain

If you *didn't* get this parable, the shopkeeper meant that the way in which you view people where you live is the way you'll view people if you move to a new location. Yes, there are certain local and regional differences among those who live in different places. If you accept the fundamental notion, however, that the similarities among people are greater than the differences, then *whatever you experience in relation to others now is what you're likely to experience some place else*. What about *acting with spirituality right where you are, right now?*

Sometimes, you see bumper stickers that say, "Practice random acts of kindness and senseless acts of beauty." I'm not sure what a senseless act of beauty is, but random acts of kindness seem particularly appropriate. Why not set as a goal to engage in some type of kind behavior toward a total stranger once a week or, if you have enough opportunities, once a day? It could be something as simple as holding the elevator door when you know someone is trying to make it in, or not giving someone a lecture when they put you on hold for a few more seconds than you would have preferred.

Here are some other suggestions. Note that all of them are small and entirely doable. Hence, your goal could be to engage in at least one of these per day:

➤ Pick up some litter in the street or in someone's yard.

➤ Let others get in line ahead of you when it appears that their need is more urgent.

➤ Write somebody a thank-you letter when they aren't expecting it.

➤ Write a thank-you note to someone you don't know who did something good for your town.

➤ Keep your word.

Taking Your Spirituality to a Higher Level

To close out the chapter, here are a variety of goals you might want to adopt in pursuit of being a more spiritual person. These are all challenging and potentially reachable, and you'll be in charge of quantifying them, such as saying you'll engage in the behavior daily, weekly, or what have you. The timeline is likely to begin now and to last for at least six or twelve months or possibly indefinitely:

➤ To strengthen my relationship with God.

➤ To reflect on and be thankful for all that has been given to me.

➤ To recognize the sanctity of all Earth's creatures.

➤ To deepen my understanding of human spirituality.

➤ To read the sacred text of my religion.

➤ To follow the teachings of spiritual leaders.

➤ To be kind and charitable to others.

➤ To be tolerant and understanding of other religions.

➤ To practice charity at home.

➤ To obey the 10 Commandments or the important codes of my religion.

➤ To dispense good will toward humankind.

The Least You Need to Know

➤ Being spiritual is synonymous with being aware of your inherent goodness.

➤ You may be religious and spiritual, but the two are not necessarily equal.

➤ Spirituality can be conveyed in small deeds, such as simply listening to someone, helping others, and looking for the good in others.

➤ Kindness and spirituality have much in common. Indeed, to act with kindness toward others is to display your spirituality.

Chapter 10

You and Your Career

In This Chapter

➤ It's not just money

➤ Oy, the pressure

➤ Making their goals your goals

➤ Women on the road to the top

Your career represents the sixth of the seven major goal areas most people have in their lives. Although I could have discussed careers in an earlier chapter, it's just as well that I waited until after I covered the mental, physical, family, social, and spiritual aspects of your life. There's no point in overemphasizing the importance of your career when it comes to personal goal-setting, because it's likely that it dominates much of your thinking anyway.

Love It or Leave It

You've got to thoroughly enjoy what you do to sustain a healthy, happy, and prosperous career. I mean, how can you make yourself get up every Monday morning, head into town, spend a good 8 to 10 hours at the office, fight your way back home, and then do it again for the rest of the week if you don't love what you do?

Could it be only for the money? Unfortunately, this is probably true for many people. They get a job for whatever reason. It's not really what they want to do, but they're stuck because of bills and other commitments and before they know it, months and then years start zipping away.

This isn't a book about changing your job or determining whether you're in the right career. It's about setting and reaching goals, and in this chapter, setting and reaching career goals. So, I'm going to begin with the assumption that you have a career that you love, or you want to get into a career that you love.

Does Your Career Support You?

Suppose that you do love your job, position, and everything about the work you do. You're making $32,000 a year. After looking at your cash flow for the coming year, you've figured out that you're going to need to be making $55,000 by the year's end to be able to afford the things your family wants and needs.

You're doing good work and you're certainly due for a raise. Historically, annual increases in your company have hovered around 8 to 10 percent for top performers. Let's see—at $32,000, a 10 percent raise would net you $3,200. You'd still be $19,800 short of your income goal! Through some digging, you find out that no company employee in the memory of anyone who's currently employed has *ever* received more than a 20 percent increase in a given year—not even top officers.

So, at $32,000, a 20 percent increase would be $6,400. That would still leave you $16,600 short of your goal.

If you're earning $32,000 annually and you need to earn $55,000, you'll need to devise a plan so extraordinary that you'll exceed the wage increase that anyone in your company has ever earned. Perhaps you could devise a new product or service plan that is so cost-efficient that it saves the company oodles of money. Perhaps your company has a bonus plan in which employees submit cost-reduction ideas that could save the company millions of dollars. Hmmm…what $1 million cost-savings ideas can you come up with?

Perhaps you could join the company sales staff and, based on a combination of salary and commission, reach the $55,000 level. If there are no such options within your organization, then whether or not you love your job, you'll have to look elsewhere to realistically pursue your income goals.

Progressive Goals for Progressive People

In Chapter 3, "The Times of Your Life," you saw that some of the best times to set goals are before and after job changes. Suppose that you're entrenched in your current line of employment, though. It's your chosen path, and you want to thrive at it. What are some goals you can set for yourself in your career area that will sustain you on a daily basis and also on the long road?

Suppose that money is not a particularly pressing issue, but the need to keep pace is. Given the rapid pace of social and technical changes in society today and their impact in the marketplace, perhaps you want to establish a goal to become a master of change so that you'll stay at the forefront of your industry. Such a quest, however, is a bit nebulous. How do you quantify it? What's the specific timeline involved?

What if you're not a technically oriented person, but you are increasingly asked to master various software programs and other technologies? Here are some specific goals you can establish to squash any technology anxiety you have:

➤ Each week, learn one new presentation or communications tool—particularly those that are already part of existing software packages you use.

➤ Read at least one article a week related to communication or presentation technology. The article can be in a PC magazine, a business journal, or your local newspaper. You don't have to pick a highly technical article.

➤ After you begin to feel more technologically at ease, consider subscribing to a technical publication. *Wired*, *PC World*, *Home Office*, *Internet Magazine*, *The Net*, *Byte*, *MacWorld*, *PC Computing*, and dozens of others are all available at relatively affordable yearly subscription rates.

You also can read back issues at the library, get on a routing list at work, or ask the boss whether the company might pay for a subscription (your initiative might even impress the boss). Often, it's best not to subscribe to a magazine until you've read it a few times and have decided whether it's for you.

➤ Once a month, read a book related to technology. Again, go easy on yourself. Pick up Nicholas Negroponte's *Being Digital* or Dan Burrus's *Technotrends*, among a variety of other books that put technology in perspective in an understandable, friendly way.

For Sure

The Complete Idiot's Guide series includes a number of insightful books devoted to software technology. Topics include the Internet, DOS, Windows, CompuServe, America Online, and PCs in general. These books are available at the same bookstore where you bought the book you're reading right now.

What Are Your Customers Using?

Find out what your clients and customers are doing with technology. Remember years ago, when faxes were becoming commonplace in offices? The first time a client said, "Could you fax it to me?" and you couldn't. The fifth or tenth time someone asked you to fax information, you had already purchased or were thinking about purchasing a fax machine. So it is with today's latest technology. Your own decisions about what technology you use and master often are based on what your clients and customers are using.

Go for the Gold!
Pay attention to what others in your industry—particularly close competitors—are using. Ask people how they're accomplishing certain tasks and what works particularly well.

If it helps, join a technology group in your area. The business page of your local newspaper will list who is meeting, when, and where. Virtually every metro area of at least 75,000 to 100,000 people offers PC and Macintosh user clubs, bulletin boards, support groups, and so on. Almost every community has at least one newsgroup that can be accessed over the Internet if you simply have the right group name. Form alliances and affiliations with people who know what you need to know, as well as those who are at the same level of technology as you.

Also, look in your local paper for upcoming technology trade shows and expositions. Again, in any metro area of at least 75,000 to 100,000 people, in the course of a year, there are at least four to six technology fairs where both hardware and software vendors display their latest products and services. The cost of attending such shows is usually free or is a nominal fee of $5 to $10. Many of these shows also have specialized seminars that are free with your general admission or require an additional nominal fee.

A Designated Weekday Evening

Go for the Gold!
It's important that you have a quiet, uninterrupted space in which to absorb new concepts and explore new ways of thinking.

Instead of attempting to absorb new information during the workday on a subject area you might not be comfortable with, designate one night a week when you'll spend two hours or so learning more about technology, becoming familiar with terminology, and forsaking the world of the technologically disadvantaged.

Remember at all times that others who felt even *less* comfortable than you mastered communication and presentation technologies to the point where it became profitable and rewarding for them. You'll be just fine.

Change Is Here to Stay

Mastering technology, and thus mastering the process of change itself, is a challenge that's likely to be with you for the rest of your career. I mean, can you conceive of a time when things are going to slow down?

Is it likely that Corel, Microsoft Corporation, Netscape Communications Corporation, or Lotus Development Corporation is going to stop issuing greatly expanded versions of its software? Is the development of applications for the Internet going to go on hiatus? If you deal directly with clients or customers, is it likely that their expectations and demands are going to level off?

Chances are, the answer to all these questions is a resounding *"no."*

By some estimates, as many as one job in three will disappear over the next few years. As vital as your role might be to your organization right now, it's conceivable that if the role itself is not a candidate for extinction, it will dramatically shift, merge, be combined with something else, and emerge as something that only vaguely resembles its predecessor.

Simply acknowledging this possibility helps you to be more prepared for the future and to set career goals accordingly.

Go for the Gold! It's often easier to have someone show you how to do something. If you work on your own, lure unsuspecting friends over to help you with various technical issues!

One of the easiest and best ways to learn new technology is to take advantage of continuing education at your local college. Does anyone learn PhotoShop, Quark, or HTLM programming on his or her own or by reading magazines or manuals with any real proficiency? The best way to keep up with the latest is to enroll in an adult education evening course.

Job Stress or Job Pressure?

Anytime you find yourself in a position of responsibility, chances are excellent that you'll be subjected to trials and turmoil that often require the best of you. Rick Pitino, the new head coach of the Boston Celtics and former coach of the 1996 NCAA Champion Kentucky Wildcats, says that he finds it helpful to "distinguish between pressure, which is healthy, and stress, which is not."

In his book *Success Is a Choice*, Pitino defines pressure as "What we put on ourselves when we set high standards for excellence."

Stress, on the other hand, according to Pitino, is negative energy that is caused by external forces when we're not focused or prepared for challenges. Pitino maintains that when you separate pressure from stress, you're less likely to be discouraged when frustration arises or difficulties present themselves. His advice is to make pressure an ally.

Pitino advises that when you're experiencing pressure, remind yourself that you worked a long time to be ready for this moment, you've done all you can do, and you're now primed to give it your best shot.

Although Pitino doesn't claim this strategy will guarantee success, he says that it will enable you to constantly put forth your best effort each time.

Replenish and Reap

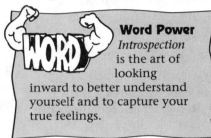

Word Power
Introspection is the art of looking inward to better understand yourself and to capture your true feelings.

I suggest that the more career-oriented you are and the more driven you are to succeed, the more important it is for you to continually stop, assess where you are, take personal inventory, and replenish yourself before moving on. Learn from introspection.

As you learned in Chapter 6, "Let's Get Physical," you need to sustain your physical self through proper nutrition, rest, and exercise so that you can perform at your best. Hence, while they're not career goals, per se, you might want to revisit some of the suggestions in Chapter 5, "Mind Over Matter," and while you're at it, Chapters 7, 8, and 9 on family, social, and spiritual goals.

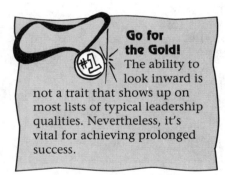

Go for the Gold!
The ability to look inward is not a trait that shows up on most lists of typical leadership qualities. Nevertheless, it's vital for achieving prolonged success.

You see, to have a career that works, you really have to approach it with balance. Author John O'Neil, in his book *The Paradox of Success*, says that many individuals who have restless personalities look for new stimuli to actually distract them from what he calls the real "business of life." Such people, in effect, substitute external change for what he calls "profound learning."

An Easy Litmus Test

One way of evaluating whether you're maintaining balance on the job is to notice how you interact with coworkers and your staff, if you manage one. If you treat your staff well,

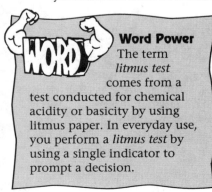

Word Power
The term *litmus test* comes from a test conducted for chemical acidity or basicity by using litmus paper. In everyday use, you perform a *litmus test* by using a single indicator to prompt a decision.

chances are you're approaching your career with a relatively balanced perspective. How about establishing some easy goals of a continuing nature to maintain effective relationships at work? You could try some of the following, for example:

➤ Leave a nice note for each staff person at least once a week. Perhaps you'll use a Post-It pad and attach the note to his or her chair. Perhaps you'll put it on a desk, in a mailbox, or send it via e-mail.

➤ Follow the time-honored tradition of praising people in public. If you have to criticize someone's performance, always do so in private.

For Sure

Management guru Tom Peters says to mind your manners. In his 1994 book, *The Pursuit of Wow!*, Peters recounts his days at the McKinsey and Company management consulting firm. A partner told him, "You'll be pushing some ideas beyond what people around here want to confront. Make sure you're irreproachable on the little stuff—show up for meetings on time, dress conservatively and so on."

Peter observes that too many people diminish their effectiveness by "relentlessly parading their brains and especially by publicly embarrassing people." "Don't be a smart aleck," he advises. Learn to hold your tongue and "don't ever embarrass folks in public."

Making Their Goals Your Goals

One of my long-term observations is that the happiest, most well-adjusted career achievers developed the habit of making the goals of their organization, department, or division their own goals. In other words, they internalize the goals that essentially have been laid out before them and make them their own.

As you learned in Chapter 1, "What Is a Goal as Opposed to a Wish?," a goal imposed on you from an external factor can become your own if you so choose. Hence, a sales manager can set sales quotas for the staff, and each and every staff person can choose to make that quota his or her goal as if setting it personally.

To the degree that you are able to adopt the goals of your organization, or your boss in particular, you can place yourself in a relatively fortunate position. This concept has been embraced by entire divisions of corporations in pursuit of serving and working more effectively with other divisions within the same corporation.

For Sure

At Domino's Pizza Distribution Company, a system developed in the mid-1980s by then President Don Vlcek regarded the division's customers as being five-fold: the parent company, the pizza store owners, pizza buyers, suppliers to the company, and the surrounding community. All goals that were created at the division level and filtered down to the personal level were geared toward meeting the needs of these five sectors. Employees eagerly internalized the goals bestowed on them, because the bonuses and advancements were tied to them, and the organizational atmosphere was one of friendly competition between one team and another.

Internalizing Goals

In your own career, wherever you're working and at whatever level, as you begin to assess the wants and needs of your boss and the department in general, take it upon yourself to make those part of your career-related goals. Besides directly asking people what they want, you can quickly and easily gather such information in other ways.

Read your organization's, department's, division's, or branch's annual reports, quarterly reports, executive reports, and so on. This literature often is available in your organization's library or on the company's intranet bulletin boards. You might even choose to buy a share of stock in your organization so that you'll automatically receive these reports.

Go for the Gold!
You can take what customers say they want and make the delivery of that service a personal goal. You'll end up shining in your department in a way few others ever will.

Often, the chairman, president, or other top officer includes a message at the beginning of such reports. These messages carry carefully crafted gems about the nature and direction of operations.

Likewise, look at the memos, reports, and notes from your own boss and coworkers within your division. The clues are all there. Obviously, any customer surveys, polls, feedback cards, and feedback data of any kind is worth its weight in gold to you and your career.

Positioning Yourself for Success

Besides internalizing goals that initially came to you via external resources, there is almost an unlimited number of ways to keep your career merrily humming along.

Chapter 21, "Steering Clear of Barriers," explores in detail the power of affiliating with like-minded people who want to help you achieve your goals—peers, coworkers, and friends; people you meet at support groups; and perhaps a mentor or two.

As you'll see in Chapter 22, "The Tom Sawyer Effect: Formally Enlisting Others to Help You," you also can practice more advanced strategies for reaching your goals, such as devising your own advisory board, attracting empowering people, retaining a career coach or life coach, and so on.

Jeffrey Gitomer, author of *The Sales Bible*, says that if you are serious about carving out a position for yourself and your organization, there are many steps you can take to propel yourself along the time frame of your choice:

➤ Learn to develop your speaking skills so that you feel comfortable in front of a small group—either inside or outside your organization.

➤ Submit letters, articles, or even column ideas to trade journals in your field or local newspapers. Visibility helps.

➤ Join or attend the meetings of the associations and groups that prospective clients attend.

➤ Expose your talents to others in the organization who may request that you be a part of their team. Stay late to help even if it wasn't requested of you.

➤ Make it easy for people to get a hold of you. If necessary, print your own business cards that include your office phone, beeper number, home phone, car phone, voice mail, and so on.

Gitomer contends that if you act on these principles until they become a way of life, soon enough you'll find that you're securely positioned in the minds of those who can help you along in your career—or, if you're an entrepreneur, those who can give a boost to your business.

Job Security or Career Opportunities?

I was surprised to read in a national survey of 500 human resource managers that the number-one concern of workers today is keeping their jobs. Yet, if you keep setting goals that propel you to higher achievement and that further the aims of your organization or serve the needs of customers and clients (because you've internalized those goals and made them your own), job security probably won't be an issue for you.

You have the smarts to continually uncover new opportunities. Here are some suggestions to further help you along in this area.

Read Client and Non-Client Publications

Read the publications of your clients as well as your industry's publications. What better way to understand the needs, fears, concerns, and hot-button issues of the people your organization serves?

Read publications that are entirely out of your field and out of the field of the customers you serve. Frequently, you can pick up ideas in publications that are otherwise totally unrelated to what you do and apply them to your own workplace. This form of borrowing concepts can help you stand out in your organization.

I go to the recycling bins in my town and grab 10 or 20 magazines off the top that I would not otherwise be inclined to pick up and certainly would not shell out good money for at a store. I flip through them at high speed and quickly detach the articles and pages that look like they will be of some interest. Then I recycle the magazines.

Later, at my leisure, I go through the articles and again determine whether they're worth my time and attention. Often, I highlight specific passages, copy the article and send it to an associate, or simply file it for future use. These articles represent a wellspring of ideas for me, and they keep my career pursuits at the forefront of my mind. Dozens of anecdotes in this book came from such sources.

Attend a Lecture Outside Your Field

Attend a lecture on a topic that normally would not interest you. Once again, you'll benefit from borrowing concepts. You'll hear ideas in totally different fields and end up finding ways to link them back to what you do. In any community of 20,000 people or more, you can open up the local paper and see a variety of groups meeting on any given night. Many of these groups have guest speakers.

Why not choose as a goal to attend one lecture per month on a topic that is not directly related to your career?

Become Interested in Other People

Ask others what they do and why they do it. Ask them what's new and innovative in their field. You can gain remarkable insights from a cab driver, housemaid, retail clerk, college student, or even a government bureaucrat. You don't have to invest a lot of time and effort in this venture.

As a goal, why not decide to simply talk with somebody totally outside your field of work for as little as five minutes? If you do this once a week, in the course of a year, you'll have had 52 five-minute conversations with people who have insights and experiences that you might never have been able to tap into.

Study the Movers and Shakers in Your Field

Look toward the people in your industry or profession who make the most profound impact. You know, the superstars—the ones who are always in the trade press and are regarded as the leading thinkers in the industry.

What do they do that's different than the rest? Study all you can about them, because, as noted author Dr. Wayne Dyer notes, "success leaves clues."

Learn from Women Who Have Reached the Top

The advances women have made as corporate executives and entrepreneurs in the last quarter of the 20th century have been nothing short of remarkable. Focusing on the top achievers among women in the corporate ranks and the top achievers among female entrepreneurs yields powerful insights and lessons for any woman—or man, for that matter—interested in establishing and reaching challenging career-related goals.

For Sure

The Evolution of Women in the Workplace

It is a plain, simple fact that women have shown themselves to be naturally incompetent to fill a great many...business positions.
—*Ladies Home Journal*, circa 1906

Women have become indispensable in business as personal secretaries.
—*Fortune*, 1938

Women-owned business is the fastest growing segment of the U.S. economy.
—*Forbes*, March 6, 1989

Based on research conducted by Edie Fraser, president of the Public Affairs Group in Washington, D.C., a vivid picture of what it takes to succeed as a corporate executive or entrepreneur emerges. Fraser studied the top 50 women in both categories.

The top 50 female corporate executives collectively manage billions of dollars as they travel the globe, consummating investment deals and building subsidiary operations for the nation's giant corporations. They are relatively young and are headed further into corporate leadership.

The top 50 female entrepreneurs are achieving extraordinary success in many lines of business, and some are preparing for family succession.

What It Takes to Become a Successful Corporate Executive or Entrepreneur

Area	Executive	Entrepreneur
Ambition	To rise to the top and be recognized as a successful executive	Fueled by the opportunity and the ability to call her own shots
Influenced By	Male mentor, corporate headhunters, or company friendships	Father or other male mentor—for example, brother or uncle; also, mother and so on
Commonality	Self-discipline, self-control, deliberateness, and long-term career plans	Creativity, risk-taking to achieve growth, high energy, and independence
Orientation to Others	Politically astute corporate animal, planned networking, team-building skills	Relationships as needed and as they develop, entrepreneurial team
Goals	Power, influence, and respect	Growth for the company "because it is mine"
Work Style	65+ hours/week, perseverance, patience to build track record, team approach	70+ hours/week, impatience, leapfrogging, opportunity and market driven
Control	Exercised by corporate culture, executive peer influence, maintaining proper image	Self-exercised, the raison d'être of the entrepreneurial career choice
Personality	Conformist	Open, gregarious
Training	MBA, management courses and seminars, project experience	On the job, business courses for younger entrepreneurs

The work-style information is a supreme example of irony. Although top entrepreneurs are workhorses, often they go into business for themselves for the flexible time.

Amidst dozens of personal and professional characteristics, 10 traits are vital to the success of both groups of women, 10 traits are prevalent among just the corporate executives, and 10 qualities are common to entrepreneurs.

Core Traits Prevalent Among Female Career Climbers

Both Groups	Corporate Executives	Entrepreneurs
❏ Ability	❏ Calculation	❏ Building
❏ Ambition & achievement	❏ Consistency	❏ Creativity
❏ Attitude	❏ Deliberative	❏ Dollar drive
❏ Commitment	❏ Discipline	❏ Dynamism
❏ Dedication & diligence	❏ Diplomacy	❏ Enthusiasm
❏ Determination	❏ Education	❏ Independence
❏ Energy	❏ Strategic planning	❏ Innovation
❏ Goal orientation	❏ Patience	❏ Passion
❏ Motivation	❏ Political savvy	❏ Risk-taking
❏ Team-building skills	❏ Power, status	❏ Vision

Top achievers in the corporate world are enthusiastic about their progress and proud of their status, as reflected in their senior positions, substantial salaries, bonuses, and stock options. They are quietly moving forward, not flaunting their success with the media.

If you thrive on change and can perceive and capitalize on opportunities, the entrepreneurial life might be your cup of herbal tea. Whereas corporate executives are deliberate, calculating, and cautious, entrepreneurs tend to be freewheeling individuals who embrace change constantly and keep an eye out for opportunity in whatever form it may disguise itself. When entrepreneurs seize an opportunity, they pour energy into making it pay off. They are overly ambitious and glad of it. Win or lose, they rely primarily on their own resources.

Whether you're a woman or a man, when you think about it, anyone can learn from the success patterns of corporate and entrepreneurial women. It's hard to argue with success, whoever achieves it.

The Least You Need to Know

➤ You must thoroughly enjoy what you do in order to sustain a healthy, happy, and prosperous career.

➤ You can establish specific goals to squash any technology anxiety you experience and actually embrace technology both at the workplace and in your personal life.

➤ One job in three may disappear over the next few years. As vital as your role may be, it's likely to shift dramatically.

➤ The happiest, most well-adjusted career achievers seem to develop the habit of making the goals of their organization their own goals.

➤ Focusing on the top achievers among women in the corporate ranks and the top achievers among female entrepreneurs yields powerful insights and lessons for any woman or man.

Chapter 11

Now for the Biggie: Your Financial Life

> ## In This Chapter
>
> ➤ I spend, therefore I am
>
> ➤ The ghost of finances past
>
> ➤ Building your nest egg slowly
>
> ➤ Making it automatic

In 1947, *Ladies Home Journal* polled thousands of American households and found that 70 percent of all their worries were about money. In five decades, little has changed.

Chances are excellent that of the seven major goal areas in your life (mental, physical, family, social, spiritual, career, and financial), you have some real challenges when it comes to getting your finances in order. It would be a Herculean task to convey everything cogent to the topic of financial goals within this short chapter, so I'll stick to the highlights!

Habitual Indebtedness Isn't Pretty (or, I'd gladly pay you Wednesday for a hamburger today!)

All of our lives, it seems, we're confronted with a bewildering array of rules and instructions for living and succeeding in this world—nowhere more so than when it comes to personal finances. The confusion about what to do with what you earn may account for some of the reasons why your savings and investment accounts aren't larger than they are. I suspect other factors may be at play, though.

Sure, I Want to Be Well Off

Most people want have enough money to live comfortably—to reasonably be able to do what they want when they want to do it. If you poll people on their financial goals, the issues that come up most often include buying a new home, providing for their children's higher education, and having a productive, prosperous retirement.

Yet, data from the Social Security Administration reveals that such "goals" are probably closer to wishes or fantasies.

U.S. Social Security Administration data from 1990 reveals that 87 percent of Americans retire with less than $10,000 per year to support them, and 50 percent have less than $5,000 per year. The average person between the ages of 45 and 54 has only $2,300 in assets.

By retirement, the typical person's assets will have grown to just $19,500. Less than 50 percent of Americans are able to participate in a company pension plan, and the average annual private pension payment is less than $5,000. At the same time, employee pension benefits are decreasing.

Medical costs are increasing and life spans are increasing. Most elderly people spend from three to five years in a nursing home or require home care with average annual costs exceeding $32,000. Of those who are 65 years old, 75 percent are dependent on relatives or charity. Meanwhile, Social Security benefits overall are decreasing!

Concern, Yes; Action, No

It seems that there is far more concern about finances than goal-attaining behavior. A recent Gallup Poll found that 57 percent of successful baby boomers between the ages of 30 and 50 in the Rocky Mountain states reported that finances are their top retirement concern and that 92 percent said they believe Social Security will be inadequate to provide their retirement financing. Yet 43 percent said they are not contributing toward a retirement plan, and 25 percent said they had no plans at all!

Something has to give!

Stopped in Your Tracks

Among the legion of excuses that otherwise rational adults offer as to why they have not set and therefore will never reach their financial goals, these often surface:

➤ "My company offers good benefits, so I don't need to do anything."

➤ "I have no confidence in making financial decisions, so I'm excused."

➤ "I did some investing once and got burned."

➤ "I don't trust financial advisors. I have hard evidence that each and every one of them is a crook."

➤ "The amount I have to save would buy a pack of bubble gum."

➤ "Who's got time?"

➤ "Retirement is just too far away to think about."

And please, if I've missed your personal favorite, feel free to record it here:

"_____."

Happiness Is a Positive Cash Flow

Suppose that your financial goals are to get out of debt, build your savings account, have money for emergencies, pay taxes as required, and maybe get a new home. Maybe to have adequate insurance in the case of loss, invest for your child's college, and contribute to your retirement fund. Where, oh where, do you begin?

On the path to controlling and then mastering your finances, achieving a positive cash flow is as good a starting point as any. A positive cash flow is as important for a family as it is for a business.

For Sure

In the 1970s when inflation was high and in the 1980s when taxpayers were able to write off the interest on debts, it made financial sense for some people to be in debt. Things were going to be more expensive if you waited to buy, and the interest you paid on acquisitions was deductible. Now, with relatively low inflation and reduced tax deductions for the interest on debt, it is no longer prudent to be in debt.

In the Red or in the Black?

Being debt free and maintaining a positive cash flow is a worthy and valid financial goal for many people, including you! Fortunately, determining whether you have a positive cash flow is simple. First, list all of your income for a typical month. Then, add up all of the dollars that are going out the door every month for your mortgage payments, insurance, housekeeper, kids' expenses, medical expenses, and so on. Are you in the black (a cash surplus) or in the red (in debt)?

Chances are that if you work with a PC and know how to run spreadsheet programs, you already have the skills to produce your own detailed cash-flow analysis.

Cash-Flow Planning 101

Skip the next several pages if you already know how to prepare a 12-month cash flow. Please follow closely if you don't know how, or it has been several years since you constructed a cash-flow analysis.

A well-developed cash-flow projection shows the timing and magnitude of your cash needs. If your cash flow shows deficiencies for any given month, beware—that is when you're most likely to rely on credit-card debt, delayed payments (along with late payment fees), and other costly maneuvers.

A Projection Form You Can Use

The following cash-flow projection form is almost self-explanatory. It is nothing more than a systematic method of noting cash inflows and outflows. As you earn income and make payments, you can compare your forecasts with actual receipts and expenditures as they occur—hence the two columns "Estimate" and "Actual." If you are a salaried employee, your earnings forecast obviously will equal your projected cash flow.

The entries listed on the form will not necessarily apply to you, and some entries might not be included that are pertinent to your specific situation, so cross out and add entries as needed.

Hopefully, your cash position at the end of each month is positive. The assumptions you make about your projected cash inflows and outflows are as important as the actual figures themselves. It is not difficult to produce a detailed cash-flow projection that is off by—yikes!—thousands of dollars. Although software spreadsheet programs can help simplify calculations, there is no substitute for plotting inflows and outflows as carefully as possible.

YEAR MONTH	Pre–Start–up Position		1		2		3		12		TOTAL		
											Columns 1-12		
	Estimate	Actual	Estimate	Actual	Estimate	Actual	Estimate	Actual	Estimate	Actual	Estimate	Actual	
1. Cash on Hand Beginning of Month: Cash on hand equals cash position in the previous month (step 7)													1.
2. Cash Inflows (a) Salary													2. (a)
(b) Commissions													(b)
(c) Fees													(c)
(d) Bonuses													(d)
(e) Alimony or child support													(e)
(f) Entitlements													(f)
(g) Other monthly inflows													(g)
3. Total Cash Receipts Sum of step 2a through step 2g													3.
4. Total Cash Available. Before cash out (step 1 plus step 3)													4.
5. Cash Outflows (a) Mortagage or rent													5. (a)
(b) Utilities													(b)
(c) Car expenses													(c)
(d) Food													(d)
(e) Medical payments													(e)
(f) Clothing													(f)
(g) Insurance													(g)
(h) Taxes													(h)
(i) Interest													(i)
(j) Other expenses													(j)
(k) Miscellaneous													(k)
6. Total Cash Paid Out. Sum of step 5a through 5k													6.
7. Cash Position. End of month (total of step 4 minus total of step 6)													7.
Enter this amount in step 1, Cash on Hand following month.													

Here is an explanation of the various components of a cash-flow projection sheet:

1. **Cash on Hand**

   Beginning of month: Cash on hand equals cash position in the previous month (step 7)

2. **Cash Inflows**
   (a) Salary
   (b) Commissions

      (c) Fees

      (d) Bonuses

      (e) Alimony or child support

      (f) Entitlements

      (g) Other monthly inflows

3. **Total Cash Receipts**

   Sum of step 2a through step 2g

4. **Total Cash Available**

   Before cash out (step 1 plus step 3)

5. **Cash Outflows**

   (a) Mortgage or rent

   (b) Utilities

   (c) Car expenses

   (d) Food

   (e) Medical payments

   (f) Clothing

   (g) Insurance

   (h) Taxes

   (I) Interest

   (j) Other expenses

   (k) Miscellaneous

6. **Total Cash Paid Out**

   Sum of step 5a through 5k

7. **Cash Position**

   End of month (total of step 4 minus total of step 6)

   Enter this amount in step 1, Cash on Hand following month

Now the great part! With a positive cash flow, you can readily identify how much money you can save each month. Some people will spend any cash surplus they have. I'm hoping that you're not among them. If you find that you can't hold on to a surplus, you might want to consider having the money automatically taken out of your income each month (more on this shortly).

Underestimating and Overestimating

As in a business, it makes good sense for you to overestimate your expenses and underestimate your income; this keeps you in a safety zone. When you're in a positive cash-flow situation, even after you've allocated a sum for savings, you should allow for emergencies.

If you get into a small car accident, for example, and your insurance doesn't cover the deductible, you can afford to pay the damages. Beyond that, strive to establish emergency funds equal to three to six months of actual living expenses. I know this might sound like a tall order, but hey, I'm giving sound advice.

A House of Cards

A major factor that makes it harder for many people to achieve positive cash flows is that they become house poor. See if this is familiar: People who bought houses in the 1980s when inflation was high and houses were appreciating now sometimes find that these houses are not worth as much as homes on the East or West Coast of the U.S., for example. At the same time, the earning power of many of these same home buyers has declined.

Are you among this group? Or, do you simply live in expensive digs without all the extenuating circumstances? Even if you've been able to refinance your mortgage and obtain an attractive rate, if the overall principal on your loan remains high, you still will be in a *house-poor* situation.

This is a potentially risky situation, because so many unpredictable things could happen. And, unless you are a bona-fide upwardly mobile income earner, remaining house poor can be a lifetime sentence. It might make sense to sell your house if you can at least break even, move to a less expensive home, and start investing the extra cash on a monthly basis.

Go for the Gold!

An emergency fund is one of the fundamental building blocks to any solid financial plan. The more uncertain your finances are (for instance, if you work on commission, own a business, or are an independent salesperson), the more important emergency funds are to you!

Uh-Oh!

CAUTION!

If you are in a house-poor situation and your money keeps going into your house, you might be contributing to one of your most lofty goals: building equity. You might not be accumulating any other investments, however. In the long run, all of your savings will be in one asset: your home.

When Spending Threatens Your Cash Flow

If being house poor is not your malady, maybe overspending is. Regardless of how much you earn, there is a simple formula for getting into a negative cash-flow position. Let the drums roll:

Spend one more dollar than you take home each month.

It doesn't matter how much you are earning; if you spend one dollar more, you are heading into a negative cash flow. If you are in debt, your number-one short-term financial goal is getting out of debt. The best way to get out of debt and improve your cash-flow situation is to develop systematic ways to limit your spending and to save more. I suggest that you carry only one credit card (and, if you can, only when you are traveling—that's the only time it's crucial to have it).

One tactic that works for some people is to leave their checkbook and credit cards at home. Then, if they see something they want, they go home, think about it for a while, and decide whether they need it. If they have the resolve to go back to the store, perhaps it is something they really wanted instead of simply an impulse purchase. Travel without the tools that allow you to impulse buy when at all possible.

Getting Those Balances to Stay Down

If you can't pay off your full credit card balance each month, a lower interest rate will save you money. If you do pay off your balance in full each month, the best bet is to choose a card with no annual fee.

For Sure

For a small fee, you can purchase a list of the most competitive interest rates and credit cards in the country and find out how to qualify for the lowest rate possible. Contact Bankcard Holders of America, 560 Herndon Parkway, Suite 120, Herndon, VA 20070, (703) 481-1100.

Credit Damage Control

If you've run into problems because of debt, you might want to know about credit-reporting agencies, such TRW, Equifax, and Trans Union. Their toll-free numbers follow:

TRW: (800) 392-1122
Equifax: (800) 685-1111
Trans Union: (800) 916-8800

You can find other credit bureaus in your area by looking in the Yellow Pages under Credit Bureaus or Credit Reporting.

Chances are that you might have to set the record straight when it comes to reports about you on file. Also, if you apply for credit, insurance, a job, or to rent an apartment, your credit record might be examined. You can make sure yours is accurate by doing the following:

➤ Get a copy once a year or before major purchases. Your report is generally free if you've been denied credit in the past 60 days. Otherwise, the credit bureau can impose a reasonable charge.

➤ Read the report carefully. The credit bureau must provide trained personnel to explain information in the report.

➤ Dispute any incorrect information in your credit record. Write to the credit bureau and be specific about what is wrong with your report.

The credit bureau then has to investigate your dispute and respond to you, usually within 30 to 45 days. Information that is inaccurate or that cannot be verified must be corrected or taken off your report.

Out of Debt

The moment you climb out of debt and get into a positive cash flow, or if you already are enjoying one, another worthwhile goal is to put your money to its best use. The key to financial independence is not necessarily working hard, being smart, or even being successful. It is recognizing that what you keep is more important than what you earn. It is putting the money where it will work the hardest for you.

Essentially, there are two currencies in life: time and money. If you don't have a lot of time, you will need a lot of money. If you don't have a lot of money but you have a lot of time, you still can reach your financial goals.

So, Joe, what will you do with your money? Buy that house, send the kids to college, or make for a comfortable retirement?

Because the desire to purchase a new home (not necessarily a "new house") is usually a short-term goal, many people can handle the calculations themselves. With the help of a mortgage banker, they can determine whether they can handle a new home purchase.

Additionally, during the loan-application process, most mortgage vendors can offer precise data on what the buyer's monthly payments will be, how much the taxes and insurance will be each year, and what kinds of income tax deductions the buyer will be able to claim as a result of making the purchase. In other words, most of the financial stuff is handled for you!

Providing your children's higher education may be further off into the future. However, this might be something you want to do in addition to purchasing a new home.

Uh-Oh!
Most people spend more time planning a party than they do their future, let alone addressing what to do with their money. Consequently, the typical 50-year-old American has only a few thousand dollars in savings. This is not a lot to show for nearly three decades of earnings.

CAUTION!

Divvying Up the Funds

Suppose that you can save $2,000 a month. You want to send your child to college, and that will start in six years. Meanwhile, your retirement is 20 years away. On top of this, you want to buy a new home. If educating your child is the most important of these three goals, allocate about half of your monthly savings toward that goal.

As a rule of thumb, the sooner your children will enter college, the more likely it is that saving for this will become the dominate goal. However, you have to be careful not to let college expenses eat into your other investments, leaving nothing for your retirement or other goals until your kids are out of school.

Dis or Dat?

The next issue: Is buying the new home more important than the retirement goal? Because the new home is closer on the horizon than retirement, it tends to be the dominant goal with most people, although it is not necessarily more important. Of the remaining $1,000 you have each month to invest, you might want to put $700 toward the house and $300 toward retirement.

If you're married, you also want to have a heart-to-heart talk with your spouse about what you both expect in retirement.

Will it be more lavish?
Will it be scaled down?
Will it be pretty much the same?

Some people have the mistaken notion that diverting all their investments to their child's imminent entrance into college will take care of that goal faster, and then in a few years they can begin saving for retirement or some other goal. However, those people end up shortchanging that future goal.

> **CAUTION!** **Uh-Oh!**
> A retirement goal is a hazy goal when you're in your early working years. As you pass your 40th birthday, though, you begin to think of your retirement with increasing frequency. A retirement goal for most people can be defined simply by looking at their current lifestyle and what it costs to maintain.

Shopping for the Right Investment Professionals

It's a jungle out there. In addition to calling around, getting recommendations, checking references, and using the questions on the next page to grill potential candidates, here's useful information to help separate the wheat from the chaff when it comes to choosing an advisor:

➤ *Certified Financial Planner (CFP)*: A designation given to an independent financial counselor by colleges accredited through the International Board of Standards & Practices for Certified Financial Planners; Englewood, Colorado; (800) 322-4237.

➤ *Chartered Financial Consultant (ChFC)*: To earn this, the candidate has to undergo a program of study consisting of six required parts plus four electives, with 10 two-hour exams.

➤ *Master of Science in Financial Services (MSFS)*: A degree awarded by the American College to those who complete advanced courses in financial planning.

➤ *Registered Financial Planner (RFP)*: A designation offered by the International Association for Financial Planning to members who prove they have had three years of full-time practice as a planner and have a business degree as well as a brokerage securities license or an insurance license.

➤ *Registered Investment Advisor (RIA)*: Indicates that this person is registered with the Securities and Exchange Commission, which signifies that the candidate has provided written information about fees, types of clients, investment specialties, education, industry affiliation, and compensation. Note: There is no requirement for formal training.

Generally, I recommend that you retain a CFP who earns a fee based on services rendered rather than commissions.

Younger people who are just starting to plan for these goals might want to start off with some continuing education classes to get an overview and an idea of where to start. Classes are offered on a wide range of topics, including managing your money, buying a house, and investing in mutual funds. Often, these classes are taught by one of these types of professionals.

Questions to Ask Your Financial Advisor

Don't be shy when it comes to getting the right guidance—after all, it is YOUR MONEY. Here some basic questions to ask:

➤ Are your firm's balance sheet and income statement available for my review?

➤ Do you have a disclosure statement that includes the names and backgrounds of management and staff, potential conflicts of interest, and methods of compensation?

➤ How long has your company been in the financial counseling business? How long have *you* been in the profession?

➤ Do you have letters from existing clients for my review?

➤ What other resources and benefits are available through your firm?

➤ What percentage of your earnings is from investment advice, tax services and planning, real estate, and commissions? What financial certifications, designations, and licenses do you maintain?

Now the Tough Questions

If the professional you are meeting with is still breathing, here are second-round questions:

- ➤ Is your firm financially sound?
- ➤ Have you ever filed for bankruptcy personally?
- ➤ Has any client ever sued you?
- ➤ Have any of your licenses or certifications ever been suspended or revoked?
- ➤ Have you ever been censored by the Securities and Exchange Commission?
- ➤ Have you ever been reprimanded by any of the professional societies or any state regulatory agencies?
- ➤ What safeguards are there in my doing business with you?
- ➤ Why should I do business with you?

Make It Automatic

Go for the Gold!
Ideally, you forget that the amount being withdrawn is yours! You live on what your resulting take-home pay is, as if that is all there ever was available. Then, one day when you are ready, you'll reap the bonanza of the continual, subtle contributions you made to your financial independence.

Regardless of who counsels you, have an automatic amount taken out of your paycheck every month. Particularly for salaried individuals, having money drawn directly from your paycheck is safe, convenient, and worry-free. Have it go into tax-deferred accounts, annuities, retirement funds, and so on, based on the mixture of financial goals you want to achieve.

By *automatic*, I mean money is invested every month without any concern or discussion on your part. The most automatic of systems is to have money withdrawn from your paycheck so that your investments keep building while you learn to live on the amount that is left after this automatic investment.

Ignore the Hype

You and/or your counselor can tie up a lot of time and concern attempting to figure out exactly when it is the right time to buy or sell. Yet, market timing is largely irrelevant.

For Sure

When you make contributions to a reputable, long-term investment fund, your return over a 15- or 20-year period (regardless of when you invest, as long as you invest on a periodic basis) tends to stay within plus or minus three-fourths of 1 percent of what everyone else earns when contributing to similar funds. The key to investing automatically is to start with an amount of money that you can safely live without for the long term; the amount you take home must adequately cover your cost of living as you have devised it.

At the end of a year, if you find that you are able to live on your monthly take-home amount with no difficulty, you can increase how much you invest each month, perhaps gradually at first.

Alternatively, if you have to scrimp and cut corners, and this causes significant disruptions in the way you live, perhaps too much is being withdrawn each month. In that case, it makes sense to roll back how much is withdrawn.

Be careful: It is easy to justify taking more money for the present and leaving less for the future.

An Automatic Benefit for Automatic Investing

Investing automatically means that you benefit from a technique called *dollar-cost averaging*. This is simply a fancy way of saying that you benefit when you put the same amount each month into the same investment, whether the stock market goes up or down in value! Nice deal, eh?

This benefit occurs because you have made regular contributions to your investment over time; whether your money went into the account on a good day or bad day, when the market was high or low, it all tends to average out in the long run.

In fact, dollar-cost averaging is recognized as one of the most sound investment strategies available!

Let's See Whether You're Serious

How much are you willing to reserve and save? Pretend that you have $1,000 right in front of you, perhaps in the form of 10 new $100 bills with Benjamin Franklin staring right at you. Now spend just a few seconds thinking about what you'll do with that money. That isn't a difficult exercise, is it? Most people can spend that money mentally, 20 times over, with no problem.

Suppose that those same ten $100 bills are in front of you, but five of them magically rise off the table into a secure, long-term investment account with your name on it. Five $100 bills still remain in front of you. Consider what you will do with the $500. Once again, it probably didn't take long to spend that money, did it?

Now, the telling question: Did you feel any worse off for having the opportunity to spend only $500? Probably not. Most people report that when a portion of their monthly increase is taken off the top, and they still have the opportunity to do what they want with 50 percent or so of the money, they still feel very good about it.

Safe, Automatic Investments

The safest portfolio you can assemble that enables you to invest your money, check it quarterly, and know that you are earning a good rate of return, is one that invests in stocks through a vehicle called *mutual funds*.

401(k) Pensions

The most common and among the safest type of automatic investment is a 401(k) plan set up at your place of employment. Essentially, a 401(k) is a type of pension plan established by an employer for employees to prepare for their own retirement instead of the company providing a pension plan for employees en masse.

A 401(k) plan is employee directed, which means that you decide how much of your pay, within limits, you are willing to contribute to it. Most 401(k) plans allow you to choose from many types of investments, so you end up deciding which types of investments constitute your plan. These often include mutual funds that may have a gross fund, bond fund, and/or fixed account fund. Some types of mutual funds are a blend of many types of funds.

With a 401(k) investment, you benefit because the money that is taken out of your paycheck is before taxes, and your employer will probably match a certain percentage of what you invest.

Mutual Funds

Mutual funds are run by professional money managers who strive for a well-balanced, diversified portfolio. The funds may consist of stocks, corporate bonds, government bonds, and other well-chosen investment vehicles.

You have the opportunity to invest in mutual funds independent of 401(k) plans. Some mutual funds represent strict stock investments, strict bonds, hybrids, and so on. The success of any mutual fund portfolio in which you invest depends a great deal on the portfolio's asset allocation.

Fortunately, there is an independent rating service that provides comprehensive information about mutual funds. It's called the *Morningstar Report*. This report is available in the Business Reference section of most libraries. Also, check out the Web site **http://www.MorningStar.com** for more information.

If you don't want to have amounts taken from your checking account, then for pities sake, pay yourself first. Make sure that you contribute to your investment each month before you pay all other bills.

You might want to create your own set of 12 envelopes pre-addressed to the company that maintains your investment account. Then, write a check and fill one envelope each month, the same as you do for mortgages, car payments, and other non-negotiable monthly payments.

If you are worried that you might not have enough to pay your bills, don't. You might not have enough in a given month, but it's not worth a huge amount of concern. You'll make the payments.

Uh-Oh!
Too many people attempt to invest automatically by doing the reverse. After they write all their checks and make other expenditures, they see what is left; then they might contribute that sum to their investment account. This kind of piecemeal method of investing over a 15- or 20-year period will yield just a fraction of what regular, automatic investments will yield.

Easy Monitoring

Monitoring your investments is easy, because each of your investments will offer you monthly or quarterly data concerning what transpired in the current period. If a particular investment isn't earning the kind of return you and/or your advisor know you can get elsewhere, in most instances you can readily shift your investment.

The Safety Component

Once your investments are in place, safeguard yourself. You don't want to hear this, but you need to have enough insurance—not just life insurance, but health insurance, of course, auto insurance, disability insurance, homeowner's/renter's insurance, and personal liability insurance. These are relatively affordable safeguards and can offer very strong and necessary protections.

Uh-Oh!
Avoid moving investments around frequently. Because you are going to have sound investments that have long and distinguished track records, you are not going to allow yourself to be influenced by momentary fluctuations in the stock market. Your simple monitoring and reviewing process only needs to be done quarterly.

Most people don't buy life insurance because they don't want to contemplate their own demise. Buying life insurance is seen as a type of personal confirmation that they will, in fact, die some day. It's the same with disability policies and other types of safeguards.

For Sure

Homeowner's insurance is becoming more difficult to obtain because of the rapid pace of natural disasters occurring in the country. The type of insurance available in some parts of the country changes monthly, so it is necessary to have access to the most current information.

All homeowners, particularly those with children, should have liability insurance. With the litigious society we live in, it is good to know that you have coverage if someone decides to sue you because they have slipped on your front step or have been bitten by your dog. These unpredictable events can wreak havoc. Liability coverage typically is called an *umbrella policy*. It is inexpensive and generally is sold with homeowner's insurance or auto insurance instead of on its own. The cost may be about $200 a year for $1 million worth of coverage.

The Least You Need to Know

➤ Don't let excuses stop you from engaging in establishing important financial goals; the longer you wait, the harder your task.

➤ A *cash-flow projection form* is a systematic method of noting cash inflows and outflows. It is the easiest place to start when you want to get in control of your finances.

➤ The moment you climb out of debt, be sure to put your money to its best use. Recognize that what you keep is more important than what you earn.

➤ You'll probably want to get guidance from a trusted, competent advisor when dealing with the dilemma of trying to invest when you have multiple financial goals.

➤ You should automatically invest every month—perhaps by having money withdrawn from your paycheck.

Part 3
Secrets of Master Goal-Setters

Now that you have a well-rounded view of the seven basic goal areas in life, let's look at another dimension of reaching your goals. What do the most accomplished people do when it comes to setting and achieving goals that perhaps ordinary men and women don't do?

All the chapters in this section—including Chapters 12, "Personalizing Your Goals," 13, "It's All in the Wording," 14, "Committing to Paper," 15, "A Question of Time," and 16, "Gotta Have a Challenge," offer tools and insights to speed you on your way to becoming a champion goal-setter and goal-achiever.

Let's start now with Chapter 12 to see why it's so important to claim ownership of what you've been asked or chosen to do.

Personalizing Your Goals

You already know about the importance of personalizing a goal, especially if it has been imposed on you by an outside source. How do you convince yourself that you want do something when at first you didn't want to do it? What are the indicators that you have in fact personalized a goal and made it your own? Read on!

Maintaining a Suitable Perspective

In the pursuit of any challenging goal, you are likely to face a fair share of second guessing and self-doubt. Even the most talented goal achievers experience doubt and concern. Here's how to sail right on through to completion.

Keep the End in Sight

Many people feel that if they don't enjoy the means, the ends can't be worthwhile, so they stop short of reaching their goals. But what worthwhile goal doesn't have its share of drudgery in the quest for its attainment? The key is to revel in the drudgery. Say what?!

Go for the Gold!
Whatever blood, sweat, and tears you braved on the path to what you wanted, revel in them, for they were yours. If you can't see that now, trust that one day you will.

Know that while you're licking envelopes or stamping widgets or spending yet another half-hour on the treadmill, there's a greater good that lies just beyond the horizon.

Think back to an activity you experienced over a prolonged period of time, such as attending and finally graduating from college. While you were in college, it seemed as if you would never get to the final semester and the final exam in the final course. Then, one day it came, and—poof!—you were out. Aren't you thrilled to be out of college today with a degree (if that was the path you chose)? I'm betting strongly the answer is yes.

Your Energy Will Be Uneven

Hardly anyone can maintain a constant pace in pursuit of anything. That's easily understood. What if you don't enjoy the particular task at the moment? If so, notice your energy level. Ask yourself these questions:

➤ How do I feel about my intended outcome?

➤ How will I feel when I'm there?

➤ Did my energy rise a little?

If your energy has increased, you're probably on the right path—no need to turn back or shift course. This Bud's for you. Whoops, I mean, this goal's for you.

Breathing Is Not Optional

If you get wrapped up in your pursuit, sometimes you stray from the basics of what it takes to stay in the saddle. Still, you get to take a deep breath whenever you want. You get to drop back and relax on occasion. You get to take a shower, you get to take a nap, you get to go to sleep at night, and you get to start again. Why?

You're not some puppet dangling on a string, forced by a puppet master to proceed at breakneck speed with no sense of ownership of your goal. In fact, proper breathing techniques are essential for entertainers, trainers, speakers, athletes, orchestra conductors, piccolo players, women in labor, presidents giving State of the Union addresses, and everyone else.

Many Goals Don't Require Perfection

For Sure

Life is not a trap set for us by God so that He can condemn us for failing. Life is not a spelling bee where no matter how many words you've gotten right, you're disqualified if you make one mistake. Life is more like a baseball season where even the best team loses one-third of its games and even the worst team has its days of brilliance. Our goal is to win more games than we lose.

—Rabbi Harold S. Kushner, in his book *How Good Do We Have to Be?*

If you find yourself with an array of goals that seemingly require perfection, remember whose goals they are—they're yours. You can loosen the screws a tad and give yourself some slack. Indeed, in some cases, you won't make it otherwise. If your goal is to lose *x* number of pounds in so many weeks and only perfect discipline, perfect meals, perfect caloric intake, perfect exercise, and so on will get you there, you *will not* get there. Most of your goals don't require perfection either. They may require constant progress but something far less than perfection in the pursuit.

You'd be better off to give yourself more time to allow for the fact that perfection not only isn't necessary in this case, but it's not desirable; worse, it can prove to be counter-productive. Ask yourself questions such as these to see whether you might be striving for perfection when it isn't necessary:

➤ Do I frequently grit my teeth?

➤ Am I able to maintain my normal demeanor?

➤ Do I feel easily frustrated?

➤ Am I sleeping as well as usual?

Thou Shalt Not Comparest Thyself to Others

If the goal is truly your own, you can proceed happily without being sidetracked by the accomplishments of others. All too often, we pursue things that we see other people have achieved.

Remember the warning in Chapter 5, "Mind Over Matter": It's okay to set goals to avoid pain, but then you have to take it further and identify the positive aspects of what your achievement will mean.

Uh-Oh!
If you want a huge house simply because there are people in your town who live in huge homes, you might one day find yourself sitting in your mansion feeling very alone.

The goal of wanting a large home must be your own and must be connected with positive reasoning. Perhaps you want enough space to build a large playroom for your children. Perhaps you've always wanted a guest bedroom (not just because I recommended it in Chapter 8, "Your Social Life and How to Have One"). Perhaps you always wanted to have your own personal library and will need lots of room to store your thousands of volumes.

All About Ownership

Commercials often talk about the pride of ownership. If you own a home, you're likely to treat it much better than if you rent it. After all, it's a long-term investment. Any addi-

Go for the Gold!
When you take owner-ship of your goals, whether they are imposed externally or internally, you tend to take better care of them. You treat them as if they will contrib-ute to your well-being and perhaps even add to your psychic equity.

tions and improvements you make to the house can only add to your equity. Same thing with any other big-ticket item, such as a car, a recreational vehicle, or a vacation condo.

In case you think that goals imposed by external sources somehow can never be truly yours, think again. Some of the greatest goal achievers in recent times essentially were following the orders of their shareholders, board of directors, constituencies, and so on.

Lee Iacocca, one of the most prominent personalities in America in the 1980s, was not an entrepreneur. He was president of Ford Motor Co. and then president and chair-man of the Chrysler Corp. As head, he certainly had influ-ence over the direction the company would take, but at the same time, he had to meet a bevy of goals imposed on him by the people to whom he was responsible.

My Fellow Americans

Uh-Oh!
Even at the highest levels of business and government, top achievers as a rule are dealing with a plethora of goals imposed on them by external sources.

Even the president of the United States has a variety of externally imposed goals that he needs to embrace and make his own. In the United States, the president is beholden to his party's platform. Once he takes office, he has to deal with an inherited national budget.

After the Cabinet members are in place, they report back to the president regarding the various constraints and limita-tions of what they can achieve given the nature of their agency, its budget, social conditions, and so on. In nearly every nation on earth, heads of state also must deal with various goals imposed on them.

You Lead, I'll Follow

While I'm at it, many goal achievers also are not innovators or leaders in their field. Instead, they take their cues from some other highly influential person, such as a religious leader, head of state, corporate CEO, and so on. Being a follower, particularly in American culture, is highly underrated. Yet, where is it written that what you want to achieve has to be your own idea?

I could get into a long, philosophical discussion about how most of what you want does not actually represent your original, unique thoughts anyway. It suffices to say that a goal you identify as being worthy of you and worth the pursuit is no less valid whether it is imposed externally or is the result of another's influence on you.

Ownership Language

Here are some phrases you can say or think to help bolster your efforts in pursuit of a goal initially selected by you or by others:

➤ I choose to do this.
➤ I fully accept it.
➤ This can be done.
➤ It's my responsibility now.
➤ I'm up for the challenge.
➤ I will deal with it.
➤ Pass it over to me.
➤ Let me get started.
➤ It is my personal quest to…
➤ I am fully participating.
➤ It is my intention to…
➤ Point me in the right direction.
➤ Just say when to…
➤ Put it on my plate.
➤ You can count on me.
➤ You've come to the right place.
➤ I accept.
➤ When do I start?
➤ It's a done deal.
➤ I'm on it.
➤ Consider it done.

I'm Handling This

Whether you initially chose your goal or it was handed to you, there are yet other indications as to when indeed it is *your goal*, and you want to achieve it.

Am I Having Fun Yet?

Somewhere along the trail, no matter how rough things get, if the goal is yours, you will experience some moments of deep satisfaction if not outright fun. This is as good an indicator as any to let you know whether you're striving for something that you do indeed desire.

Is My Approach Organized?

When a goal is yours, you organize yourself in ways that support that goal. You know where the related files are. If somebody asks you how you're doing, you can pull out your files or chart, point right to it, and tell them where you are and where you're going to be tomorrow.

No Waiting for Deadlines

Another possible clue as to when a goal is yours is when you don't need a deadline to serve as a motivator. Indeed, for many of the long-term and continuing goals you set for yourself, waiting until one minute before the deadline would be counterproductive. You can't accumulate vast sums of cash at the last moment, nor can you lose significant amounts of weight or finish reading so many great novels.

Uh-Oh!
If it's easy for you to shrug off the blame, disassociate yourself, and pretend you didn't have any input, chances are you were never really committed to a goal in the first place.

A Willingness to Take Responsibility

Another indication that a goal is truly yours is when you're willing to take responsibility for the outcome, whether good or bad. If others come along and ask who's responsible, and you tell them you are, the goal is indeed yours.

Can They Take It From Me?

A wonderful way to determine whether something is your goal is to think about a situation where the goal is taken from you. Suppose that you could no longer proceed down your chosen path. Suppose that all activity in pursuit of a certain goal had to cease. Would you

➤ Be outraged?

➤ Object?

➤ Fight for your right?

If so, it's your goal.

Alternatively, if you could take it or leave it, if you wouldn't be that upset, if it all would be forgotten by the next day, chances are it's not *your* goal.

You could undertake this exercise right now with any goals you've set for yourself, especially those that are in motion. Pretend your goal is about to be taken from you.

If its loss does not cause any concern on your part, perhaps you ought to let it go entirely. If it's a goal imposed by external sources, you have not yet internalized it, and you have no opportunity but to do so, go back through the ideas I presented in this chapter so far and find ways to make it your goal.

Bend Me, Shape Me

Perhaps you have some leeway in the situations you encounter and can engage in the *shaping* of your goals.

Suppose that you have to complete your entire store inventory by the end of the month. You can do plenty of things to make your task more enjoyable and rewarding and ultimately make it your own goal. Perhaps you can tackle the job one aisle at a time. Or, you might begin with all high-priced items. You might devise other methods for proceeding that enable you to retain some measure of control.

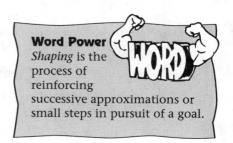

Word Power
Shaping is the process of reinforcing successive approximations or small steps in pursuit of a goal.

Make It Like a Game

I sometimes have helpers assemble packages that need to be mailed. Anyone might surmise that this job is boring. After all, if you have hundreds of envelopes in front of you that need to be stuffed, sealed, and mailed, you might think the next hour or so is going to pass as slowly as molasses.

I tell my helpers about different approaches they can take to make the time pass more quickly and enjoyably. For example, how many envelopes can they stuff in the next five minutes? Now it becomes a game instead of a chore. Almost everyone who has ever done this for me accepts the challenge.

Then, in the following five minutes, they see whether they can beat their previous best. How many times can you psyche yourself up for a five-minute period?

By approaching an externally imposed task in this way, you can view almost anything in a different light and internalize it as your own goal.

The Japanese Way

If time tests are not your thing, perhaps the art of kaizen will inspire you. *Kaizen* means *continuous improvement* and refers to a Japanese philosophy about how one approaches work.

Suppose that whatever task you undertook, no matter how insignificant or mundane, it became a challenge of sorts? If you had to sweep the decks, for example, you'd figure out how to sweep them most efficiently. If you've ever been to a hockey match and you've seen the Zamboni machine used between quarters, you'll know what I'm talking about.

Looking for More Ways

For whatever goal has been imposed on you externally, you have the option of approaching so many facets of it in so many ways.

The seasoned kaizen practitioner first looks for ways to make improvements that will offer the most immediate and dramatic paybacks. Veterans know that such results spur one on to look for even more methods of improvement. Like stuffing as many envelopes as you can in a five-minute period, the art of seeking continuous improvement is challenging and in many cases fun.

Here are some ideas for attaining improvements. Can you often make your product, service, or concept…

❑ Higher ❑ Remote

❑ Compact ❑ Faster

❑ Automatic ❑ Systemized

❑ Less expensive ❑ Modular

❑ Backed-up ❑ Lighter

❑ Portable ❑ Invisible

Making It Yours Through Role-Playing

Role-playing is like acting. You define a desirable behavior and then act it out. Suppose that you're trying to achieve something you've never attempted. Or, suppose that something has been imposed on you and you know you have to do it. How do you get to that hallowed ground? How do you make it yours? Assume the role of someone who wants to do it. Role-playing will help you master new behaviors.

Dr. Tony Alessandra, who defined the seven basic goal areas, says that role-playing can be done alone or with a partner and only takes a few minutes. As with other pursuits, the more you practice, the better you will become.

Play-Acting

One form of role-playing is getting together with a friend and *play-acting*. Define a situation and the desired behaviors. Then run through it, trying your best to act as you would like to in real life. Suppose that your goal is to increase your sales. You've identified that you're not really relaxed in front of customers, and you feel that they sense this and it diminishes the power of your presentations.

So, you and a friend set up a situation in which you play the salesperson and your friend plays the buyer. You then interact with the buyer in ways that enable you to relax more than you have in the past. You might practice using more eye contact, holding your body in a relaxed posture, listening more, joking with the buyer, and so on.

Go for the Gold!
Role-playing is an excellent way to introduce new behaviors in a relaxed, non-threatening atmosphere.

Afterward, you and your friend should discuss how each of you felt during the exercise. Repeat this exercise over and over until you feel that you've made notable progress.

Let's Pretend

Imagine a sales situation in which you were not relaxed, such as when asking someone for an appointment. How did you feel? Terrified? Someone with a fear of asking people for appointments typically might think, "Why should I ask? He's going to reject me," or "If he rejects me, I will be devastated."

Suppose that you start role-playing new thoughts in the old situation. Instead of your negative assumptions and thinking, you can substitute this:

> *I'm going to ask because I have a good chance of getting the appointment. I'm going to expect acceptance and will get it. I'm going to invite acceptance through my attitude. If I get rejected, I'll move on to the next person who may want to schedule me!*

By using such mental role-playing, you can practice what you want to achieve in real life and become adept at securing appointments (see Chapter 19, "Visualization Techniques").

Go for the Gold!
The great philosopher William James once said, "If you act a certain way long enough, it becomes you. When you act loving, a funny thing happens. You start to feel loving."

Similarly, if you act confident, you start to feel confident. When you act as if a goal is your own, you start to feel as if it's your own.

Personal Influences on the Goals You Establish

On the way to owning your goals, did someone or something serve as an initiating or sustaining influence?

As the story goes, the famous novelist Stephen King sent three manuscripts to an editor over more than a two-year period only to have all three rejected. He was working at a laundry at the time, was married, and was barely able to keep his head financially above water.

One night he became so distraught that he threw his fourth manuscript, which was in progress, into the garbage can. His wife, Tabitha, took it out the next morning and admonished him for giving up. He got back into the writing groove, averaging about 1,500 words a day, and when he was done, he sent the complete manuscript to the editor.

A Multimillion-Dollar Retrieval

King was certain that this manuscript would be rejected like the others, but instead he got a deal and a $2,500 advance. The novel was *Carrie*, and it went on to sell five million copies and became a box-office smash in 1976. As you may know, King's previous three manuscripts were published years later, and each of them fetched healthy profits.

By taking the manuscript for *Carrie* out of the garbage, Tabitha King literally committed an act worth millions of dollars. How is that for a sustaining influence?

Hear My Song

Singer Luther Vandross, a Grammy award winner, acknowledges David Bowie for providing the turning point in his career. Bowie overheard Vandross singing and invited him to be on what turned out to be a hit album for Bowie, *Young Americans*.

As a result, Vandross went on tour with Bowie and gained valuable experience, maintained resiliency, and ultimately become his own cheerleader, provider, and partner.

A Lasting Impression

Dr. John Hope Franklin acknowledges Professor Theodore S. Currier at Fisk University as being his initiating influence. When Dr. Franklin was an undergraduate, he heard Currier give two lectures on contemporary civilization. Franklin says,

> *I was quite impressed and wondered if the impression would hold over the course of the entire term. [My impression] not only held, but the excitement of exploring historical problems and witnessing the ebb and flow of the historical process turned me away from an earlier plan to study law and to a determination to make the study of history my life's work.*

Dr. Currier then helped Franklin enroll in seminars and reading courses to make certain that Franklin would have the educational foundation to pursue graduate work at Harvard University. Currier even went so far as to borrow money to pay for Franklin's tuition at Harvard.

I'd Rather Talk Than Write

In my own experience, I had the good fortune of meeting Jefferson Bates, author of *Dictating with Precision*. I already had a couple of articles published, but I wrote them out in longhand and always found writing to be laborious—this was before the days when everyone had a PC.

Bates encouraged me to use dictation equipment and from that point on, the skies opened up. I began dictating articles, entire chapters of books, and then entire books. Currently, I can dictate 20 to 30 pages in one sitting, whether in a comfortable chair, a lounge seat by the pool, or in any other relatively quiet location.

I'm eager to use voice-recognition technology, which will enable me to simply talk while my computer translates what I say into a word processing file and then saves it to my hard drive. I'll then be able to eliminate the pocket dictator, the transcription, and a ton of expenses. As voice-recognition technology is perfected, and then super powerful chips enable notebook and laptop computers to take on the task, I suspect I'll be writing and publishing books from around the globe.

If Jefferson Bates had never loaned me his pocket dictator for a few minutes, who knows—I might be the world's fastest typist by now.

The Least You Need to Know

➤ In the pursuit of any challenging goal, it is natural to experience some second guessing and self-doubt.

➤ Hardly anyone can maintain a constant pace in pursuit of any particular goal; of course, perfection usually isn't required.

➤ Some of the greatest goal achievers in recent times essentially were following the orders of others.

➤ It's likely that you have some leeway in the goals imposed on you and that you then can shape them.

➤ Acknowledge the influences that helped you initiate or sustain a goal.

Chapter 13

It's All in the Wording

In This Chapter

➤ Staying positive through thick and thin

➤ Busting through the fear

➤ From negative to positive

That second day or second week after you embark on a worthy goal, you can count on something creeping up that will get in the way of your progress if you let it. As you learned in Chapter 12, "Personalizing Your Goals," that something is *doubt*. In this chapter, you'll look at the importance of using positive wording when devising your goals, using positive language when referring to them, and maintaining a positive outlook so that doubt has nary a foothold.

The Human Predicament

No matter what goal you're seeking, whether it's something that will take you a day, a week, a month, or many years, along the way, all kinds of reasons will begin to appear as to why you will not be successful.

These thoughts will arise because you are a human being and it's natural, not because you're deviant or negative or don't truly want to achieve your goal.

Forewarned Is Forearmed

Armed with the knowledge that negative thoughts and perceptions will creep up, you're better prepared to handle them. Doubt, you see, is like a small break in a dike. It might start as a crack or a small hole, slowly becoming larger, and then, if you're not careful, opening up into a major break. Before you know it, all the water rushes through, and your quest for a desired outcome is flooded.

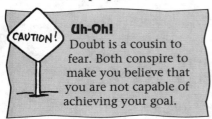

Uh-Oh!
Doubt is a cousin to fear. Both conspire to make you believe that you are not capable of achieving your goal.

Why, you ask, do you have to experience these feelings at all? Actually, the human organism essentially thrives on *homeostasis*—achieving a comfortable balance in life.

Careful! Subconscious at Work

Undoubtedly, you've heard that the mind contains both conscious and subconscious realms. The subconscious realm ingests information about your life and concludes that the way things are is how they ought to be. Consider these examples:

➤ If you smoke, your subconscious is convinced that you want to continue to smoke.

➤ If you weigh a certain amount, it concludes that you want to weigh that amount.

➤ If you're fearful of going out in public, it concludes that you want to stay away from public places.

Name anything that you do or think on a habitual basis, and sure enough, you'll see that your subconscious is at work perpetuating the status quo.

When you have a goal to improve yourself or to better your life, even though, on a conscious level, you might truly want to move, your subconscious concludes that, yup, despite what you're saying, you really want to stay right here. Hence, you tend to continue to think how you've been thinking, continue to act how you've been acting, and continue to be how you've been.

So, what you've always done will get you where it has always gotten you.

Your Subconscious in High Gear

Consider the situation in which a spouse has suffered long-term physical abuse. Ninety percent or more of battered spouses are women, so let's focus on a situation in which a woman is the battered spouse.

She wants to leave the relationship and has made plans to do so several times. She knows that it's never going to improve. Worse, the physical abuse has been escalating. Sometimes, she doesn't know how she can stand it, but after a couple days of calm, it doesn't seem so bad after all.

One night, she is beaten badly and decides that this is it. There's no way she's going to stay in this relationship. She stays at a friend's house or with her mother—anywhere but with her physically abusive spouse.

The friend, mother, or advisor has long implored her to get out of the relationship. Many times, it seemed as if she was going to, but then, to her own amazement, she finds herself continuing on. What is going on here? How could she possibly continue on when she knows on every level that the relationship is doomed?

As you guessed, the reason why she can't leave is because, on some level, her subconscious has concluded that this situation is what she wants. It sounds almost maddening, doesn't it?

Fear of the Unknown

To her subconscious, leaving the relationship represents fear. Her subconscious has concluded that her ability to leave, to venture off on her own, and perhaps to develop a new relationship is doubtful. However bad it is here, at least there are knowns. I mean, the guy does settle down—sometimes for weeks at a time.

As potentially nonsensical as it may seem, the fear of the unknown is much greater than the fear of staying in the relationship.

Your Subconscious Is Busy Planting

As you guessed, the same phenomenon occurs all the time—not just in an abusive partner situation.

It might be helpful to think of it this way: Your subconscious plants fears and doubts when you select a goal that represents forward movement. Your subconscious shuns change and so does its darnedest to keep you right where you are.

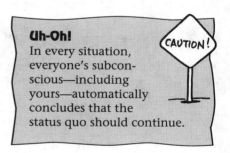

Uh-Oh!
In every situation, everyone's subconscious—including yours—automatically concludes that the status quo should continue.

Into Its Clutches

In acknowledgment of the relentlessness of your subconscious, the need to form positively worded goals becomes paramount.

If you choose to avoid something, as in the goal "I seek to quit smoking permanently by the end of this month," the subconscious surveys the situation, sees that smoking is still part of the goal (even if it's to quit smoking), and summarily concludes that what you actually want to do is continue smoking!

The Resume Smoking Campaign

When there's one week to go before the end of the month, and for three weeks you've been doing marvelously, guess what? Your subconscious isn't sure whether you mean business. So, to give you another chance to keep smoking, it decides to test your mettle.

Uh-Oh!
Your subconscious knows how to get to you in ways that are most effective. It waits and waits and waits and then springs its trap, catching you at a point of vulnerability and launching its campaign for maximum impact.

It starts installing tripwires all around your life. If you walk into a room and people are smoking, all of a sudden, you think to yourself how good it would be to take a quick drag. If, during lunch, you walk down the street and see an attractive member of the opposite sex smoking, you think to yourself, "Sure, why not?"

With three or four days to go, the subconscious shifts into high gear. If you're flipping through the pages of a magazine and you see a circle, you might think of Lucky Strikes, or if you see a cowboy, you might think of the Marlboro Man.

So Why Bother?

If even half of what I've just described is true, by now you might be wondering why you should even bother to ever set a goal. "Aren't the cards stacked against me?" You know that I would never leave you hanging.

The Answer You've Been Waiting For

The antidote, the magic elixir, the cure, the winning formula for overcoming homeostasis, for vanquishing the subconscious' quest to maintain the status quo, is here. Are you ready for this?

It's to steep yourself in the positive:

➤ Positive thoughts
➤ Positive deeds
➤ Positive outlooks
➤ Positive words
➤ Positive everything

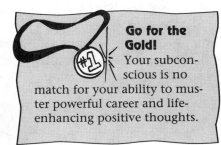

Go for the Gold!
Your subconscious is no match for your ability to muster powerful career and life-enhancing positive thoughts.

The late Reverend and inspirational speaker Norman Vincent Peale said in *The Power of Positive Thinking* that when you maintain a positive outlook, you benefit from the power of positive thinking.

Each Word Carefully Chosen

If you want to quit smoking by the end of the month, you start with a carefully worded positive goal that becomes your rallying cry.

"I choose to have clean, clear, healthy lungs."

If you've been smoking for many years, chances are clean, clear lungs might not appear by the end of the month. If you've given up smoking for a month, however, you certainly will be on the road to having clear, clean, healthy lungs.

For Sure

Nature is very forgiving. In the case of smoking, you could have abused your lungs for 10 years or more, but in as little as one year of abstinence, you can achieve nearly miraculous results. In two years, many people can almost eradicate the effects of all the years of abuse (given that permanent damage has not taken hold, such as lung cancer).

The goal of having clean, clear, healthy lungs points you in a positive direction, and your subconscious doesn't know what to do at first. After all, you haven't mentioned cigarettes as part of the goal, so it waits and it watches, looking for the opportunity to drag you back to what it thinks you need to do.

Day By Day

Day after day, you affirm your goal. Perhaps you refer to a poster placard or a wallet-size card. Maybe you put up posters that show breathtaking mountain scenery or the beach at dusk. You flood your conscience and subconscious with images of strong, deep breaths.

In time (at least 21 days, the experts tell us), the new habits begin to take hold. Positive, healthy habits. Your subconscious has been waiting all this while for its chance to make a move. Oddly, it doesn't see the opening it usually sees. "Hmmm, maybe this time, Ed or Edwina is serious. It looks as if clean, clear, healthy lungs are what he or she wants. Okay, I can support that."

Break on Through to the Other Side

Congratulations! Welcome to the world of winners. You've stuck to your positive goal *long enough for your subconscious to get the message that this is the new status quo*—the new you. Your subconscious actually begins to support you automatically, as it supported you when it thought you wanted to keep smoking.

How did this process start? It's all in the wording—the language you use both for goal statements and in your everyday life. Even the language in your head.

I'll Be Happy to Handle That

George Walther, an author from Seattle, Washington, says that even the most subtle phraseology can have a dramatic impact on you and the people around you.

Think of the last time you called a company and were told something along the lines of, "I'll have to look that up." What would the impact be on you if instead you heard, "I'll be happy to look that up for you"?

More important, what is the impact on the person who abandons a grudging response and replaces it with a friendly one? The effects are dramatic. If you're in a customer service position and answer the phone all day, your life can seem like drudgery as you have to look up one thing after another for the people who call.

Suppose that you'll be happy to look these things up day after day, week after week, month after month, however. What does your subconscious conclude? That you enjoy your work, that you like to help people, and that looking things up makes you happy. Guess what happens as a result? Looking things up *does* make you happy, and helping people *keeps* you happy.

Language That Uplifts

No matter what you're doing and in what capacity, the *language you use* will impact your view of what you do and can help create an upward spiral. You begin to look forward to doing what you do because it can make you happy.

Go for the Gold!
Use positive, uplifting language anytime you set or seek to support one of your goals.

Although you might not necessarily skip down the halls of your organization shouting about how happy you are to have clear, clean lungs, you might harbor such thoughts, as well as these:

➤ I enjoy having clear, clean lungs.

➤ I am feeling more energetic each day with clear, clean, healthy lungs.

➤ I constantly seek activities that enable me to maintain clear, clean, healthy lungs.

In essence, you say yes to the goal you've chosen—yes to the choices you've made.

Positive Words for Positive People

Now for affirmations. Much has been written on this topic, and it's often misunderstood. Affirmations can be…

➤ Said out loud as a form of positive self-talk

➤ Read out loud

➤ Thought silently

One of my long-term and continuing goals is to be more productive every day. I also seek to see opportunities in what I used to regard as adversity. For the first time, I posted an affirmation on the dashboard of my car, in my kitchen, near my PC, and in my appointment calendar. It says in big letters,

> "Today is going to be a great day."

The wonderful thing about this affirmation is that it doesn't matter whether any given day turns out to be a great day. And indeed, what is a great day? Assessment always is highly subjective anyway.

A Solid Observation

Since I posted my affirmation, I have noticed that I am more effective each day in measurable ways, whether it's completing a speech outline in a given amount of time, handling a given quantity of phone calls, or performing other tasks. I have noticed a discernible, cumulative buildup. Each time my subconscious sees the phrase "Today is going to be a great day," it concludes that this is where my interests lie.

My subconscious goes to work for me to find ways to "make it a great day." If this all sounds like positive self-talk blather to you, rest assured that it once did to me as well. I'd see people who would go around always feeling super, and I'd say to myself, "Oh, great, just what I need, another positive thinker."

Little did I know that regardless of how *they appeared to me*, the benefits *they were deriving* were both significant and extraordinary. Perhaps some of the people I encountered who maintain this demeanor came off as too zealous. I've always thought that if somebody is *too* anything, it isn't an affectation I care to emulate. Now I understand that there are few substitutes in life for using positive language and engaging in positive thought. Thus, I've decided that affirmations are wonderful tools.

Record and Reap

If you're so inclined, you can even go as far as to create your own cassette tape. In your own words, record affirmations that you can play back each day to further increase the amount of positive self-talk you hear.

Word Power
An *affirmation* is simply a positively worded phrase that supports a goal.

Go for the Gold!
It's productive and useful to constantly have reminders all around you of your competence, intelligence, and resourcefulness so that you can tip the self-talk scales in favor of the positive.

163

You could record such statements as these:

➤ I am a highly resourceful person.

➤ I am confident in my abilities.

➤ I willingly meet career challenges.

➤ People look to me as a source of inspiration.

➤ I accept my role as a leader.

➤ I am able to discern the opportunities that come with change.

➤ I am constantly adding to my storehouse of knowledge and wisdom.

When recording such statements, leave lengthy pauses so that you can repeat the statement to yourself before the tape plays the next statement. That way, each statement sinks in on a deeper level.

For Sure

Studies show that if you play a tape of affirmations for 21 consecutive days (maybe each morning while you're getting dressed, for example), you will actually begin to notice changes. You will feel different, and you will gravitate toward these affirmations you've been making so that even others will notice.

You also could create a tape of affirmations that specifically encourages you to behave in a certain way. Suppose that your goal is to have confidence and assert yourself when situations call for it. On your tape, you might include the following statements:

➤ I feel confident when I encounter someone who is highly attractive to me.

➤ I feel confident when I encounter someone whose experience or formal education is considerably more than mine.

➤ I feel confident in the face of near impossible deadlines.

➤ I feel confident that I can handle life's challenges.

➤ I can easily make myself heard and understood.

➤ I speak up at appropriate moments.

➤ I know how and when to stand up for myself.

Go for the Gold!
Think of yourself as a work of art in progress. When noted Supreme Court Justice Oliver Wendell Holmes, Jr. was asked why, at an advanced age, he was reading the voluminous text *The Lives of Plutarch*, he responded, "To improve my mind."

Positively Contagious

Although the effects of having positive goals, using positive language, and creating affirmations are easily demonstrable in everyday life, we often can't see the forest for the trees. Think about a manager or supervisor you've worked with who is able to get people to perform at their best.

What was it about this person that invoked in others a willingness to go beyond the routine? Often, it's the fact that the manager uses language that is uplifting, nurturing, and supportive. Yet the manager doesn't come across as some type of rah-rah motivational speaker but instead has an upbeat style to his or her language pattern and sentence structure.

It's Even on the Walls

I've seen companies in which a positive, upward spiral begins to feed on itself. As new employees are brought into the fold, they immediately seek ways to help the company beyond what anyone asks of them. They help alleviate many of their bosses' tasks, and in turn, it becomes easier for their bosses to manage or lead the employees.

The supportiveness that surrounds the new employees reinforces what's expected of them and at the same time makes them feel good about exerting the extra effort.

Such organizations have motivational posters on their walls. They've made a surprising discovery: The posters work. They tell employees that together they can achieve more, and—you know what?—together they do achieve more.

Here are additional uplifting phrases you might want to use or modify for your personal use in your work setting:

➤ We mean what we say, and we say what we mean.

➤ We can do more to help each other, and we do.

➤ Yes, we can!

➤ Each person puts in more than he or she takes out.

➤ Winning is a group accomplishment.

➤ We give our best every day.

➤ Excellence is spoken here.

➤ The more we accomplish together, the more we can accomplish.

➤ We'll handle it!

Make the Question an Affirmation

Suppose that you're up against a problem or a tough challenge, and you want to use language that will help you instead of leave you in a quandary.

If you've recently been promoted to a leadership position, for example, it might be your earnest goal to be effective in your new position. You might want to ask yourself this question:

"How can I be an effective leader?"

What happens, however, when you change the question from "How *can* I?" to "How *will* I?" or "What *will* I do?", as in

"How *will* I be an effective leader?"
or
"What *will* I do to be an effective leader?"

Just by slightly rephrasing your statement, you may identify a host of answers. You can even change a generic type of question, such as "What *can* I do about this issue?" into a powerful inquiry that will inspire prompt answers when you state it as "How *will* I handle this issue?"

Go for the Gold!
Suppose that your goals include being a more loving member of your family and running a more effective business. Instead of asking "How *can* I make time for both my family and my business?", ask yourself "How *will* I make time for both my family and my business?"

Climbing Your Way Out of the Negative Spiral

Suppose that you are steeped in negativity. You don't believe that a certain goal is possible. Doubts and fears have reared their ugly heads. Your subconscious is working overtime to keep you where you are instead of where you want to be. How do you break out of the box in such situations?

Go with the Flow

One technique you might use involves acknowledging the situation at hand. Suppose that you're overweight. You choose to have a lean, trim, and healthy body. For many of the reasons discussed in this chapter, however, you find yourself stymied time after time. In this case, try the following.

On a piece of paper, write down what your negative commitment is, such as "I'm committed to staying overweight." Now, below that, write all the things you dislike about being overweight (given that there are items you can cite). For example, you might say

> ➤ I can't stand not being able to fit into some clothes I bought earlier in life.

> ➤ My low energy is frustrating.

> ➤ I am frustrated with my appearance.

> ➤ It is difficult to not be able to move everywhere with ease.

> ➤ I am worried about potential health problems related to being overweight.

Lay It on Thick

To make this strategy work, you want to lay it on thick. Write down everything you can't stand or have ever hated about your current situation. After you complete the list, go back and read each item. That alone might shake something loose.

What Would the Opposite Be?

Now concoct the opposite of each statement you've written. If one of your statements is "I can't stand not being able to fit into some clothes I bought earlier in life," next to that, write "I will be thrilled to fit into those clothes."

Similarly, go back and create the positive statement that represents the counterpoint to each of your earlier statements.

Surprise! You've now devised a page of highly positive affirmations. Throw away the first half of the page and dwell on what you've just created. You now have as fine a description of your positive goal as you're likely to develop!

Keep Reading Your Statement

If you find that you still are steeped in negativity and don't have a clue as to how to get out of it, take the simplest approach: Just continue to read your positively worded goal statement. Look over what you've written, even if your mind doesn't fully accept it.

On some level, you're making progress. If you look at your goal statement often enough, it begins to take effect. Never mind the how.

The Least You Need to Know

➤ Even though, on a conscious level, you might truly want to change, your subconscious automatically concludes at first that you want to stay right where you are.

➤ Your subconscious is no match for your ability to muster powerful career and life-enhancing positive thoughts.

➤ An *affirmation* is a positively worded phrase that supports a goal and can be read silently or out loud.

➤ You can't afford to use negative language or to harbor negative thoughts if you intend to make swift progress toward positive goals.

➤ When steeped in negativity, keep reading your positively worded goal statement, because on some level you're making progress.

Chapter 14

Committing to Paper

In This Chapter

➤ Carving out a little quiet

➤ Turn on your printer

➤ Reminding yourself what you've chosen

➤ Hey, goals can change

In the movie *Jerry Maguire*, Tom Cruise shakes hands on a major deal. The deal is to represent a Heisman Trophy winner as he is about to sign a professional contract with a National Football League team. The only problem is that Jerry doesn't get any type of agreement down on paper.

I'm sure you've already seen the movie, so I won't be giving away the plot by telling you that the football player's father ends up being influenced by another agent and signs an agreement with that agent. Jerry loses the chance to earn a 6 percent commission on $20 to $30 million. In one fell swoop, he blows the opportunity to earn more than $1 million.

As a result, he finds himself in dire financial straits, is ditched by his volatile fiancée (which proves to be a fortunate development), and finds himself scrambling for months on end to keep his professional and personal life intact.

In this chapter, I'll walk you through the oh-so-important need to commit your goals to paper. I'll tell you why, without such a commitment, you might as well be whistling in the wind.

I Commit—Therefore, I Achieve

A magical thing happens when you commit your goals to paper: You increase the probability of achieving them. Yet, if you're like most people, you might have some trouble when it comes to making commitments.

My college roommate of many years ago, Martin Horn, is senior vice-president of the Strategic Planning and Research division in the Chicago office of DDB Needham Worldwide. Each year, Marty helps conduct DDB Needham's lifestyle study, which tracks what drives the American consumer. The study has been ongoing since 1975.

In the late 1990s, some highly revealing data emerged from the lifestyle study. In essence, the study found that Americans wanted gain without pain. Check out these findings:

➤ *Healthful eating:* After years of learning that it's important to eat more of this and less of that, people are paying less attention to nutrition and diet. For more than 10 years, the percentage of people who make an effort to increase their vitamin intake or fiber content and to reduce additives, cholesterol, salt, sugar, and fats has fallen rapidly.

Although people say they want to have more healthy eating habits, the reality is that more people are taking no action and are actually moving in the *opposite* direction.

➤ *Fitness:* At the beginning of the study, more than half the consumers surveyed thought they were in good physical condition. That percentage, however, has been falling for more than 20 years.

Although people say that exercise is a good idea and they should do more of it, there's little indication that most people are doing much about it. Most forms of exercise have declined as regular activities.

➤ *Environmental issues:* Near the end of the 1980s, nearly 70 percent of men and women said they would support pollution standards "even if it means shutting down some factories." Ten years later, that number is starting to fall.

Twenty years ago, more than 60 percent of men and women said they would accept a lower standard of living to conserve energy. Twenty years later, these numbers have dropped drastically.

➤ *Traditional values:* Although an overwhelming 85 percent of men and women indicate that they have "somewhat old-fashioned tastes and habits," an increasing number of people support the legalization of marijuana. An increasing number believe that couples should live together before marrying, and on many other issues, an increasing number of people have moved away from the "traditional values" they originally said they embraced.

Uh-Oh!
People might want to be environmentally conscious, but the truth is they're taking less action and are actually moving in the opposite direction.

Marty says the pendulum is swinging toward satisfying one's self, and that's why people will embrace traditional values only as long as they don't interfere with convenience, practicality, or individualism.

Say One Thing, Do Another

Far too many people say they want one thing but then do another. Is it likely that, en masse, they're going to achieve their goals? Not!

If you wish upon a star or say one thing but do something entirely different, is it likely you're going to achieve any of your goals? The answer is a big NO.

For Sure

Lee Iacocca says that "writing something down is the first step toward making it happen." In conversation, you can get away with vagueness and nonsense often without realizing it. But there's something about putting your thoughts on paper that forces you to get down to specifics. That way, it's harder to deceive yourself—or anyone else. (*Forbes*, March 11, 1996)

The Best of Intentions

You can have all kinds of wonderful intentions. You can be willing to. You can want to. You can strongly desire to accomplish something. Unless you put it in writing, though, your chances of achieving your desired outcome are very small—with one exception.

The one exception is when you have one major goal and nothing else, and it is so clear, so much on the front burner of your mind all the time, that all your thoughts and activities propel you in the direction of achieving that goal. However, because you're a multifaceted, complex creature, the chances that you have one major goal and nothing else on your agenda realistically are next to nothing. Therefore, you're going to want to keep reading.

Quiet on the Set!

The dean of management consultants, Dr. Peter Drucker, has observed that most busy executives and managers have at best only one or two hours a day to focus on the important tasks that are crucial to accomplishing their goals. With all the distractions that abound today, you can be pulled off-course easily and routinely. It is harder still to carve out the time you need when devising goals in the first place. Drop-in visitors, phone calls, faxes, and e-mail messages all can vigorously compete for your time and attention.

You might find that you do your best goal setting away from your office or place of work. For me, an airplane seat works well. While I'm flying from one speaking engagement to another, I'm able to examine my existing goals, modify them, and create entirely new ones in ways that I simply can't sometimes when I'm back on the ground.

If you don't fly often, there are other locations, such as a park bench, a seat at your local library, or even a seat in the far corner of your organization's conference room when no one else is around. I don't know of anyone who's good at committing goals to paper when plagued by noise, interruptions, distractions, and general chaos.

If you're fortunate enough to have an administrative assistant or other type of helper, perhaps he or she can schedule quiet time for you. During this time, your phone calls are taken for you, no appointments are made, and no visitors are allowed.

Granted, if someone walks by your office and looks in, it won't look like you're doing much. After all, when you're contemplating your goals, nothing much appears to be happening to an outside observer. In your head, however, a couple million neurons are firing in intricate patterns.

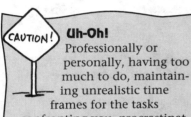

Uh-Oh!
Professionally or personally, having too much to do, maintaining unrealistic time frames for the tasks confronting you, procrastinating, and being disorganized are among the dozens of reasons why carving out even a few minutes here and there to get your goals on paper may seem like a monumental task.

Go for the Gold!
You might find it desirable to schedule some quiet time for each day. It wouldn't hurt to develop the habit of setting aside some time to think about what you're attempting to achieve, what your progress is, and what modifications you might need to make to the goals you've set.

Printing and Posting

The fastest and easiest way to commit your goals to paper is to continue working with what you already are using. Most people maintain some type of to-do list. That's as good as any document for getting started. In my book *The Complete Idiot's Guide to Managing Your Time*, I discuss at length the power of having an extended to-do list. I'll summarize it here, because it is so applicable to the notion of committing your goals to paper.

One Strategy: The Super List

I maintain a 12-page to-do list! I have hundreds of things on my to-do list arranged by major life priorities. How do I keep from going crazy? Most of the items on the list are medium- to long-range activities. The first page of my list represents only the short-term activities. In fact, the first items on the list represent things I've chosen to do now or this week. I continually draw from the other 11 pages and move items to the top as it becomes desirable or necessary to tackle them.

It is a dynamic to-do list in the sense that it contains everything on earth I want to get done, but there's only one page I need to look at, and that's always the top page. I don't worry about all the things on the list, because I know I can only get so much done in a day, a week, and so on. I periodically review the entire list and continually move items from, say, page 8 up to page 1.

Maintaining such a long to-do list also helps me to be more proficient in pursuing long-term or maintenance goals. If something represents a long-term project, I can continually draw from it those portions that can be handled in the short-term and move them up to the front page. Likewise, if something is a repeat or cyclical project, something that I need to do every month or every year, I can move the portion I choose to get done in the short-term up to page 1.

Get Out Your Highlighters

If you are among those who maintain some type of to-do list, whether long or short, you can avoid some writing tasks by using a highlighter. Highlight those three or four goal areas that are most important to you right now. Or, if you maintain such a list on disk, perhaps you could use the redline, bold, or italic function or add stars, capital letters, or a larger point size to those key areas you've identified.

You always have the option of copying the few key goal areas onto a separate page, printing that page, carrying it with you, making multiple versions, and posting them in strategic locations so that you'll constantly be exposed to the goals you've set for yourself.

For Sure

High achievers routinely commit their goals to paper. At the tender age of 24, Curtis Carlson founded the Gold Bond Stamp Company. He committed to paper his goal of earning $100 a week, which was a lot of money during the Great Depression. Carlson maintains that he carried the piece of paper with his goals at all times, until it was dog-eared and disheveled. Carlson was once quoted as saying, "Writing out a goal crystallizes it in my mind. I can quickly evaluate whether decisions will take me toward that objective or away from it."

More than 60 years later, the Carlson Company generates revenues exceeding $9 billion and ranks among America's largest privately held corporations.

Realistically, other activities will always arise that seem enticing. Then, too, projects that are easier to complete and perhaps offer more immediate rewards will tug at your mind. If they do not support your chosen goals, it's far easier to ignore them if you have a sheet of goals that you've already committed to and are there for you to read in black and white.

Written Format Optional

When you write your goals on paper, the form they take is up to you. You can record your goals in many, many ways. You can maintain charts, matrices, and so on (much of which is covered in Chapter 15, "A Question of Time"). Here are a few options, one or more of which may strike your fancy.

Goals and Subgoals

For every goal you write down, you might want to add a variety of subgoals to support your overall goal. If your goal is to finish a huge project on time and under budget, for example, your subgoals might include completing so much of the project each week and scheduling the time of experts you'll need, such as a project reviewer, an editor, and a technical specialist.

If your goal is to achieve some specified athletic performance, your subgoals might include retaining a coach, practicing so many hours a day, and meditating or visualizing so many hours per week (see Chapter 19, "Visualization Techniques").

You might want to write your goal on the left side of the page and the subgoals on the right side of the page.

Goal A _____	Subgoal A1 _____
	Subgoal A2 _____
	Subgoal A3 _____
Goal B _____	Subgoal B1 _____
	Subgoal B2 _____
Goal C _____	Subgoal C1 _____
	Subgoal C2 _____
	Subgoal C3 _____
Goal D _____	Subgoal D1 _____
	Subgoal D2 _____

Listing your goals.

Or, you might just simply list the subgoals under your goal with associated timelines to the left.

Goal A _____	
Subgoal A1 _____	Month 1 _____
Subgoal A2 _____	Month 2 _____
Subgoal A3 _____	Month 2 and 3 _____
Goal B _____	
Subgoal B1 _____	Month 2 _____
Subgoal B2 _____	Month 4 _____

Listing your goals, alternative format.

Reliable and Unreliable Indicators

For goals that otherwise are seemingly difficult to quantify, such as having a better marriage, being a better friend, being a better trainer, and so on, you might want to list each goal on a separate piece of paper followed by what I call *reliable indicators*.

Reliable indicators are observable, quantifiable phenomena that tell you you've achieved your goal. Suppose that you are a management trainer, and your goal is to improve your training performance. You routinely pass out rating sheets and ask participants to rate you from 1 to 10, with 10 being the best. They rate you based on various categories, such as ability to communicate clearly, quality of information, pacing of presentation, and ability to answer questions.

Then, you simply compare the scores you receive in one training program with the scores you receive in the most recent program to see whether you are improving based on the feedback you obtain from attendees.

Performance Indicators

When committing your goals to paper, you might want to write down your own performance indicators in advance. These are observations that will let you know whether you're making progress toward your goal.

Go for the Gold!
Selecting performance indicators is important. What you write down on paper will guide how you actually deliver your training program. After all, when you're committed to meeting these performance indicators, you'll consciously or subconsciously proceed with these indicators in mind.

In the case of seeking to be a better trainer than you were last year, performance indicators might include the following:

➤ No one walks out on your session.

➤ At least one quarter of attendees asks a question.

➤ You are invited back again within one month.

➤ Three or more attendees remark afterward that they wish their coworkers, spouse, or friend could have been in attendance.

➤ You receive at least four unsolicited letters of praise.

There are many performance indicators. The ones you use now could change as time goes on. You might learn of yet other performance indicators that are more valuable in terms of your assessment.

The Action Plan

Another variation when committing your goals to paper is to devise a simple action plan. This can take the form of a matrix with three columns and three or four rows to represent the goals you've chosen for yourself.

In this matrix, each goal in the leftmost column is supported by subgoals, resources, and a timeline (I focus on timelines in Chapter 15). Note that the third column, which contains identified resources for each goal, could be extensive.

In other words, instead of listing one resource per goal, you might want to list as many as eight or ten. You can make this matrix as simple or as complex as you want.

Goal	Subgoals	Identified Resources	Timeline
A	A1	1.	
		2.	
		3.	
	A2	1.	
		2.	
B	B1	1.	
		2.	
		3.	

Listing goals via a matrix.

Keep It Simple

My strong recommendation is to keep such charts as simple as you possibly can. The fewer goals of significance that you're pursuing at any one time, the more likely you are to give your devoted time and attention to each. If they're challenging but reachable, quantifiable, and have specific timelines and you've committed them to paper, you're way ahead of the crowd.

The Reality of Your Pursuit

When you commit your goals to paper, a curious thing happens as you initiate action. Some timelines begin to appear unrealistic, because factors change. Perhaps you find that you can reach some of your goals in a remarkably easy manner.

At any rate, once you get into a project, factors that you could not have anticipated often emerge. Hence, it's important to understand that goals can change, although I'm certainly not giving you carte blanche to shift things around for purposes of mere convenience.

Go for the Gold!
It's up to you how you want to commit your goals to paper—whether it's a simple list, a chart or matrix, or a complex chart using computer software. Just remember that the simpler you keep it, the more likely you are to achieve your desired outcome.

What Are You Committed To?

Without a strong commitment, it's difficult to reach a challenging goal. Your mental and emotional commitment leads to commitment on paper. So often, particularly within the context of large organizations, you'll read a values declaration or mission statement that says something about being committed to the health and well-being of it's employees. But if you were to poll the employees, you'd see that the organization is committed to anything but that.

Some organizations commit to offering extraordinary products or services. Some commit to being the industry leader or other such blather. I need to make a clarification here. Merely writing down what you may be committed to is not analogous to committing to your goals on paper. Indeed, they're two separate notions.

The former may lead to the latter, and if so, the organization or individual making the commitment and converting it to a goal on paper has a much better chance of achieving that desired outcome. Otherwise, a commitment put on paper without being converted to a goal statement is largely a hollow gesture.

The only benefit a commitment might have, comes from prominently posting it so that everyone sees it on a regular basis. Then, it might sink into some level of subconscious, and people might automatically begin to work toward its accomplishment. It would essentially serve as a form of group affirmation.

Still, it won't have the same power that it would have if the commitment were posed in the form of a goal statement that is quantifiable with clear timelines.

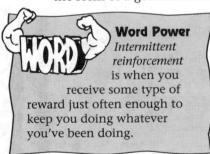

Word Power
Intermittent reinforcement is when you receive some type of reward just often enough to keep you doing whatever you've been doing.

Reinforcing Your Commitment

No matter how well you've crafted your goals, written them down, put them in chart form, posted them, and examined them every day, you'll need some type of reinforcement to keep you going.

The strongest type of enforcement is called *intermittent reinforcement*.

Mr. Pavlov and His Dog

Suppose that your next-door neighbor, Mr. Pavlov, has a dog. Pavlov decides to set up a simple experiment with his dog. Every time he rings a bell, he then offers the canine a dog biscuit. Soon enough, every time he rings a bell, the dog begins to salivate. Why? The dog has learned quickly enough that closely following on the heels of the bell comes a yummy dog biscuit.

Pavlov decides to change the experiment a little. He rings the bell but doesn't give the dog a biscuit each time. In fact, he starts to give the dog a biscuit on the average of every three or four times. Still, each time the bell rings, the dog salivates. Why? The dog has learned that hearing the bell means a dog biscuit will be forthcoming—perhaps not every time, but enough of the time. Hence, the dog has been intermittently reinforced.

Go for the Gold!
Research by many psychologists has shown that intermittent reinforcement keeps you engaged in a specific behavior to a far greater degree than other schedules of reinforcement.

More Rings, Less Biscuits

Suppose that every single time the bell rings, the dog receives a biscuit. Then, for no reason, 15 times in a row, after the bell rings, the dog receives no biscuit. The sixteenth time the bell rings, the dog may conclude that the bell no longer signifies that a biscuit is coming. Hence, he stops salivating.

Alternatively, if only three or four more bell rings come after the last biscuit, the dog is still in the game. In time, even if 10 or 20 bell rings in a row are not followed by a biscuit, guess what? The dog keeps salivating. Why? He's learned that, although he's not sure exactly when, if the bell rings often enough, at some time, he will receive a dog biscuit.

This phenomenon works exactly the same with you when in pursuit of goals that you've committed to paper. In its simplest form, if you compose a chart to trace your goal of achieving your target weight, it's likely that there will be many days when you will not be able to indicate a downward weight progression and progress toward your goal. Indeed, there may be some days that you gain a pound or two.

If your progression is flat or upward for too long at the start, or flat for several weeks into your program, you might give up and say "What's the use? This is as far as I can go. I don't see the opportunity to create greater progress."

However, if even one day out of three, four, five, or six (the threshold is different for everyone) you're able to record the loss of one pound, that intermittent reinforcement might be enough for you to continue.

For Sure

In the long run, the ability to record a one-pound weight loss as infrequently as once a week will actually result in a magnificent achievement of your target weight loss, because one pound per week is a safe and achievable outcome for anyone pursuing such a goal. If you lose one pound per week, in half a year, you'll be down 26 pounds.

Stand By Your Plan

Here's a brief list of activities where seemingly nothing is happening. Yet, with each of them, if you hang in there a little longer, you may well achieve your desired outcome:

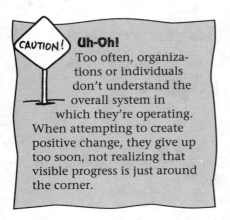

CAUTION! **Uh-Oh!**
Too often, organizations or individuals don't understand the overall system in which they're operating. When attempting to create positive change, they give up too soon, not realizing that visible progress is just around the corner.

➤ Charting your weight

➤ Fishing

➤ Running a series of ads to attract more business

➤ Taking a course on public speaking to be more persuasive

Hereafter, in pursuit of any goal you've committed to paper and are following based on some type of chart, stick to your guns. Don't be disheartened by periods of apparent lack of progress. Sometimes, you're merely going through a phase where good things are happening but they're simply not visible at the moment.

The Least You Need to Know

➤ You need some quiet time to reflect on the goals you've set and the goals you'd like to set. No one does his or her best thinking amid clamor and commotion.

➤ When putting your goals on paper, you have many options, including simply listing them or creating one of a variety of charts. Pursue only a few goals at a time and keep things as simple as possible.

➤ When pursuing a goal, remember that factors may change. Modify your commitment as necessary on paper and get right back to the pursuit of your goal.

➤ When tracking your progress, don't be disheartened if nothing seems to be working initially. The good that is taking place is probably not visible yet.

Chapter 15

A Question of Time

> **In This Chapter**
>
> ➤ Everyone needs a little push
>
> ➤ Plotting your course with charts
>
> ➤ Giving yourself some slack

Have you noticed that the phones are quiet on August 15 each year? Have you noticed they're quiet on October 15 as well? It's no coincidence: The number of people who file for extensions for personal income tax returns is on the rise. Normally, April 15 is the day of anxiety for broad masses of the American public. However, because of the opportunity now to file for a four-month extension, millions have now shifted this anxiety to August 15. And, if you pay something both to the federal government and to your state government, you can actually hold up the works until October 15.

Whether it's paying your taxes or attempting to accomplish almost anything else, if given the opportunity, people will opt to push back a timeline. This chapter is all about establishing and holding fast to timelines for your goals.

When Any Time Will Do

Without a strict timeline, a challenging but reachable goal that is quantifiable is too nebulous. Worse, the lack of a specific timeline often results in a lack of a focused approach to attaining your goal. You don't have a clear idea of the degree to which you need to marshal your energies, because the goal is open-ended.

Suppose I say to you, "I'd like you to finish that report as soon as you can." In essence, what have I just done? I've given you the opportunity to turn in the report whenever you will, because "as soon as you can" literally equates to whenever you are physically able. If anything else comes up that commands your attention, you won't be able to finish. Hence, you only need to turn in the report at *some* time, virtually *any* time, in order to meet my request.

"Ah, but wait," you say. "If I'm requested to turn in the report as soon as I can, isn't there an implied assumption that I will turn in the report with all due haste?" Perhaps, but not necessarily. What if in telling you to turn in the report as soon as you can, I don't realize that you have several other pressing deadlines? Hence, "as soon as you can" means "after all the other items are taken care of." From your perspective, given what you're facing, turning it in eight days from now might be as soon as you can.

Uh-Oh!
You may have heard stories about people who set goals without timelines and achieved spectacular results. You may have even had a few such experiences yourself. We are talking probabilities here, though. Generally, people need timelines. The probability is much higher that you'll achieve a goal if you attach a timeline to it than if you don't.

If you want to lose those proverbial 10 pounds, you'd better attach a date to your desired outcome. Otherwise, those 10 pounds can sit or maybe drop down to eight or nine, balloon up to 11 or 12, drop down again to seven or eight pounds, but never reach the 10-pound mark because you never gave yourself a timeline.

Because this is a book on the simplest way to achieve your goals, let's stick with the notion of attaching timelines to everything. Later, if *you master setting and reaching your goals*, and you feel you *no longer need to attach timelines*, *you have my permission* to experiment without timelines.

Until then, you're not excused.

No Timeline Equals No Commitment

As a self-litmus test, if you're not willing to devise a specific timeline for your quantifiable, challenging, and reachable goal, you probably need to examine your commitment to achieving that desired outcome. (Also see Chapter 14, "Committing to Paper.")

Go for the Gold!
Even the smallest action pursued toward some long-term goal is far better than nothing.

If there is something you'd like to achieve but haven't chosen when, and you use the super to-do list I described earlier in the book, it might make sense for you to shift your goal to the long-term portion of the to-do list and simply park it there.

Small Steps Do Add Up

Suppose that you want to make a major job change entirely out of your field into something you've never attempted. Instead of contemplating week after week, month after month, and even year after year of how it will be when you make the change, accomplish one small task in pursuit of your desired outcome starting now.

One man wanted to be a movie scriptwriter but didn't know how he would ever make the transition from his job as a foreman in a manufacturing plant. So, he initiated a three-year goal of leaving his job to become a full-time scriptwriter. During the interim, he established a daily goal of spending a minimum of 15 minutes working on scripts. Some evenings, he was able to get two or three pages completed. Some evenings, he was able to get only as far as a paragraph. He attended scriptwriting seminars and workshops, read articles and books on the topic, and even joined an association of scriptwriters.

A year and a half into his program, he still checks in every day at the manufacturing plant, and still draws 100 percent of his pay as a foreman. Yet, he is enthusiastic about the progress he's making and is mustering a growing potential for making his living as a movie scriptwriter.

Using a Time Log

Some people find it helpful to use a time log to record exactly how they use their time in a given day or week to see how that aligns with the goals they've set for themselves.

A time log can be as simple as a two-column chart down the page that chronologically lists each activity and how much time you engage in it as you proceed throughout a day. See the next page for an example of a time log.

If it's helpful and convenient for you, separate your time log into personal time versus professional time; before work, during work, and after work; or any other division that suits your purpose.

What Do You Notice?

Often, after reviewing several days or weeks of time logs, you'll notice some trends. Nothing eye popping or earth shaking. Nevertheless, for many people, a curious phenomenon is at play. *Those things that they've selected as important to achieve—their goals—do not seem to be getting the time and attention they deserve based on the time logs.*

Uh-Oh!
Most people see little correlation between their stated goals and how they spend their time on any given day. Some find that they have to simply drop activities altogether in order to pursue what's truly important to them.

❑ ARISE, SHOWER, AND DRESS FOR WORK	30 MINUTES
❑ EAT BREAKFAST, READ PAPER	30 MINUTES
❑ COMMUTE TO WORK	45 MINUTES
❑ REVIEW IN-BASKET MAIL AND E-MAIL	45 MINUTES
❑ MEET WITH STAFF	25 MINUTES
❑ DICTATE THREE LETTERS	30 MINUTES
❑ CONTINUE ADDING TO PROJECT REPORT	90 MINUTES
❑ LUNCH AT DESK	30 MINUTES
❑ CONTINUE ON PROJECT REPORT	35 MINUTES
❑ MEET WITH DIVISION BOSS	15 MINUTES
❑ ATTEND EXPANSION PROJECT MEETING	60 MINUTES
❑ MAKE PERSONAL CALLS	10 MINUTES
❑ CONDUCT ONLINE RESEARCH	20 MINUTES
❑ FOOL AROUND ONLINE	10 MINUTES
❑ RESPOND TO TODAY'S MAIL	20 MINUTES
❑ COMMUTE HOME	45 MINUTES
❑ PICK UP A FEW ITEMS	15 MINUTES
❑ HAVE DINNER WITH FAMILY	35 MINUTES
❑ REVIEW PROJECTS FROM WORK	30 MINUTES
❑ INTERACT WITH CHILDREN	20 MINUTES
❑ WATCH TELEVISION	60 MINUTES
❑ SPEND TIME WITH SPOUSE	15 MINUTES
❑ SPEND TIME LEISURE READING	10 MINUTES
❑ GET READY FOR BED	15 MINUTES

What Gets Dropped, What Can Be Combined?

If your time log is in conflict with your goals, it's time to make choices. Watching television is relaxing, for example, but is it as important as exercising during that time? I've found that certain activities lend themselves to doubling up, such as exercising while you watch television.

Go for the Gold!
Because you don't need to give your sharp attention to the television set, you can concentrate on exercising. Just consider anything worthwhile you do pick up from the show as gravy.

Your Undivided Attention

When does it not make sense to double up on activities? When *compromising your attention is risky*. You don't want to shave or put on your makeup while driving, as so many people do in the mornings on the way to work. Driving requires sharp attention, and putting on makeup or shaving also requires sharp attention; you can't give your sharp attention in two different directions.

You may drive and listen to a CD or cassette, or you may drive and talk to others. As I elaborate in *The Complete Idiot's Guide to Managing Stress*, many people fall into the trap of routinely doubling up on activities in the quest to get more done. However, this seldom brings the benefits they initially sought.

If you read at the kitchen table while you eat, you don't taste and enjoy your food to the degree you could, and you don't absorb what you're reading with the retention rate of which you're capable. Nevertheless, you're not going to bounce off a highway guardrail if you eat while you read, so if this is one of your pleasures, keep at it.

Assigning Times to Your Goal

Assigning times to your goal is not a complex issue. In some cases, a deadline is imposed from an external source. Or, you may be engaged in an activity for which the timeline is obvious, such as if you're participating on a team in sports, engaging in some work-related contest, and so on.

Uh-Oh!
If you set too short a timeline for a challenging but reachable goal, you may render that goal as unreachable. Conversely, if you allow too much time, the goal may no longer be challenging.

Be Prepared to Shift

Like the pilot of an airplane who constantly must readjust during the flight, you may find yourself shifting timelines as you become more knowledgeable of the realities of accomplishing your desired goal. Again, this is not an excuse to change your timelines at will but simply an acknowledgment that *planning* to pursue a goal and actually *pursuing* it represent different kinds of activities.

Budget a Little More Time Than Usual

Paradoxically, highly successful people have the habit of sometimes underestimating the time it will take to accomplish things, because they've accomplished so much in the past. If you fall into this category, cut yourself some slack when you assign timelines.

If you think an activity is going to take 10 hours, perhaps it would make sense to budget 1.2 to 1.5 times the time—in other words, 12 to 15 hours. Then, if you finish earlier, you'll feel good. Conversely, if you attempt to handle a 12- to 15-hour project in 10 hours, you may feel rushed and anxious the entire time.

Allow for Contingencies

Allow for downtime, particularly on maintenance and continuing goals. Suppose that you have to turn in reports every Thursday afternoon by 4 p.m. as a standard part of your job responsibility. To meet that recurring deadline, it makes sense to allow for contingencies.

Murphy Is Alive and Well

Sometimes, things will go wrong—and more often than any of us care to have happen.

➤ What if your PC goes haywire?

➤ What if the power goes out?

➤ What if your car breaks down on the way into work?

These and a variety of other nagging occurrences require that you put some backup systems in place, such as always backing up your hard disk, having an alternative means of transportation, and even having a laptop computer with its own battery fully charged and ready to go. It also means scheduling your time so that you won't finish at 3:55 p.m. but rather 2:55 p.m., more preferably 1:55 p.m., or even early that morning!

Do You Call Instead of Appear?

When I have an appointment with someone at 3:00 p.m. and that person calls me at 3:00 to say he'll be late, I cringe. The reason? A call at 3:00 p.m. to say you'll be late is already too late. If you were the least bit courteous and professional, you'd call the moment you knew you'll be late.

For those who call me at 3:00 to tell me they'll be late for a 3:00 appointment, I always wonder what other *lack of contingencies*, inability to build in some downtime, and other shortcomings they will exhibit when it comes to honoring timelines.

In case you're thinking, "Well, an appointment is a relatively small thing in the grand scope of life," I agree. Often, however, calling in late is the harbinger of other difficulties when it comes to meeting timelines.

Think about the people you know who are always running late. Aren't these the same people who are continually frustrated and anxious of missing deadlines, taking on too much, and not scheduling their time accordingly? How good a job will they do when it comes to assigning timelines to challenging but reachable, quantified goals that are important to them? My guess is they won't do well at all.

Time Tools

With each day that passes, the world gets more technological. So too, tools to assist you in maintaining the timelines for your goals are becoming ever more sophisticated and powerful. Let's take a look at the timing tools available, starting with traditional, non-technical varieties of charts and graphs, and then moving to more sophisticated project-management and scheduling software.

Using Gantt Charts

One of the most basic charts you can employ, and one that you probably have already used at some time, is called the *Gantt chart*—also known as a *milestone chart*. Suppose that in the area of your career, you've established a goal of increasing your earnings by $5,000 at the next salary review coming up in six months.

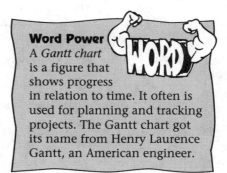

Word Power
A *Gantt chart* is a figure that shows progress in relation to time. It often is used for planning and tracking projects. The Gantt chart got its name from Henry Laurence Gantt, an American engineer.

In support of that goal, you've identified five subgoals:

1. Finish the XYZ project one month early.

2. Get an article published in a key industry journal that highlights both me and my organization.

3. Complete the pilot program for training new hires.

4. Establish an 800-number hotline program so that customers can call my organization directly.

5. Attend the major industry convention to make key contacts and gather critical information for my boss.

All these activities and events will occur in the next five months. How can you most efficiently allocate your time, energy, and resources to effectively accomplish all these items and position yourself to get the $5,000 raise you're seeking?

By plotting what you need to do and when on a Gantt or milestone chart such as this one, you have a clear, graphic representation of the timelines and sequencing of the five major subgoal areas you want to pursue.

Milestone or Gantt Chart						
Item	Month 1	Month 2	Month 3	Month 4	Month 5	Month 6
XYZ Project						
Article Published						
Pilot Program						
Hotline Program						
Attend Key Conference						

In this chart, the most basic information is conveyed, including the subgoals/project or task area, the start time, and the completion time. In the case of developing a pilot program for new hires, for example, there are multiple start and stop times because the subgoal is multifaceted.

You can use other symbols to add detail to your chart:

➤ A broken line can denote germination.

➤ Numbers can refer to footnotes at the bottom of the chart.

➤ Initials can refer to other people with whom you need to cooperate to accomplish the subgoal.

You also can use colors to denote various aspects of your progress:

➤ Red can represent a critical phase.

➤ Green can represent the initiation of tasks.

➤ Blue can represent completion.

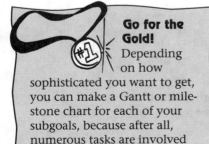

Go for the Gold! Depending on how sophisticated you want to get, you can make a Gantt or milestone chart for each of your subgoals, because after all, numerous tasks are involved in achieving your goals.

You can make similar charts for goals in the other areas of life, including mental, physical, family, social, spiritual, and financial goals. With project planning and scheduling software (discussed later in this chapter) you can even plot the timelines for all goals and all subgoals in all areas of your life on one master chart.

My advice, however, is to *keep things as simple as possible.* Pursue only a handful of key goals at a time, and increase the probability of magnificently achieving them all.

Using Flowcharts

You've seen flowcharts since you were in the third grade. Your teacher might have drawn a big circle on the board, and then an arrow to another circle, a square or triangle, and then perhaps another arrow from that figure to yet a third figure.

Although flowcharts traditionally are used to convey a process (for example, how something happens), you also can use them to stay on target in terms of meeting your goal based on your specific timelines.

A flowchart can flow downward, to the right, or in any direction. Let's use the traditional direction, which flows downward.

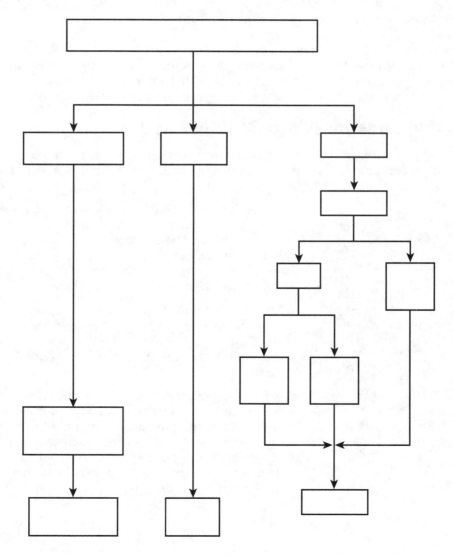

You can use colors on a flowchart much like on the other charts. Different shapes often are used to convey different types of information when constructing flowcharts:

➤ Squares—Information

➤ Circles—Connecting points

➤ Triangles—Yes/No decision

Other symbols often are used to convey information as well:

➤ Straight lines—Direct connection

➤ Broken lines—Partial or one-way connections

➤ Squiggly lines—Interrupted or tenuous connections

As with any chart you create, you can devise your own symbols as well. Initials of another party could represent the need for their input. Stars, Xs, check marks, and other symbols can convey other information. Just make sure that you're consistent throughout your chart and that you keep a key handy so that you don't forget what the symbols mean!

Using the Calendar Block-Back Method

Of all the ways to ensure that you reach your goals based on the timelines you've set, the *calendar block back* is my favorite. With this method, you use your calendar in your appointment book or a large wall calendar to plot out your campaign.

CAUTION! **Uh-Oh!**
If you attempt to plot too many subgoals and associated activities, your calendar sheets quickly become hard to follow. Nevertheless, the calendar block-back method is a highly useful tool, because when you proceed in reverse through the monthly calendar, you establish realistic interim dates that reflect not only your available resources but also weekends, holidays, vacations, time away from work, and other downtime.

If you're considering a six-month campaign, it makes sense to post the next six months of calendars on your wall so that they're all visible. Then, starting from the ending date (in other words, the deadline for completing your goal), work back to the present, indicating the subtasks or specific activities you need to undertake by when.

In the case of striving to achieve a $5,000 increase in salary, each of the five key subtasks you've identified would be listed according to their starting and ending dates. You also should list any interim steps in the completion of one of the subtasks.

The following example shows only one calendar month of the six months of your overall campaign. If you need to deliver the first test program to new hires by the 31st of the month, for example, you'll need to schedule the conference by the 22nd. Also, you'll want to have your training manual critically reviewed by the 9th, proofread by the 15th, and assembled by the 19th.

190

MONTH ___*March*___ YEAR _____

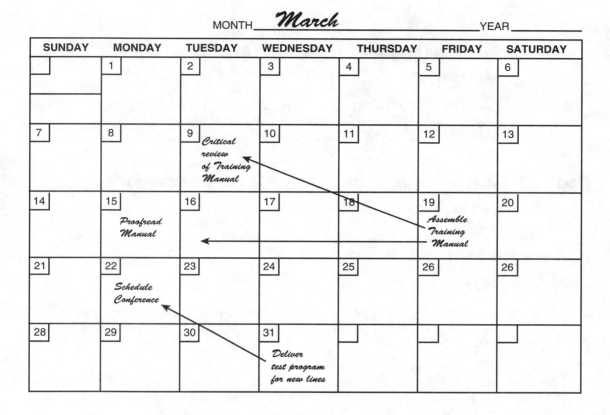

SUNDAY	MONDAY	TUESDAY	WEDNESDAY	THURSDAY	FRIDAY	SATURDAY
	1	2	3	4	5	6
7	8	9 *Critical review of Training Manual*	10	11	12	13
14	15 *Proofread Manual*	16	17	18	19 *Assemble Training Manual*	20
21	22 *Schedule Conference*	23	24	25	26	26
28	29	30	31 *Deliver test program for new lines*			

Likewise, with all the other activities in pursuit of this subgoal and all the other activities and interim due dates in pursuit of the other five subgoals, you would mark up your calendar accordingly.

Once again, you can use the symbols and colors that help you to stay in control.

Focusing on the End and Working Backward

With some goals, such as retiring by a certain age with a certain size nest egg, beginning with the end in mind is in many respects the *only practical way to proceed.*

If you want to have $450,000 in savings by age 65 and you're currently 37 (assuming a certain rate of interest, inflation, and accounting for taxes), it is entirely possible to determine how much you would have to save per year and more specifically how much you would have to save per month.

Starting with the end in mind also works well in the other goal areas of life. The calendar block-back method helps make your goal pursuit tangible, because you can look at your calendar and see what needs to be done by when.

For Sure

Any of the office superstores and other office-equipment stores in your area carry a variety of wall charts to aid you in your quest to achieve your goals, whether you use a Gantt chart, flowchart, or calendar block-back method for plotting and monitoring your progress. Many such charts are erasable if you use a highlighter or soft-tip felt marker.

Project-Management and Scheduling Software

With each passing month, the sophistication of project-management and scheduling software increases. So, no matter what I describe to you now, it will be superseded quickly. In general, however, scheduling software, calendar systems, and other types of project organizers share some common principles.

Common Denominators

All such software provides some type of calendar system you can use to keep appointments, readily identify schedule conflicts, and alert yourself as to when you need to engage in some critical activity.

Project-scheduling software enables you to choose the form of chart—whether it's Gantt, flow, calendar block back, and so on—that's most convenient for you. Using pull-down menus, familiar icons, and drag-and-drop techniques, you quickly can cue in the subgoals and associated tasks or activities in the desired sequence, indicate start and stop times, and add various other symbols and colors to give yourself a vivid portrayal of the timelines you've established and your overall progress.

All programs enable you to print your charts. Most give you the capability to toggle on buzzers, bells, and alarms that remind you to send a fax or e-mail, make a call, or engage in any other activity that supports your overall goal progress.

Nothing Is Foolproof—Yet

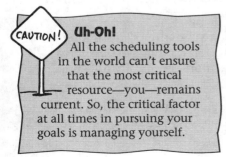

Uh-Oh!
All the scheduling tools in the world can't ensure that the most critical resource—you—remains current. So, the critical factor at all times in pursuing your goals is managing yourself.

As with all project-management and scheduling software or any other manual system for monitoring your goal progress, if *you don't keep your chart or graph current*, the whole process may quickly become ineffective.

Although the scheduling tools can help, you alone have to make critical decisions as to where to proceed and where to drop back. If you attempt to take on too much at once, the tools may help you realize that you've done so, but largely it's up to you.

The Least You Need to Know

➤ If your timelines are too stringent, any goal quickly can grow out of reach; if they are too lenient, you may lose focus.

➤ After you begin pursuing a goal, you'll have a clearer notion of how long things will take.

➤ Build some slack into your schedule and allow for contingencies.

➤ Charts enable you to more effectively establish timelines, monitor your progress, and reach your goals.

➤ Any sophisticated project-management or scheduling software will let you down the moment you don't keep it updated.

Chapter 16

Gotta Have a Challenge

In This Chapter

➤ Goals to move you further

➤ Maintaining the wonderful you

➤ Prodding yourself along

➤ Now for some challenges

To close out Part 3, "Secrets of Master Goal-Setters," I'm going to focus on the critical notion of making your goals a challenge—stretching yourself and reaching for what you might not have attempted at an earlier time. To see why this is so important, read on!

Goals to Move You Forward

Your subconscious—as you learned in Chapter 13, "It's All in the Wording,"—tends to give you more of what you already have, summarily concluding that what you're doing now is what you want to keep doing forever. In many respects, your subconscious works almost as a robot or a highly sophisticated computer that keeps acting on the program it was originally fed.

Taking Advantage of the Situation

The inability of your subconscious to pass judgment, something you might consider to be a limitation, can actually be used to great advantage. If you respond with joy to the news that you're receiving a $10,000 advance, for example, or that you simply are getting a $10 refund from a purchase, in both instances your subconscious regards the events as positive and, most curiously, equal.

Although the events differ greatly as to financial ramifications, they both register the same on the "Richter scale" of your subconscious. Hence, when you strive for a highly challenging goal broken into subgoals and achieve each subgoal, your subconscious works on your behalf. In simple terms, it concludes that this is a good thing, and it helps you go on to the next subgoal and the next, until you achieve your larger goal.

To the Outer Limits

The top managers at many progressive companies apparently understand the workings of the subconscious. This is shown in part when they schedule executive or team-based retreats into nature, where cooperation is essential for a successful experience.

For Sure

Dr. Maxwell Maltz, in his 1960 work, *PsychoCybernetics*, tells how the subconscious not only continues to maintain the status quo but also lacks the ability to differentiate between a significant or insignificant event, something that you deem as good or bad, and in general passes no judgment on anything you do.

Organizations such as Vision Quest and Outward Bound are in business expressly for the purpose of providing their customers with a strong dose of nature and teamwork. The challenges the participants face—whether it's trekking through mountains, rafting, or making or breaking camp—impart to each of their subconsciouses that they are capable of meeting great challenges. Routinely, total strangers leave the programs feeling like long-time comrades. In fact, many maintain their relationships for years thereafter.

An executive or work-related team that goes through such an experience returns to the workplace having a stronger bond with one another. Sometimes, they bond in a way that didn't happen in all the years of each person's employment there and might not have happened in all the years to come.

Because the subconscious is not good at differentiating experiences or the magnitude of such experiences, success during a retreat is fodder for the subconscious. Back at work, continued success adds to the fodder.

Although a sojourn into nature might not be in the immediate future for you, the principles and payoffs remain the same. If you accept a challenge, masterfully reach each of the subgoals, and complete the goal itself, you give your subconscious a powerful message: You routinely set and reach challenging goals.

If you set and reach challenging goals often enough, guess what? That becomes the status quo. Your subconscious has no choice but to conclude that what you're all about is achieving what you set out to achieve.

Therefore, as it goes to work on whatever level of goal achievement you are operating, your subconscious simply does its thing. This phenomenon explains why high achievers in various arenas of life often are able to set and reach challenging goals in other areas. So, the highly successful CEO also happens to be a crackerjack tennis player, a mover and shaker in his community, a deeply spiritual and religious person, and so on.

Out-of-Balance Achievers

True enough, there are numerous examples of people who have set and reached challenging goals but otherwise lack a balance in life. This is the man or woman who proverbially puts all his or her eggs in one basket. Here is perhaps the most surprising information in this book:

The person who excels in one particular arena of life to the detriment of all other arenas nevertheless has vast potential for excellence in those other arenas. Why? Just as you reach challenging goals in one arena, so can you proceed in other arenas.

It's all a matter of planning your course of action, writing down what you want to achieve, determining the steps or subgoals, and acknowledging your successes as you proceed so that your subconscious gets a clear message and goes to work for you in the direction in which you're already proceeding.

Success Breeds More Success

This is where it gets really exciting. Identify where in life you consistently reach challenging goals. Then determine why you've been consistently successful. Now you practically have a ready-made formula for achieving goals in other arenas of your life.

You're not like the people who never bother to examine what makes them successful in one arena; you're much more inquisitive. You recognize that you have the opportunity now, right before you.

Uh-Oh!
Some people never engage in such introspection and self-assessment. Some do it only after completing a major milestone (see Chapter 3, "The Times of Your Life").

Go for the Gold!
When you consider your successes, look at them with an almost third-party detachment to discern precisely why indeed you reached such challenging goals. Then, take out those transferable elements for use again and again.

Tony Robbins, in his cassette series of "monthly power talks," discusses the importance of expanding your frame of reference. Often, we simply traverse the same circles day after day, week after week, year after year. Robbins suggests visiting your town hall, fire station, or any place that represents something out of the ordinary to you.

From an expanded frame of reference, goals that once seemed unreachable, as well as new goals that you might not have ever considered, often seem to be more within your reach. As you'll see in Chapter 19, "Visualization Techniques," if you can see, hear, taste, and touch objects that signify the attainment of your goals, you're that much more likely to achieve your goals.

Spreading Yourself Too Thin

The counterpoint to wide-focus goal achievement is that if you try to take on too much too fast in too many arenas of life, you might overstress yourself or even reach a stage of burnout.

Unfortunately, contemporary society seems bent on increasing the number of images of the supermom, superdad, and superexecutive shown to us daily. Such images show up in movies, television shows, print media, and everywhere in-between.

For Sure

The portrayal of life as it "ought to be" started with Norman Rockwell. He set a marker in society. Rockwell paintings depict an idyllic way of life. Today, models of all varieties flood us with notions about how we're supposed to look, walk, talk, act, dress, and so on. Even highly educated and respected adults sometimes get caught up in the flood of images and forget some of the basic realities of life.

Word Power
Other-directed refers to individuals who are more concerned about what others think of them than what they think of themselves.

The term *other-directed*, coined by Dr. David Reisman, author of *The Lonely Crowd*, describes vast numbers of the American population. Too many people today are caught up in the pursuit of what they merely have been programmed to want. Many will live their entire lives not even realizing it. You need challenges, but they need to be your own challenges, internally chosen for internal reasons.

Taking Calculated Risks

In *The Luck Factor*, author Max Gunther tells us that among the many traits that converge to help us be "lucky," the ratchet effect is the most compelling. The *ratchet effect* means that if you reach for a goal and fail, instead of losing everything, you fall back to a position, like a ratchet in a wrench and socket set, from where you can regroup. Then, in short order, you can resume your campaign.

Benefiting from the Ratchet Effect

The ratchet effect routinely guides top executives of digital gamemakers, such as Nintendo and SEGA. Before a new software game is shipped to stores, such companies employ *bug catchers*. These are people who spend every waking hour trying to find the flaws in a program before it's distributed.

For Sure

The great gamemakers know that to achieve the challenging goal of establishing a large market for the latest innovation in gameware, they need to employ bug catchers to find anything that might be wrong with the product, even if it means scrapping it entirely (which rarely happens). Then, when the games are ready to ship, the manufacturers have some sense of security knowing that they did all they could to ensure that their customers receive a solid product.

One executive at a top game manufacturing company says that when the director of bug catchers calls her, she feels like "hanging herself." On the other hand, after the game passes the internal tests and is ready to be shipped by the thousands, the company is left with an acceptable, calculated risk. The risks they now face are normal in the market-place—will there be delays in shipping, will customers buy in the numbers projected, will someone usurp their creation?

Raising the Odds of Reaching Your Goal

Successful risk takers have almost an ingrained capability for lowering the odds of failure. Dick Rutan flew an amazing 325 combat missions over Vietnam. When he was ready to board the *Voyager* with fellow pilot Jeana Yeager, although the trip seemed to be fraught with perils, Rutan knew exactly what he was doing.

The aircraft had been tested and tested and then tested again. Professor Jefferson Koonce, an expert in human-factors engineering at the University of Massachusetts, said "It wasn't done blindly. The design was feasible and they climbed on board with fairly high confidence."

The Risk Taker in You

In your own life, right now, think about the times when you engaged in appropriate risk taking, when you ventured way out on a limb, yet because of your knowledge, experience, and background, knew that the odds were pretty good that you'd succeed.

Maybe you decided to take a leadership position in some group, even though you had not held one previously. Perhaps you set out to accomplish something and although it seemed as if you had precious little time and resources, you prevailed. Or, maybe you went head-on against stiff competition but nevertheless came out on top.

List three times when you engaged in what you consider to be appropriate risk taking in pursuit of a highly challenging yet reachable goal:

1. _____
2. _____
3. _____

While reviewing your brief list, reflect on the common denominators of these successful risks. Did you have a contingency plan, for example? In other words, if things started to go badly, would you have been able to shift gears, perhaps follow a different plan, and still have the situation turn out all right?

Did you engage in extensive planning or preparation prior to engaging in the behavior or task? It's one thing to just step into the ring against the heavyweight champ. It's quite another if you've been vigorously training for six months with the world's top coaches and already have fought successfully with highly skilled and respected sparring partners.

Finding an Edge

Were you able to gather some knowledge about the situation—perhaps hard-to-get information that gave you an edge? Consider the company that uncovers a small but key weakness in the product of its main competitor or the baseball coach who detects a flaw in the delivery of the opposing pitcher and hence is able to alert the batters on his team to their ultimate advantage.

Did developments or trends in the environment prompt you to believe that your chance of success would be greater if you proceeded at the right time? Successful contractors dealing with large entities, such as national governments or multinational corporations, often close deals based on the twists and turns in the political, military, social, or economic environment.

For Sure

The popular, high-priced trend-letters, such as *The Naisbitt Report*, *The Kiplinger Washington Letter*, *Hull's Financial Digest*, and a slew of others stay in business because of their subscribers' eagerness to learn of changes in the external environment. For a comprehensive directory of all such newsletters and trend-letters, visit the reference section of your local library and peruse the latest volume of *The Oxbridge Directory of Newsletters*.

All About Maintenance Goals

Another type of goal exists alongside goals for which you strive, achieve, and then move beyond. These other types of goals are called *maintenance goals*. A maintenance goal is something you want to continue to achieve. The simplest examples of maintenance goals are those related to wealth, health, weight, and leisure. Let's spend a little time focusing on how you can set maintenance goals in each of these areas.

Wealth-Related Maintenance Goals

A wealth-related maintenance goal could be as simple as deciding to save or invest a fixed amount of money each month (see Chapter 11, "Now for the Biggie: Your Financial Life").

Although some people mistakenly believe that their annual gross earnings will lead to wealth, it's not how much you *earn*—it's how much you *save* and *invest*. Stories abound of domestic workers who were able to retire with grace and ease, put their children through college, and even travel the world, although their meager hourly earnings or annual salaries would seem wholly insufficient to an outside observer. Conversely, if you're earning $30,000 a month, but your expenses total $31,000, you don't need a calculator to determine that you're going to be $1,000 in the hole every month.

Go for the Gold!
For every person who wins the jackpot or receives a major inheritance, there are many more who earn their wealth through periodic saving and investing. Such wise individuals realized at some point along the trail that putting away a little at a time as early in life as possible would enable them to benefit from compounded interest and growth.

Go for the Gold! Those who are adept at setting wealth-related maintenance goals seem to share some common characteristics—the most visible being that they are frugal with each and every dollar.

You or I might whoop it up following a $10,000 windfall. Those who have long-term goals related to wealth, however, maintain and apply the same discipline to virtually all funds that come their way. It's as if these individuals have an ingrained notion and profound realization that some portion of every dollar that comes their way contributes directly to their personal net worth.

Instead of regarding themselves as miserly or austere, they actually gain a sense of deep satisfaction, if not joy, as they continue to build and build and build toward their desired financial outcome.

Health-Related Maintenance Goals

Becoming wealthy is a habit. Becoming healthy or maintaining health is no less a habit. If you could follow a healthy person around for a day and observe what he or she does, invariably you'd observe some common behaviors and characteristics.

Sure, some people have good health as a result of heredity. Sweeping those aside for a moment, however, the healthy people among us seem to have an active set of maintenance goals that prompt them to do such things as

➤ Drink plenty of water each day.

➤ Take vitamins.

➤ Engage in some type of physical exercise.

➤ Get proper rest.

➤ Eat an average of at least two square meals a day.

➤ Take time out to stretch and relax.

➤ Avoid known *carcinogens* (cancer-causing agents).

As I discussed earlier in the book, your body is often forgiving. If you engage in unhealthy activities or behaviors, even for an extended period, once you turn the corner and start exercising regularly, eating more nutritious foods, and getting proper rest, your body will begin to respond in kind.

In a matter of days, you'll begin to feel better; in a matter of weeks, you'll notice a marked change for the better; in a matter of months, you'll feel like a new person; and after years of engaging in health-maintenance activities and behaviors, you may be among the most healthy and fortunate individuals in society.

For Sure

Abraham Lincoln once said that after age 40, a person's face is determined largely by what that person does. One could make the same observation about one's waistline, blood pressure, posture, and even skin tone.

Do you want to set some challenging health-related maintenance goals for yourself? Any maintenance goals in a world that beckons you to overindulge on junk food, foods heavily laden with preservatives, alcohol, and other harmful substances are challenging.

When the television stations beseech you to watch them at all hours of the night, and everywhere you turn, more information and more choices are competing for your time and attention, beware. Concurrently, when you're asked to do more and more at work with less resources, maintaining your health is a worthy, appropriate, and highly challenging goal.

Weight-Related Maintenance Goals

On the heels of health come weight-related maintenance goals. I covered this extensively in previous chapters, so I'll be brief here. After getting out of college, if you add the minute amount of a half pound every six months, by the time you're 42, you'll be 20 pounds overweight; by the time you're 62, you'll be 40 pounds overweight.

Conversely, if you hold the line this week, next week, all month, the next month, and so on, you can actually go through your whole life at the same weight. Because weight is something you can monitor simply by standing on a scale, devising a chart that plots your weight is a simple and effective exercise.

At the same time, you don't want to fall into the trap of believing that minor fluctuations in your weight indicate a long-term trend in one direction or the other. Usually, the fluctuations represent water weight. All too many of those diet programs you see on television and in books make outrageous claims.

Gentle reader, nobody loses four to eight pounds in a week, unless it's related to water loss. Indeed, that much weight loss in a week is unhealthy and potentially dangerous.

Uh-Oh! CAUTION!

Like compound interest in the financial world, small gains in weight tend to add up quickly. Worse, combined with a sedentary lifestyle and a lack of desire to exercise, added weight can have a compound effect on you by inhibiting your desire to exercise.

Uh-Oh! CAUTION!

Too many people put their scale in the bathroom, where it does less good than if it were placed in the kitchen. If you step on the scale and notice that you're not at your desired weight, that's a pretty good indication that perhaps you should have smaller portions for the next few meals.

It would be a supreme challenge to lose only one pound a week, and more realistically, one pound every two weeks—hence, two pounds a month and 12 pounds in six months.

Leisure-Related Maintenance Goals

It is a fallacy to believe that you can force leisure between periods of otherwise frenzied activity. I often see stressed-out career professionals who think they're going to get all "caught up" on their leisure time over the next long weekend.

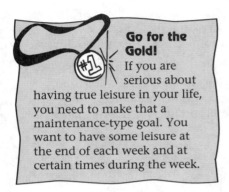

Go for the Gold!
If you are serious about having true leisure in your life, you need to make that a maintenance-type goal. You want to have some leisure at the end of each week and at certain times during the week.

Unquestionably, three days away from work with complete rest and relaxation will offer immediate benefits. However, if it has been weeks or months since you've given yourself some leisure time, don't expect miracles. Like sleep, weight maintenance, health maintenance, or wealth maintenance, you can't "catch up" all in one weekend.

If you're a career type who frequently works late and then takes work home from the office, perhaps you can establish a goal of having one night a week as a work-free night. On Wednesdays, for example, you might choose to have fun regardless of what else you're facing in life. This is the night when you'll go to the movies, take a long walk, have an ice cream cone with your kids, or whatever.

On weekends, you'll carve out true leisure for yourself instead of pretending that an hour watching the ball game and another taking your kids to the mall will meet your needs.

If you're committed to having true leisure time in your life, you'll start setting goals that support your quest to have vacations that yield substantial leisure benefits. You'll be on the lookout for ways to engage in self-renewal. Perhaps you'll even get to the point where you're comfortable going entire days with no agenda!

Uncorking Some Real Challenges

Sticking with the four areas discussed in this chapter (health, wealth, weight, and leisure), what are some highly challenging, maintenance-related goals you might set for yourself? The following are suggestions. You'll want to modify these goals to fit your own situation or add others if the spirit moves you.

Challenging Wealth-Related Goals

Here are but a handful of challenging goals that may be right for you:

➤ To save $500 every month, starting this month, for the next 20 years

➤ To join an investment club this month that requires an investment of *x* amount per month over five years

➤ To direct my employer to deduct an automatic sum from my paycheck, which will go directly into a savings account that I cannot touch without severe tax penalties

➤ To identify a savings/investment partner, preferably my spouse, with whom I will invest a matching amount of no less than $250 per month until December 31, 2010

Challenging Health-Related Goals

Among many health-related goals you might want to take on, here are some suggestions:

➤ To meet with a nutritionist or dietitian within the next 10 days and establish a plan I will follow for six months and then renew or modify accordingly

➤ To sign up for exercise, aerobics, swimming, or other classes at the local YMCA that require three workouts of at least 45 minutes per week for the next six months and, thereafter, to renew my enrollment

➤ To walk for at least 20 minutes every evening for the rest of my life

Challenging Weight-Related Goals

There are an endless number of weight-related maintenance goals. Here are a few you might want to adopt:

➤ Hereafter, to buy clothes only in the size that corresponds to my target weight

➤ To move my bathroom scale to the kitchen, weigh myself every morning, record my weight on a chart, and maintain the chart for a complete calendar year, after which I will begin again

➤ Starting now, to begin buying fat-free or reduced-fat versions of the products I have normally been consuming

➤ To read the nutrition labels on all products and to not purchase anything that contains greater than a 40 percent fat content

➤ To team up with a partner who seeks to reduce his or her weight by the same amount that I do and to report our respective weights to each other on a daily basis

Challenging Leisure-Related Goals

Among the many leisure-related goals you may choose, here are a handful:

➤ Starting this Wednesday, to take no work home from the office on any Wednesday hereafter, regardless of what work-related situations I face

➤ To schedule a relaxing weekend trip with my family once per month that involves a minimal amount of travel, an optimal amount of sleep, and at least two 30-minute periods of complete solitude

➤ To have at least one leisurely lunch per five-day work week—including not rushing to or from lunch, slowly and carefully digesting food, and not having any work-related thoughts

The Least You Need to Know

➤ When you strive for a highly challenging goal broken into subgoals, as you achieve each subgoal, your subconscious works on your behalf and helps you go on to the next subgoal.

➤ If you set and reach challenging goals often, your subconscious eventually accepts that as the status quo.

➤ Successful risk takers have an almost ingrained capability for lowering the odds of failure.

➤ Any maintenance goal in a world that beckons you to overindulge in every aspect of your life is challenging.

➤ If you're serious about having true leisure time, you need to make that a maintenance goal.

Part 4
Bring In the Reinforcements

Being a member of the species Homo sapiens, you're subject to a well-developed set of faults and foibles. No matter how well you've set your goals and regardless of the progress you're making, you're likely to run into some obstacles along the way.

The five chapters in Part 4 focus on specific elements for generating reinforcement for yourself as you pursue your chosen goals. Chapter 17, "Contracting with Yourself," focuses on devising a contract with yourself to keep on course. Chapter 18, "All About Deadlines," focuses on harnessing deadlines to ensure that you reach your goals on time.

Chapter 19, "Visualization Techniques," is all about using visualization—using your senses to draw yourself closer and closer to your goals. Chapter 20, "Affiliating with Others: Capitalizing on Those Around You," tells you about the vast assistance you can get by having other people support your goal efforts. Finally, Chapter 21, "Steering Clear of Barriers," will help you steer clear of the barriers that are likely to arise someplace along the trail between where you are and where you want to be.

Let's get started with Chapter 17, which presents simple but profound notions you might never have encountered previously. Hereafter, don't be surprised if you use this technique again and again.

Contracting with Yourself

In This Chapter

➤ Beyond writing out goals

➤ Get your pen ready

➤ Who sees and keeps a copy

➤ Reviewing and renewing your contract

"I've already written down my goals and made them challenging, reachable, and specific, with clear timelines. Why do I have to write anything else?"

As you set some goals, you might find added incentives to reach them by devising a contract for yourself. This technique is simple, powerful, and optional. You don't have to do this; you could skip the whole chapter if you are so committed to your goals that devising a contract with yourself doesn't seem worthwhile. There are champion goal achievers who have never used this technique.

You might be among those who gain a winning measure of support from this technique, though. So, who am I to deny you from learning all you can about it?

Beyond Writing Out Goals: Developing a Contract

I first learned about contracting with yourself from author Dennis Hensley, who called the process "advancement by contract." According to Hensley,

> *A contract takes precedence over everything else. For example, you make your monthly house payment rather than use the money for vacation because you have to make that payment: The contract allows the bank to foreclose on your home if you do not fulfill your obligation.*

Likewise, there are many other kinds of contracts in your life, whether they're for automobile loans, employment, marriage, house additions, or business partnerships. In all these cases, you sign a document agreeing to do such and such—whether it's to make payments, render a product or service, perform at a certain level, or simply be responsible for certain types of behaviors.

The party with whom you've entered into a contract or agreement might have similar responsibilities or obligations that complement yours.

Easier Than You Think

Contracting with yourself is a much easier deal! You get to word the contract however you see fit. You can use language that is familiar and inspiring to you. You can load it up with clauses and make it look like legalese, or you can keep it simple, sparse, and easy to follow.

In any case, the contract is uniquely yours. You're going to use this valuable tool to prompt achievement of important goals in a timely manner.

Especially for Nagging Issues

You're probably not going to devise a contract with yourself for goals that you can handle via standard routines. No sir. You're likely to take this extra measure because you want to achieve something that continues to elude you. Perhaps you've tried other approaches, but your efforts fizzled out. Maybe other responsibilities diverted your attention and the efforts your goal needed.

A Constant Reminder for Faster Achievement

Another possible reason for contracting with yourself is that the goal in question requires daily, continual monitoring. Sometimes long-term goals require a series of interim or short-term steps; hence, you want to prominently post your contract as a constant reminder.

When I sign a performance contract to deliver a lecture series, write a book, or record a cassette, I often take the essence of the contract I've signed, such as the time these key elements need to be completed and the quantities of anything I've promised, and put this information on its own page in the front of my appointment book.

I then can review the key elements of the contract on a regular basis. This provides reinforcement above and beyond simply plotting contract milestones on a chart or using scheduling software. The constant hard-copy visual reminds me of the key elements of the contract and helps me stay focused and committed.

How to Write a Contract

Dennis Hensley suggests including three to five carefully selected and major goals in your self-contract. This is not a bad idea if you've used this technique successfully in the past. I suggest that you begin by focusing on one goal, however. After you master using self-initiating contracts, you can think about pursuing more than one goal at a time with this method.

It's okay to have subparts that support your major goal. If your goal is to lose 10 pounds by six months from today, for example, the subparts might include the following:

➤ To buy a small food scale

➤ To visit a nutritionist

➤ To join a health club and work out three times per week for at least 30 minutes

➤ To substitute margarine for butter

➤ To buy a bathroom scale

➤ To create and post a weight chart

Each of these subparts also would have a timeline.

Step Into the Showroom

To give you an idea of what a self-initiated contract looks like, here are some models.

I, Jeff Davidson, agree to accomplish the following goal before the 30th of this month, and hereby do formally contract myself to these purposes. This goal is challenging but reachable, and I willingly accept the challenge:

_____

_____

_____

Signature: _____   Date: _____

This contract represents the simplest of the simple. No adornment, no subparts, no official language. It only needs to exist and be posted prominently.

The next contract, though, might be your cup of tea. You include subparts that elaborately lay out the various things you need to support your overall quest. It's your contract—it's up to you! You might want to list these subparts in the sequence in which you'll undertake them. You also can assign timelines to each subpart; I recommend it.

I, Jeff Davidson, agree to accomplish the following goal before the 30th of this month, and hereby do formally contract myself to these purposes. This goal is challenging but reachable, and I willingly accept the challenge:

_____

_____

_____

In support of this goal, I will undertake the following activities:

➤ Buy a small food scale

➤ Visit a nutritionist

➤ Join a health club and work out three times per week for at least 30 minutes

➤ Substitute margarine for butter

➤ Buy a bathroom scale

➤ Create and post a weight chart

Signature: _____   Date: _____

The next contract could be effective for you if you're motivated or inspired by something that actually looks and feels like a contract—something that has stilted language that appears stern and foreboding.

I, Jeff Davidson, being of sound mind, formally agree to devise this contract with myself expressly to accomplish the following goal before the 30th of this month, and do hereby declare that this goal is challenging yet reachable, and that I willingly accept said challenge:

_____

_____

_____

Part and parcel to this contract, subgoals as delineated below shall be added, each of which shall be completed by or before the aforementioned schedule:

➤ Buy a small food scale

➤ Visit a nutritionist

➤ Join a health club and work out three times per week for at least 30 minutes

➤ Substitute margarine for butter

➤ Buy a scale to bring to work

➤ Create and post a weight chart

Signature: _____ Date: _____

Backup Systems

Undoubtedly, you'll have a file on your hard disk that contains your contract. Print one to several copies of your contract to place in any one of the following locations you choose:

➤ Inside the front of your appointment book

➤ On or near your nightstand

➤ On or near your bathroom mirror

➤ In the front of the file folder that you check daily

➤ On any door or wall where you'll see it frequently

If it helps, make several copies and mail one to yourself each week. If you use scheduling software, initiate the reminder functions so that you'll see your contract every Thursday at 10 a.m. or at some other interval.

Specifically, if your goal is to lose weight, post your contract someplace in the kitchen.

Go for the Gold!
Get creative when it comes to arranging your day and life so that you'll constantly be exposed to the contract. If you want to achieve this goal, you can't overdo it!

Who Sees and Keeps a Copy

Go for the Gold!
The power and potential of giving someone else first-hand knowledge and an active role in helping you achieve your goal can't be understated.

The issue of who sees and keeps a copy of your self-initiated contract is significant. If you're like me, the only person who would see the contract would be yourself. My feeling is that if I'm going to undertake the effort to devise this, I sure as heck intend to accomplish my goals. I don't need to let anyone else keep a copy of the contract. Still, there are compelling reasons to share your contract with a spouse, friend, mentor, coworker, child, or a combination of people.

For many people, being in partnership with another is the critical difference between achieving and failing when it comes to goal setting.

A Little Agreement Here

If you choose to issue a copy of your self-initiated contract to your spouse or significant other, it makes sense to have some ground rules:

➤ Get the support of the other person before actually forking over a copy of the contract. You need to have your partner's full cooperation and participation for this plan to work.

➤ Tell him or her that you want to be held accountable for what you've put in your contract, but you don't necessarily want to be nagged.

➤ Devise a schedule whereby your partner periodically asks or reminds you about your commitment.

If it's a goal to lose weight, perhaps your partner can observe you as you weigh yourself once or twice per week. Some people find it effective to simply have a scheduled five- or 10-minute discussion with their partner about the goal. Or, perhaps your partner can serve as a sounding board, advisor, or coach (coaches are covered in Chapter 22, "The Tom Sawyer Effect: Formally Enlisting Others to Help You").

When you feel stymied or frustrated, use your confidant to help you smooth out the wrinkles and carry on. The relationship you develop is entirely your choice.

You and Someone from Work

If you choose to share your self-initiated contract with someone from work, whether a coworker, boss, mentor, or other trusted individual, perhaps you can keep in touch by phone, fax, or e-mail if the trusted individual is physically apart from you.

I've encountered situations in which two people shared self-initiated contracts with each other and used each other as sounding boards. In this manner, they were able to increase their level of mutual commitment and accountability. (For more information on these types of maneuvers, see Chapter 20, "Affiliating with Others: Capitalizing on Those Around You.")

When choosing a partner for your self-initiated contract, you might want to consider these types of people:

➤ Someone close to you or someone who knows you well

➤ Someone who likes you

➤ Someone who willingly chooses to participate

➤ Someone who will hold your feet to the fire

➤ Someone who has a vested interest in your achievement

➤ Someone who has a reciprocal need

➤ Someone who has helped others in a similar fashion

A prime consideration when selecting a partner for your self-initiated contract is to find someone who has a vested interest in your success.

For a career-related goal, your boss may well be the appropriate party. For business-related goals, choose business partners, potential suppliers, creditors, or professional advisors such as bankers, lawyers, and attorneys. There are people all around you who could serve as appropriate partners in this process.

> **Go for the Gold!**
> If your spouse wants you to lose 10 pounds and can serve as the right type of partner for this process, proceed at full speed! If your spouse will nag more than listen and encourage, think again.

Holding Your Feet to the Fire

Here's an entirely optional feature for using self-initiated contracts that may or may not be right for you. Suppose that you add a clause at the bottom of your contract that delineates some consequences if you do not achieve your goal in the scheduled time frame. When you sign a contract for a home loan or a business venture and you default on the contract, there are usually consequences you'd rather not experience.

Dennis Hensley notes that if you default on a contract in the business world, you can be sued, go unpaid for work you've performed to date, or surrender valuable property or equipment.

What might you include as consequences of your not meeting the terms of your self-initiated contract? It's up to you and the person who is helping you in this process. Here's a roster of potential consequences to help stimulate your thinking:

➤ The other person will not believe anything you say again.

➤ You will go a week, a month, or some other time period deprived of something you enjoy.

➤ You will donate $1,000 to the other person's favorite charity.

➤ You will put $2,000 in escrow, and the other person will receive it if you do not make good on your goal. (This is more economically palatable with a spouse rather than someone outside your family.)

➤ You will have to engage in some other unpleasant task for a defined period of time for that other person.

Consequences of Little Use

Now here are a few consequences you don't want to use, because they're likely to cause more trouble than they're worth:

➤ Increasing the stakes if you default in some way on your self-initiated contract—for example, adding even greater consequences for not reaching your goal by a new period of time. This only puts more pressure on you and is not a good idea.

➤ Allowing for some sliding-scale consequence based on what percentage of the goal you reach. If you sought to lose 10 pounds and you only lost eight, for example, your consequences are less severe. You want to avoid this because it gives you an out; it actually constructs a scenario in which you might not strive to lose the entire 10 pounds, because you know the consequences are less severe if you make some progress toward the goal.

Avoid Built-in Escape Hatches

CAUTION!

Uh-Oh!
If you continually achieve only 60 to 80 percent of the goals you set for yourself, you risk violating your own sense of personal integrity. Ten pounds is 10 pounds. Eight pounds is not 10 pounds.

Beware! You'll encounter many books and articles on goal setting that say it's okay to set a challenging goal and achieve 80 percent of it because, after all, that's 80 percent farther than you were before.

I pose to you an essential question: How serious are you about reaching the goal you specifically set to reach? If you sought to lose 10 pounds and you only lost eight, what other goals will you shortchange? Moreover, what's the probability that you'll lose the additional two pounds unless you take time to reestablish and commit to a new goal?

Reviewing Your Contract

In addition to posting your contract in places where you'll often encounter it, you might need to review your contract; you might find that certain words you originally used need to replaced with more appropriate words. When seeking to lose 10 pounds, you might say, "I seek to be 10 pounds lighter by September 30th of this year." You might want to modify that phrase to "I seek to be 10 pounds lighter by September 30th of this year and stay at my new weight for a minimum of six months."

Too Low, Too High

While pursuing your goal, you might find that you were too ambitious or not ambitious enough. If you wanted to achieve a 20 percent increase in something, but you find that 30 percent is a more worthwhile goal, it makes sense to modify your self-initiated contract or to rewrite your contract altogether. Remember that you're in charge.

You might find that your contract was too ambitious. Although 20 percent seemed challenging but reachable, it became evident that 12 percent is the maximum attainable, so 20 percent is out of the question. This isn't the same as waffling on your goals as discussed previously. Instead, you are acknowledging reality, which prompts you to make a change.

Perhaps your timeline is too long or too short. Again, don't review and modify your contract based on whims or personal convenience. Do it based on new knowledge you've attained that prompts you to change terms.

A New Ball Game

Here is a list of some external factors that could prompt you to change contract terms:

➤ New technology is introduced that dramatically impacts a critical procedure.

➤ New legislation is enacted that dramatically enhances or impedes your progress.

➤· Someone close to you becomes seriously ill.

➤ A key resource suddenly becomes unavailable.

Renewing Your Contract

You renew your contract when you've successfully completed your original contract. If you wanted to attain level X, and you did so, devise a second contract and target level 2X. If your goal was one of maintenance, and you're able to achieve it over a defined time period, renewing your contract and identifying a new timeline can be more reinforcing than merely hoping to remain in a maintenance mode.

Wordy and Unwieldy

If your former contract was elaborate and wordy, you might want to tone down the amount of prose in your renewed contract. Maybe you don't need to list the subparts.

If you included a clause delineating consequences, perhaps you want to change the consequences so that the clause acquires greater vibrancy. You might find that you don't need a consequences clause at all.

Best Time to Renew

The best time to renew your contract is a few days before the old one expires. The risk of waiting until the day it expires or a few days after is that you might wait several days or weeks to embark on the new contracted quest.

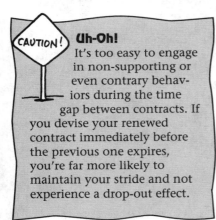

CAUTION! Uh-Oh!
It's too easy to engage in non-supporting or even contrary behaviors during the time gap between contracts. If you devise your renewed contract immediately before the previous one expires, you're far more likely to maintain your stride and not experience a drop-out effect.

Renewing with a Partner

When you renew your contract, you have the option of renewing with your current partner or selecting someone else.

The value in selecting someone else is that you get new types of input and a different interaction than you had with the original person. Also, let's face it, the original partner might not want to sign on for another hitch.

Although self-initiated contracts aren't for everyone, you might be pleasantly surprised by your initial trial and find that self-initiated contracts are what the goal-achieving doctor ordered.

The Least You Need to Know

➤ As you set some goals, you might find an added incentive for reaching them by devising a contract for yourself.

➤ It's best to have subparts that support your major goal.

➤ Sharing your contract with a spouse, friend, mentor, or coworker may bolster your efforts in reaching your goal.

➤ If you're serious about reaching your goal, you won't shortchange yourself by settling for less.

➤ For maintenance goals, devise a new contract immediately before the previous one expires to maintain your stride and avoid a drop-out effect.

Chapter 18

All About Deadlines

In This Chapter

➤ Dealing with no-choice situations

➤ Making the best of deadlines

➤ When you face constant deadlines

➤ Systemizing your efforts

Do you hate to face a deadline? Many people do for a variety of reasons:

➤ The deadline has been imposed by someone else.

➤ The deadline is unrealistic.

➤ The deadline is unrelenting.

In this chapter, you'll explore your relationship with deadlines, how they've stifled you in the past, and how you can use them to accelerate your progress toward goals.

We Must, Therefore We Will

Did you see the movie *Apollo 13* staring Tom Hanks and Ed Harris? In the movie, which is based on James Lovell's book, *Lost Moon*, the crew of space capsule Apollo 13 find themselves in a desperate situation. Something has gone wrong on their attempted moon mission, and the mission will have to be aborted before they reach their destination. They will need to steer their capsule back to earth. Their oxygen and fuel supply will last only three more days—barely enough time to make it back and live to talk about it.

Ed Harris plays the character in charge of the Apollo 13 flight operation back in Houston. Harris and his staff quickly determine that the only way the Apollo 13 crew has a chance of returning to earth is to bypass the moon, get into the moon's orbit, and use a sling-shot effect—that is, going all the way around the moon and heading back to earth.

Portraying Life

I was utterly amazed when *Apollo 13* did not win the Oscar for best picture; I think it was the best picture of the decade. Nowhere else in life have I seen such a vivid and gripping portrayal of something that captured every minute of an audience's attention.

Apollo 13 was fascinating from the standpoint of setting and reaching goals, because there was an intractable, absolute deadline that the flight and ground crew had to meet. If they failed to do so, three astronauts would die. Therefore, everyone poured their energy into steering the capsule into earth's atmosphere at a precise angle and within a narrow time frame.

The flight crew reconfigured its interior. They stripped the capsule of everything that would not be needed to accomplish the mission. The ground team in Houston operated around the clock to ensure that the astronauts could maintain an adequate oxygen supply, have the requisite electrical voltage to restart a dormant engine at a critical juncture, and otherwise battle the elements.

Simulating the Predicament

An original crew member was prevented from going on the mission because he may have been coming down with the measles. He was summoned out of bed in the early morning the day the mission went awry. At the flight center, he asked to be placed in a prototype capsule with the same equipment, the same resources, and the same operating room as the space crew. He assumed the responsibility of devising a solution to his compatriots' electrical problem using only what they had available in space.

Similarly, engineers and communications specialists tackled one problem after another using only those same resources available in the capsule. If you see the movie, you'll have a good understanding of the potential power you can harness to meet deadlines—yours or those imposed on you—to reach your goals. The rest of this chapter discusses using deadlines to help you set and reach goals.

Have Someone Waiting for You

Since early in human civilization, having someone waiting for them to turn in their results has motivated human beings to set and reach their goals. In the dead of winter, the hunter often was faced with cornering his prey, killing it, and bringing it back to his family's cave. Today, if you're an adult with dependents, your task may be less hazardous but no less heroic. You might face tasks such as these:

➤ Completing homework

➤ Taking tests

➤ Turning in term papers

➤ Paying monthly rent or mortgage

➤ Paying taxes

➤ Registering your automobile

➤ Completing professional certifications

➤ Getting to work on time

➤ Getting back from lunch on time

➤ Voting

➤ Meeting a quota

➤ Meeting a budget

➤ Making a plane flight

➤ Paying off a car loan

➤ Filing an income tax extension

➤ Registering for courses

➤ Paying bills

FOR SURE

For Sure

As an author and speaker, I've found that although deadlines might seem unappealing, they have largely contributed to my productivity. My 25 books were all products of having specific deadlines and having someone waiting for my work. The Alpha Books division of Macmillan, a highly organized, professional organization, requires me to turn in manuscripts one quarter at a time instead of submitting a single manuscript at the end of a contract period.

Domestic Deadlines

Think about the deadlines you have to meet in your own life and career and the actual benefits you get from meeting them. Undoubtedly, you pay rent or contribute to a mortgage. What would happen if your landlord or mortgage company said you can pay them every six months or once a year instead of paying them monthly? Realistically, how comfortable would you be with that payment plan?

Would you be able to cough up the requested sums at the end of six or 12 months? Sure, you could write a check to yourself each month, invest the money, have the interest grow, make your payment, and have a little change to boot. Most people can't or won't do this, though. You'd probably be scrambling to find the funds, feel anything but balanced, and deprive yourself of relative simplicity. You certainly wouldn't be taking an incremental approach to paying for your premises.

Deadlines at Work

How about at work? If you're in sales, you already know about meeting quotas. If you're not in sales, there's some volume of work you need to present within some time interval on a regular basis.

Indeed, a capitalist society is structured on a time versus money tradeoff. You take X amount of time to deliver a product or service, or to achieve some performance level that others deem valuable. Those others might include your boss, clients, or anyone who's willing to pay you for your services.

For Sure

In recent decades, global economic competition has intensified. If a manufacturer can hire cheaper labor elsewhere, that manufacturer will use the cheap labor. Ultimately, the worldwide effect of cheap labor is that you may be working harder and longer just to stay even, regardless of whether you're in a white- or blue-collar position.

When Deadlines Are Constant

If you are employed in an industry or profession, imposed continual and rigorous deadlines can be nerve-wracking and may seem pointless. Suppose that you're a newspaper reporter covering a local beat. You may have to turn in a column each or every few days in words that conform to certain style guidelines and meet the approval of your editor, publisher, and subscribers.

For Sure

In nearly every American city, within a block or two of the city's major newspaper, there's a familiar watering hole where reporters head out after work on Fridays. If you've ever been in such a place, you might have been aghast at these hard-boiled types who seem to drown their sorrows because of demanding and gut-wrenching deadlines.

Whether you are a reporter facing daily deadlines, a sales representative facing a weekly quota, or any other type of white- or blue-collar professional who has to complete so much by some imposed time interval, there are ways to make deadlines work for you.

Here are a variety of techniques and steps to help you maintain control and better harness the power to be derived for having to meet deadlines. Not surprisingly, the first elements include maintaining balance, proceeding with relative simplicity, and taking an incremental approach. Let's see how these apply.

Maintaining Balance in the Face of Deadlines

If you're in an occupation in which you continually have to meet deadlines, the first order of business is to recognize that there is no use in pretending it's any different. Then ask yourself these questions:

➤ To what degree do I seek to attain balance in my life and work?

➤ Do I give myself a good eight hours of sleep each night?

➤ Do I eat a balanced meal or two each day, or do I load up on fast food and short-term energy boosters that leave me drained?

➤ Do I take vitamins and nutritional supplements regularly?

➤ Do I frequently stretch, take walks, and simply take breaks?

Tell me how rigorous and restricting your deadline is, and I'll still gently explain to you the ways you can maintain some semblance of balance in the midst of the fray.

Go for the Gold!

In the most challenging occupations, there are people who maintain their fitness level and weight, take regular and strong, deep breaths, leave work at the end of the day with enough energy to enjoy their evening, and actually prosper. You have the tools and the plan to do the same.

Maintaining Relative Simplicity in the Face of Deadlines

Suppose that you're in an occupation with imposed deadlines that are complex, multifaceted, and downright tricky. How can you maintain relative simplicity in such a scenario? The first thing to do in accordance with what I discussed earlier is to look at the most successful people in your line of work. Ask yourself these questions:

➤ How do they conduct themselves?

➤ What time do they arrive?

➤ What time do they leave?

➤ What equipment do they use?

➤ What are their work habits?

➤ When and how often do they take breaks?

➤ What other resources do they employ?

Another step toward achieving relative simplicity that is ignored by too many people is to identify what is not necessary to meet your deadline. Look around your office and determine everything you have that doesn't support what you need to accomplish you goals. These items could be equipment, furniture, books, files, information, or desk items. If you've read either of my earlier two books, *The Complete Idiot's Guide to Managing Your Time* or *The Complete Idiot's Guide to Managing Stress*, you know that I'm a strong advocate of working in a relatively clutter-free environment.

What about simplifying your communications? Do you have three different e-mail accounts when one would do the trick? Do you dispense your cellular phone number to everyone when only a few key people need to have it? Do you try to get your best work done in the middle of a hyper-hectic office that makes the New York Stock Exchange look like a pastoral setting? If these or other aspects of your work situation prevail, you might be operating in an environment that is more complex than necessary.

Go for the Gold!
The more effective you are in managing your surroundings, particularly flat surfaces in your office, home, or car, the more effective you'll be overall. It's too easy today to be awash in material things. Evaluate, sort, and filter your surrounding items so that you can work more effectively.

Systemize Things

To achieve relative simplicity in pursuit of a constant deadline, systemize work elements that lend themselves to such a process. For example, consider the following:

➤ Do you find yourself having to frequently enter text onto your screen that is derived from other sources? If so, perhaps you can simply buy a scanner that reads the text and converts it to your word processing system.

➤ Do you regularly need to send information to the same parties by snail mail? If so, prepare a healthy supply of addressed, stamped envelopes to the regular recipients.

➤ Can you produce a chronological or functional checklist to aid you in your performance? (Chapter 15, "A Question of Time," discusses using charts and goal-related software.)

➤ Are there modular elements to what you do? If your work involves assembling component elements on a recurring basis, is there a way to systemize that?

As a professional speaker, I'm frequently called by parties who want to see my demonstration video, price list, and letters from previous meeting planners who have retained me. Instead of rounding up these things all over my office, I've assembled a bin system that has slots in which I can easily store these items. When someone requests information, I can efficiently gather the components and compose a professional package.

Reuse What You've Already Done

Are there ways to draw on what you've already done in meeting past deadlines to meet current deadlines? In several of my books, I've discussed the time-honored notion of making your work count twice. That involves looking for ways to reemploy what you've already done.

Suppose that you're a management consultant who develops a financial report at the end of each engagement. These reports usually stretch out to 20 or 30 pages. Are recommendations you made for a previous client applicable with slight modifications?

> **Go for the Gold!**
> If you have to write management reports in general, are there four- to five-page stretches within previous reports that are relevant or critical to what you're currently working on? If so, you have a wonderful opportunity to make your work count twice.

Assemble What You Need

Perhaps the single most important observation I can offer is this: The way to meet your deadlines and still have a life is to ensure that you meet those deadlines with the appropriate level of resources. As an equation, it looks like this:

Challenges Faced = Resources Allocated

This is as simple as it gets. By using this equation, you never need to find yourself in a time deficit again. It drives me crazy to see all these time-management gurus telling people all these things they need to do to stay in control of their time. Look at the situation you're facing, determine what's required, leave work on time, have a life, come back, and do it again.

First, identify the challenge you face. You might laugh this one off and say the challenge you face is obvious. Is it, however?

CAUTION! **Uh-Oh!**
Would-be authors frequently ask for my advice about writing a book, getting it published, and getting it marketed. Many are aghast when I tell them that writing the book represents only one-third of the overall effort needed to make the book successful. These people did not have an accurate picture of the challenge they face in this pursuit.

In your own career, can you specifically define what is required of you? Is it simply turning in a report every Thursday by 4 p.m., making 10 calls each morning before noon, or handling all the items in the lot by the end of the day? Without knowing specifically what you do, here are other likely elements I'm guessing you might want to consider:

➤ Handle your work with flair. Put a little pizzazz into your work so that the customer, client, or end-user gains a little something more than merely a timely delivery.

➤ Troubleshoot as you go. Ensure that there won't be problems down the pike because you were so rushed to meet the deadline that you didn't handle important details.

➤ Complete all the internal reporting. In addition to delivering the goods or services on time, you usually need to complete many other kinds of procedures. Perhaps you need to complete a time log. You might have to update a file folder. Perhaps there's something to check off or send out.

➤ Create a clearing for your next effort.

Clear the Decks

I worked for Smyth Manufacturing Company the summer before heading to college. They made book-binding equipment. It was my only time in a factory, thank goodness, but I learned many lessons that have stayed with me to this day.

One lesson I learned was how important cleaning is in an industrial setting. Before I left for the evening, I oiled my machine, wiped the floor and counters, and cleared out extraneous items so that I was ready to begin the next day without impediments. The craftsmen with whom I worked often elaborately cleaned and reorganized items in the middle of the day as well as they switched from one job to another; everyone's safety depended on it.

No matter how quickly these job shop professionals worked, they continually maintained control of their immediate environment, because they understood its importance on many levels. They also were acknowledging the full measure of the daily challenges they faced.

In case you think they were being overly cautious or were paid some admirable hourly wage, guess again. These workers were paid by the piece, and they were commonly known as *piece workers*. Any one of them easily could have increased his output on a given day by slacking off on cleaning and maintenance procedures.

After all, if you can turn out seven pieces in a day while spending 30 percent of your time cleaning and maintaining, you might be able to produce more than 10 pieces if you completely concentrate on your output. In the short term, you could make much more money. In the not-so-short term, you could get injured, injure others, create more waste, shorten the equipment's life, or get fired.

Line Up Your Ducks

Challenges Faced = Resources Allocated

Allocating resources is the other side of the equation. If you've accurately identified the challenge you face, following procedures and protocols, coming in on time, and giving it your all seems sufficient. Unfortunately, this is rarely enough.

Suppose that you earn $40,000 annually. You then get a raise. How much of that increase will you use to maintain balance and simplicity in your life as when you were performing and were expected to perform at a level commensurate with a $40,000 wage?

It is critical for you to take some portion of your pay increase and use it in the manner that best supports your efforts. Perhaps there's personal equipment you can buy, or perhaps you need a weekly massage. Maybe you'll spend some of the money on a career coach who can help you perform at your best (more on this in Chapter 22, "The Tom Sawyer Effect: Formally Enlisting Others to Help You").

> **Uh-Oh!**
> CAUTION!
> Too many professionals accept a responsibility increase and (hopefully) a pay increase but fail to acknowledge the need to reserve some of the money for their personal well being.

Ask yourself these questions:

➤ What elements or resources does my organization provide that I might redirect or reallocate to meet the continuing challenges I face?

➤ Do I have a staff that could be used in more supportive ways?

➤ Am I using my staff to my best advantage now?

➤ Do I have equipment being used in limited ways?

➤ Are there mentors, subject matter experts, and trail blazers in my organization that I can draw on to assist me in my quest to meet recurring, rigorous deadlines with relative simplicity? (For more information, see Chapter 20, "Affiliating with Others: Capitalizing on Those Around You," and Chapter 22.)

Taking an Incremental Approach

Four summers after working in a job shop, I got a summer job before entering graduate school working for a large moving company. Talk about working under imposed deadlines! Each day the drivers and helpers (I was a helper) left the company parking lot at 6:30 a.m.

However varied the assignments, everyone's daily goal ultimately boiled down to the same thing: finishing the move by the day's end. If we were moving office equipment or entire offices, the deadlines often were based on the closing times of loading docks, secured parking lots, and office buildings. If we were doing household moves, we wanted to finish before dark or by about 9 p.m. at the latest.

The movers, or *lifers*, as they were called, came from all kinds of backgrounds. It was a demanding, exhausting, and unrelenting line of work. Most of the lifers were visibly aging faster than normal.

Incremental If You Want to Live

These movers understood the importance of meeting their daily deadlines with an incremental approach. In the moving business, you simply cannot make a hurried move. For one thing, you'd start dropping items, bumping into other people, and putting things in the wrong rooms.

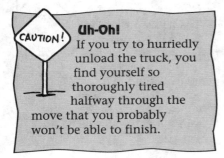

Uh-Oh!

If you try to hurriedly unload the truck, you find yourself so thoroughly tired halfway through the move that you probably won't be able to finish.

We therefore unloaded our trucks in an almost methodical fashion. I caught on from the first day largely because I had no choice. It also made great sense. Those first couple of days, I was so sore every evening that I couldn't proceed any faster, not even if I wanted to. By about the second week, I started to build up some muscles and could maintain the required pace.

Item by item, the lifer and his helper would lift items off the truck or roll them onto dollies. Office moves were easier than household moves because buildings had loading docks, freight elevators, and long, tiled hallways. Houses, by contrast, had narrow doors, heavily carpeted living rooms, winding stairs, and other irritating impediments.

Overwhelming on Purpose

One technique I've never forgotten represents the reverse incremental approach. With a simple nod to one another, lifters and helpers working on the move began to unpack the individual items in boxes at a furious pace. At first, the family was pleased to see such vigorous efforts.

After a couple of minutes, as one box was opened after another, and hundreds of items started pouring forth, the family typically panicked. They realized that if they let the movers go unchecked, every box in the house would be open and every item they owned would be parked in the far reaches of the house. So, families routinely asked us to stop.

They wanted to open the boxes at their own pace and regain the ability to make incremental progress themselves. We always feigned perplexity. We'd say something like, "Are you sure you don't want us to do any more unpacking?" They were sure, all right. They could hardly wait to see us go. They signed off on the moving contract and displayed signs of great relief as we made our way to their front door.

Your Incremental Strategy

Now how can you approach some of your recurring deadlines on an incremental basis knowing that chipping away at what you do is a method for meeting the deadline? Here are some suggestions:

➤ Remember to stop and take deep breaths.

➤ Identify natural breaks in the process beforehand and use them to your best advantage.

➤ If it's helpful, monitor your progress with checklists or charts.

➤ Remember to give yourself small rewards for incremental progress. Rewards might include allowing yourself to call a friend, eating the other half of your bagel or bran muffin, or composing some e-mails you've been wanting to send.

The Least You Need to Know

➤ Deadlines often accelerate your progress toward goals. Model yourself after others who are effective at meeting deadlines.

➤ Strive to improve your work or become a specialist so that you can charge more or earn more and break free from the traditional time versus money tradeoff.

➤ To help achieve relative simplicity, identify what is not necessary to meet your deadline.

➤ To avoid getting into time binds, meet the challenges you face—such as deadlines—with the appropriate level of resources.

➤ Give yourself small rewards for incremental progress on important deadlines.

Chapter 19

Visualization Techniques

In This Chapter

➤ See it, feel it, touch it

➤ Establishing a routine

➤ Tales of the extraordinary

A powerful way to reinforce your progress toward achieving your goals is to use visualization. Even though the word *visual* might seem to refer directly to your sense of sight, you can draw on one or more of your senses to visualize the attainment of your goal. Let's see how this works.

See It

Undoubtedly, you've heard or read about Olympic athletes who have used visualization techniques to enhance their performances. Have you ever tapped in to this powerful goal-reinforcing technique yourself? You don't have to be an Olympic athlete in pursuit of a gold medal to engage in this process, but an example from the Olympics is a good place to begin the discussion. Olympian Dwight Stone, a high jumper who represented the

United States in the Olympics some 25 years ago, was one of the most avid and prominent users of visualization techniques in the sport. His method was so precise and so observable that he influenced the generation of high jumpers that followed him.

Every Step of the Way

Prior to every jump, during practice or actual competition, Stone took his place a measured distance away from the high-jump bar and paused for several seconds. He then mentally envisioned himself taking every step on the way toward his launch over the bar. During televised competitions, particularly the Olympics, you could see Stone moving his head up and down as he visualized each step and where his foot would fall on his approach and takeoff.

When he mentally got to the final step before the jump, you could see him contemplating the angle at which he approached the bar, where he'd plant his foot, and how he'd use his arms and upper torso to create an upward thrust. Stone's head movements told you in advance of his approach that he planned to rise over the bar easily, land on his back in the proper position, and be quite pleased with his efforts.

Often enough, Dwight Stone used visualization techniques to help achieve record-setting performances in the process. Certainly, he didn't clear the bar at every height every time. In fact, many of his jumps were misses; he knocked over the bar, and in some cases failed to make the jump altogether. Such misses and failed attempts are never the point when it comes to using visualization to reinforce your goal progress. The fact that you use visualization helps you to increase performance, accelerate your progress, and reach your goals in ways that people who don't use visualization will never be able to appreciate.

Whirling Dervishes

So, the high jump is not your sport, huh? Let's look at figure skating instead. In a sport like the high jump, you can miss a couple of times, but as long as you clear the bar by the third time, you can stay in the competition and move on to the next height. In figure skating, however, your routine has to be nearly perfect to win.

However long you're on the ice, whether it's during compulsories or artistic impression, every eye in the arena is on you for every second. Judges, pencil in hand, are ready to mark down the slightest fault—a landing that doesn't hit the mark, a wobble, or any other mistake.

Did you know that some professional skaters visualize their entire routine before actually going out on the ice? Even for a four-minute routine, which requires a lot of visualization, these skaters run through every twist, every turn, every triple axel, and every landing.

For Sure

Visualization works *even when you're not in practice*. A growing body of evidence indicates that using visualization techniques can aid in one's performance—even in the absence of practice sessions!

Basketball free-throw percentages have been dropping for several years at the pro and college levels. A study of basketball players revealed that visualization during time away from practice enabled 50 percent of one team to increase its foul-shot percentages above those of the other half of the team, *who participated in uninterrupted practice with no visualization!*

A More Accomplished You

How much better will you do on the job or at home in pursuit of your goals if you use visualization techniques? Right now, I'd like you to write down three areas in which you might be able to enhance your progress toward goals by using visualization:

1. _____

2. _____

3. _____

I'm guessing that the three areas you wrote down, if you wrote anything down, focused on some type of physical performance. Yet this need not be the case. Suppose that you want to have a better relationship with your son. Lately, you've argued every other time you've encountered each other. Can you visualize having a pleasant, five-minute conversation?

If it has been your ongoing goal to remodel one of the rooms in your house, how about visualizing your efforts in making this a reality? See yourself stripping the old wallpaper, painting or putting up new wallpaper, changing the rug, putting in a new light fixture, and so on. Go ahead—visualize that you've completed all the work and that the room is now sparkling.

Establishing an Environment for Visualization

Many people don't use visualization techniques because they don't foster a climate in which they can be practiced. To give you an extreme example of when visualization doesn't occur, imagine that your house is being assaulted by a 120 mile-per-hour hurricane.

What's the likelihood you're going to envision turning in some superior performance at work or on the athletic field? Pretty low, huh? You're occupied at the moment with prevailing atmospheric conditions.

On the other hand, when you give yourself a little space (such as sitting in a big, comfortable easy chair or on your living room couch), you can foster an environment in which you're more easily able to use visualization, although it isn't absolutely necessary. You can use a plane seat, a bus seat, a park bench, or a beach blanket. Like Dwight Stone, you can even use visualization techniques while you're standing.

Probably, however, you're just starting to use this valuable technique, so you'll begin while sitting.

A Few Moments for Yourself

In addition to a little space, you need to give yourself a little time. Although it's possible to have visualizations that last only a few seconds, to get the full benefit, give yourself at least a couple of minutes. Mentally and emotionally allow yourself to dwell in that arena where you want to do well.

Go for the Gold! Precisely how much time do you need to get the full benefits of your visualization? It differs from person to person. A second-to-second match is ideal but not always practical. If you skate for a four-minute routine, then visualize the entire routine for the full four minutes. It's possible, however, to visualize what you want to achieve in far less time than you actually would spend in its execution and still derive great benefits. A solid five- or ten-minute visualization as to how you're going to perform can yield an admirable payoff.

I'll talk about drawing on other sensory inputs momentarily, but the more fully immersed you can get in the environment in which you're going to actually perform, the stronger your visualization. If you were a boxer and you could hear the announcer at the end of the match say, "And the winner and still champ...you!" it would add to your overall incentive.

If you're going to be delivering a one-hour lecture 30 minutes from now, find five minutes of quiet someplace. Those five minutes can mean the difference between being incisive, motivating, and stimulating and simply being there with the audience tolerating you.

A Private Space and Time

Political campaign advisors often coach their candidates before a campaign rally by telling them to go to the public rest room, find a far stall, sit down, and spend a few minutes in quiet contemplation.

I once saw a candidate and her advisors pull up in a limo alongside the curb just outside the building where she was going to be giving a campaign speech. I was several paces behind the limo, and I think I was out of sight. Even though the limo's glass was tinted, I knew exactly who was inside—I mean, who else is going to pull up in a limo prior to a scheduled campaign speech?

When the candidate got out of the car along with her advisors, I could see that she was quite composed. She gave a pretty good speech that day, and although she might have given a good speech anyway, I like to think that those few minutes in the limo before-hand paid off.

Quiet on the Set, Please

The third element for effective visualization is a little quiet. The quiet I'm suggesting doesn't mean you have to be surrounded by absolute silence. Far from it. You can find "quiet" in the middle of a cheering crowd at Yankee Stadium. You can find quiet before it's your turn to get up and take care of that spare during your weekly bowling league game.

The quiet to which I'm referring means closing down your information receptors and retreating to that motionless inner part of you that has the ability to focus on one thing at a time. If you're literally sur-rounded by quiet, that's fine too.

The reason why you can find quiet in otherwise noisy situations is because the roar of the crowd, the con-stant sound of bowling balls hitting bowling pins, the hum of your washing machine's spin cycle, or the white noise of a fan or air conditioner does not com-pete with your ability to focus within.

Classical or soft music, the purr of a well-oiled engine, a baby's babbling, and a gurgling brook all allow for focus within.

> **Uh-Oh!**
> Too often in our overly noisy society, our visualization is hampered by the TV playing in the next room, your neighbor's dog barking, or some other penetrating noise. Most television programs, many forms of music, highly audible conversations, and a ringing telephone are all likely to impede your progress.

Feel It

"Feel It" is defined as your ability to gain a specific sense of accomplishing your goal by "feeling" some object that represents that achievement.

When writing this book, for example, it would have been easy for me to stop and lament several times in the middle of any particular chapter and conclude that the project was hopeless.

"I'm never going to finish this." Macmillan wants 350 pages. Yikes! That's like writing 35 10-page term papers. I didn't do that my entire four years in college or two years in graduate school!"

"How did I get into this line of work? Maybe I ought to call them right now and tell them I can't do the job."

Just kidding! What if those were the thoughts I harbored, however, while proceeding from chapter to chapter? Is it likely that I would have ever finished my book?

Suppose that you have some large report to turn in at work. How far will you get if you keep thinking about how much you have to go? No, my friend, the key is *to visualize the report* (or, in my case, the book) *already completed*.

As I was writing this book, I thought how wonderful it would be when it was finished. I could "feel" the book in my hand. I saw the cover with my name on it; the familiar orange motif; all those sparkling pages; the little characters the Macmillan artists draw; my long, proud biography on the inside of the back cover; the width of the spine; and all the things that go into this book.

I felt the weight of the book when I mailed it off to the *New York Times* after they decided they wanted to do a major book review on it (remember that I'm using visualization techniques here!).

Name That Accomplishment

What do you want to achieve right now? What tools or objects do you want to use to achieve these goals? Can you mentally feel those objects in your hands? If your pursuit is an athletic achievement, perhaps you can feel the baseball bat or basketball in your hands, the skates on your feet, the football helmet, or the volleyball kneepads. Perhaps you can feel the trophy, the blue ribbon, the banner, the award certificate, or the check for $10,000!

If it's an achievement at work, maybe you can feel the finished report, the letter in your hand from the satisfied client, your boss's hand as he shakes yours and says, "great job," or the goose bumps on the back of your neck when everyone stares at you with admiration for your outstanding performance.

If it's a domestic goal, maybe you can feel the texture of the new wallpaper in that room you're going to complete, the steering wheel of your new car, the steering wheel of your old car that you've just tuned up and cleaned to perfection, or the big kiss from your spouse for completing who knows what.

Too Much Sight and Sound

Too often in this hectic, over-stimulated world, we rely heavily on our sense of sight or hearing to gain cues from our environment. Touch and taste, along with smell, are important senses as well. I know that you can use these senses to aid in your visualization and reinforce your progress toward goals. In fact, I'll prove it to you.

I want you to think back to the last time you had Thanksgiving dinner at your parent's home. It might have been last Thanksgiving, or, if your parents have passed away, it might have been many, many years ago. You're sitting on one of the strong dining room chairs. Can you feel it beneath you? The table is covered with one of your mother's better tablecloths. Put your hand on the tablecloth.

Your mother's best plates and the best silverware are in front of you. Pick up the fork. Now, as your father, or mother, or someone carves the turkey, they ask for your plate. Pick it up. Extend it so that they can put that big drumstick right smack in the middle. Put your plate down now, and pick up your glass. Take a drink and put your glass down. Now, with your knife and fork, put a little of that succulent turkey into your mouth.

Welcome back! Where have you just been? Certainly, you didn't physically leave your location as you were reading that last paragraph. Yet I'll bet you "felt" everything I described. In this case, you were experiencing something from your past—Thanksgiving dinner. Miraculously, marvelously, visualization works just as well in projecting the future.

Projecting, Not Predicting

Notice that I said *projecting* the future, not *predicting*. When the future unfolds, it might not be quite what you envisioned. Often it isn't. However, to the degree that you can get a clear sensation of how you'd like things to be, using the strength of your mind to engage your senses, you increase the likelihood, if even slightly, that what you envision will come to pass.

This is not wishful thinking or daydreaming, as I discussed in Chapter 1. You're using visualization techniques in pursuit of a challenging yet reachable goal that is quantifiable and has a specific timeline. To the best of your ability, you're going to stay balanced in pursuit of your goal, maintain relative simplicity, and take an incremental approach, even though your progress might not turn out to be incremental at all.

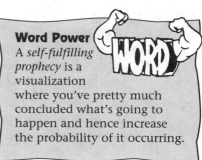

Go for the Gold!
The more often you engage in profound, prolonged visualization techniques, the greater your progress. If you get to the point where you can visualize every nuance of your desired goal, who's to say that soon you won't be right there?

Dwell On It

The late Earl Nightingale, in his award-winning cassette, "The Strangest Secret," observed that, indeed, the strangest secret of the human experience is that we tend to become what we dwell on. It's called a *self-fulfilling prophecy*. If you dwell on the successful completion of your goals, you automatically move in that direction. If you dwell on failure, be prepared to experience failure in abundance.

Word Power
A *self-fulfilling prophecy* is a visualization where you've pretty much concluded what's going to happen and hence increase the probability of it occurring.

Norman Cousins, who wrote *Anatomy of an Illness*, once said, "People are never more insecure than when they become obsessed with their fears at the expense of their dreams." Your mission is to focus on what you want, not what you want to avoid. If you can feel some object that represents the accomplishment of your goal, all the better.

For Sure

The great Milwaukee Braves pitcher Warren Spahn once lamented that at a critical juncture of a baseball game, his manager or pitching coach came out to the mound to discuss how Spahn would face the next batter. The manager said, "Don't give him any high and inside pitches," and then promptly ran back to the dugout.

Spahn was confused. Because he was told what to *avoid* instead of what to aim for, Spahn was left without a definite line of action. Perplexed by his manager's negative description of what course of action he should take, he went with his instincts and sure enough served a high and inside pitch, which the batter promptly smacked.

Touch It

When Bill Clinton was a teenager, he had the opportunity to meet the president at the time, John F. Kennedy. This encounter—shaking the hand of the president of the United States of America—was a defining moment in Clinton's life. Deep within him, Clinton concluded that he too could be president, and as his biographers have dutifully noted, he began preparing for that eventuality.

Regardless of what you or I might think of him, it's highly revealing to consider that long-term visualization sparked off by a touch, such as that experienced by Bill Clinton, led 30 years later to one of the most magnificent achievements an individual can experience on this earth—being elected to head what is arguably the most powerful nation on earth.

Touch Means Much

Perhaps one of the reasons why people shake hands in the Western world as a method for initiating a business or personal relationship is because it affords an instant opportunity to touch another individual in a socially approved way. Touch differs from feeling in that *with feeling, you envision something* such as a trophy, a report, or some object that represents your accomplishment as actually being in your hand.

With *touch*, you *initiate the process of visualization* because of your physical contact with some person, object, or symbol (you physically put your hand on it) and gain clarity, insight, and even inspiration in pursuit of some lofty goal—even a goal you might not have thought of yet.

Touching Makes It Real!

The first thing astronauts in training seem to want to do is to touch a space shuttle. Wannabe professional speakers come up to the front of the room and put their hands on the lectern or touch the microphone when they're attending another person's presentation.

Young children seem to want to touch everything. My daughter, Valerie, is athletically inclined, and whether it's roller skates, roller blades, a tennis racquet or tennis balls, soccer shoes or a soccer ball, she wants to touch it all as a prelude to engaging in and mastering the sport.

Sculptors often intimately touch their clay, stone, or wood long before getting down to the business of creating a work of art. Bakers sometimes needlessly knead the dough beyond what's purely functional in the process of creating their delights.

Reach Out and Touch

This is, of course, personal and private, but what could you touch at work, at home, and in between to help you initiate or solidify progress toward some goal you deem worth reaching? Here are some suggestions:

➤ Your boss's high-back, swivel chair

➤ Your boss's wood-grained desk

➤ The plaques on the wall in the reception area of your organization's offices

➤ The fine material in the suit worn by a friend

➤ An expensive watch

➤ A notebook computer with the works

On a more domestic and personal basis, here are more suggestions:

➤ Wood at the lumberyard before you start that new addition to your home

➤ Faucets at the home supply store

➤ A canvas at the art supply store

➤ The strings on an instrument at the music store

Naturally, you'll be discreet about all this. However, anytime you have the opportunity to touch an artifact which, for you, represents an element of what you'd like to achieve, seize it.

For Sure

Because most pianists cannot cart or ship their own piano around to their concerts, they need to become familiar with the piano available for their performance. Here's where touch takes on utmost importance. Beyond determining whether all the keys are in tune and that none stick, what do the keys feel like? What about the seat? No accomplished pianist would think of giving a performance without getting to know the instrument in advance via touch.

Establishing a Routine

The more you can use visualization techniques to reinforce your goals, the faster and more regular your progress will be. If you're good at visualizing on-the-fly, congratulations and keep at it.

For most people, at least at the outset, it's best to establish some sort of routine. Depending on the particulars of your work and home life, perhaps there's a room you can find with a favorite chair, away from the maddening crowd.

It might help to close your eyes. As in the case of Dwight Stone envisioning his way toward the high-jump bar, though, depending on what you want to accomplish, it might make sense to keep your eyes open.

Before or as You Arise

You might be among those who are particularly adept at engaging in visualization at the start of the day. Perhaps you can do it while you're still in bed. Perhaps you can engage in such contemplation while taking a shower, shaving, putting on your makeup, or brushing your teeth.

I prefer to not be otherwise physically engaged in some activity because of the potential distraction and lack of focus. For me, lying down on a bed or couch, sitting in a chair, or simply standing and pausing works best.

Afternoon Delight

Some people use lunch time or the early afternoon for extended sessions. You can engage in short-term visualizations that last a few seconds to perhaps a few minutes at any time. You might find lunch to be an opportune time to engage in visualization.

Perhaps you favor visualizing after lunch when your body goes into a heavy digestion mode and you might not be as focused as you are at other times of the day. This preference varies widely from person to person, so you'll have to experiment with times of the day to see what works best for you.

In the Evening

Things are hectic at work for you, and you seemingly never have a spare moment. Go ahead—visualize in the evening. After you get home, take off your business clothes and loosen up a bit, and you might find that the time is right to let your imagination soar. You can even visualize while taking a stroll.

That Time of the Week

There might be certain days and times in the course of a week that are better for you than others—perhaps Friday evening, Saturday morning, Sunday evening, or some point in the middle of the week. You don't have to schedule visualization sessions on your calendar, but if you do, more power to you.

Go for the Gold!
Your mind is a marvelous contraption that will serve you in ways you might not have tapped. Visualization is one of the fastest and easiest ways to put your mind to work for you in positive, stimulating ways.

Tales of the Extraordinary

Ted Williams was a baseball player for the Boston Red Sox from 1939 to 1960. In 1941, he hit .406 and became the most recent man in baseball to do so. Surprisingly, at the ripe old age of 39, 19 years after his .406 season, he led the American League with an average of .388, flirting with .400 for much of the season.

Ted Williams was remarkable in other ways—one of them being his ability to hit home runs. He spent two and a half years in the service of his country during World War II and another two years in Korea, which pulled him away from the game he loved. Although this service came in the prime of his career, he still managed to whack 541 home runs— good enough to be among the career leaders.

Baseball fans have long debated how many home runs he would have hit if those four and a half seasons of prime time were added back to his career.

Perhaps the most remarkable thing about Ted Williams is that at the age of 42, with his last swing in the last game of the last season of his career, he hit a home run. Although today, athletes routinely play professional sports in their 40s, back in the early 1960s, it was extremely rare for a baseball player to still be succeeding at age 42.

Tell Us the Secret

Williams often was asked for his secrets for hitting a baseball. He reported that he did as little reading as possible, explaining that he could not afford to strain his valuable eyesight reading fine print. In fact, he only read the *Sporting News*, a weekly publication that lists all the baseball players' statistics.

He needed his superb eyesight, he said, to literally see the stitching on the balls pitched to him. *If this is true, it is astounding.* Pitchers throw a fastball at anywhere between 80 and 95 miles per hour. The notion that someone could actually see the stitching on the ball, gauge the rotation of the ball, and then instantaneously decide whether to swing is extraordinary.

What if, just what if, you could visualize the stitching on the pitched ball? Perhaps Williams was only visualizing his ability to see the stitching. Today, four decades since his last at bat, there's no way of proving or disproving his claim.

Bird's House

In his book *Friendly Persuasion*, Boston attorney and sports agent Bob Woolf tells a re-markable tale about former Boston Celtic great Larry Bird. It seems that Bird would visit an opposing team's court hours before the game and certainly hours before anyone else was in the gym.

Bird practiced going up and down the floor dribbling the ball here and there so that he knew exactly where the dead spots were (places where the ball doesn't bounce as high).

Woolf says that Bird even practiced falling on the floor so he would have a clear sensation of this experience if the situation arose in games, such as when he was scrambling for a loose ball. These are remarkable insights. Here, one of the greatest players of the game "touches" every aspect of the opposing team's court, the backboard, the rim, and the floor. He even falls on the floor to achieve a clear and vivid sense of the court's nuances and how he can use that sense to take control during a game.

Imagine how Bird must have visualized taking shots, making passes, dribbling past opponents, and even accepting his three Most Valuable Player awards and three NBA Championship trophies.

Chicken Soup for Success

My friend, Mark Victor Hanson, had already written several books when he and Jack Canfield devised the concept for *Chicken Soup for the Soul*. Yet, before they created the title, they envisioned what Mark called a "million dollar title."

After many weeks, the title *Chicken Soup for the Soul* emerged. Mark took a copy of the *New York Times* best-seller list and, using the same font and point size, pasted "*Chicken Soup for the Soul*, by Mark Victor Hanson and Jack Canfield," over the number-one posi-tion for nonfiction books.

Mark then posted his "best-seller" list on the wall, where he saw it all the time, and from which he continually drew dynamic energy. The rest, as they say, is history, and Mark remains one the best examples of someone who clearly envisioned himself a spectacular success.

The Least You Need to Know

➤ The top achievers in the world have the habit of visualizing success before it actually happens.

➤ Using other mental imagery such as "feeling" an object that symbolizes your success accelerates your progress.

➤ Sometimes, touching a person or object can help initiate and clarify the goal-setting process.

➤ Finding a little space, a little quiet, and a little time helps in your visualization.

➤ You can practice visualization even in the midst of a crowd of 60,000 people. It's all a matter of going within.

Chapter 20

Affiliating with Others: Capitalizing on Those Around You

In This Chapter

➤ The power of like-minded others

➤ Peer groups and support groups

➤ Team members and mentors

➤ Other resources

So far, you've learned about some strong goal-reinforcing techniques, such as contracting with yourself, using the power of deadlines, and employing visualization techniques. Now you'll learn that affiliating with others—capitalizing on those around you—can mean the difference between reaching your goal or not.

Think Alike, Act Alike

"Birds of a feather flock together."

"United we stand, divided we fall."

"Either we all hang together, or we all hang separately."

As you learned in Chapter 17, "Contracting with Yourself," giving a copy of your self-initiated contract to a spouse, boss, peer, or another person who has a vested interest in you achieving your goal increases the probability that you will realize your achievement. In that scenario, you are the driving force, and the other party is largely a monitor of your progress who also may provide some pithy observations along the way to help you succeed.

When you share your self-initiated contract with like-minded individuals, you summon resources beyond those offered by a randomly selected person. A like-minded other could be someone who is attempting to achieve the same type of goal you're seeking, or the same goal itself. Perhaps you're members of the same athletic team or work team.

As people have known for ages, there is something encouraging, stimulating, and even inspiring about being affiliated with others who are seeking to achieve the same goal or types of goals as you. The following factors do not need to be present to reach your goals by affiliating with others, but they can certainly help:

➤ You are striving for the same goal at the same time. The classic example here is two students studying for an exam. They're in the same class with the same teacher, so they obviously have to take the same exam at the same time.

➤ You share the same level of intensity. When affiliating yourself with others, it helps if members of the team, whether it consists of two people or more, proceed with the same intensity toward pursuit of the goal.

➤ You have a geographic proximity with those you want to affiliate with. The closer you are geographically to those with whom you are affiliated in pursuit of a goal, the more support you can derive from one another. Certainly, with the advent of the Internet and global e-mail, the geographic barrier is not what it used to be.

Go for the Gold!

For most goals of shorter duration, affiliating with someone from the same regional or metro area makes it easier for you to benefit from all the sparks that can fly as a result of your face-to-face interaction. As real-time computer video and video phones become more popular, technology will add a new and highly worthwhile wrinkle to people's ability to affiliate with one another in pursuit of their common goals.

Word Power

Skunkworks, a term made popular in the book *In Search of Excellence*, refers to a group of individuals purposely assembled to tackle a tough or challenging assignment.

Here are a variety terms that could relate to individuals affiliating with each other in pursuit of common goals:

Affiliates	Friends	Partners
Comrades	Team	Colleagues
Principals	Joint venturers	Co-venturers

Cohorts	Collaborators	Classmates
Helpmates	Compadres	Mates
Founders	Crew members	Staff members
Contributors	Cronies	Associates
Accomplices	Helpers	Group members

Here are some terms that could relate to a group of individuals working together toward the same goal:

Band	Teammates	Crew
Union	Unit	Assembly
Conglomerate	Party	Council
Task force	Skunkworks	Commission
Committee	Board	Advisory board
Cabinet	Congress	Parliament

Peer Groups

Of all the possible people you could affiliate with, your peers are the easiest to identify and join in partnership. Your peers consist of friends, coworkers, relatives, people in your neighborhood, people in your line of work, and generally anyone who offers you a rather natural and easy communication channel.

Peer group members tend to change more often than members of other groups. However, peer groups can be as powerful as any of the other types of groups discussed throughout this chapter. Undoubtedly, you already belong to one or more peer groups consisting of two or more people.

Name That Peer

Now take a minute to list at least two different peer groups you belong to and the members in that peer group (don't include your own name in these lists).

Peer Group #1

1. _____
2. _____
3. _____
4. _____

Peer Group #2

1. _____
2. _____
3. _____
4. _____

It's possible for the same person to be in two different peer groups of yours. The groups might meet for different reasons at varying times with different pursuits. When I was in high school, for example, one of the members of my peer group, Don, ended up attending the same college that I did—the University of Connecticut (Go Huskies!). Coincidentally, Don also lived in the same dormitory that I did during my sophomore and junior years. Hence, Don was part of the peer group I had in high school, as well as part of the peer group I had in college.

When Peers Reappear

Go for the Gold!
Ask yourself what you're facing right now that a member of your peer groups might be facing as well. Ask yourself who can help you by virtue of the fact that he or she has already been down that path.

At work, you might find that Mary is one of the people you naturally hang around with, and she also happens to have work expertise in a certain area of interest to you. Perhaps because you're drawn to her as a friend or you're both in the same department and work together a great deal, you end up drawing on her knowledge frequently. In that regard, Mary is part of your informal peer group, as well as part of your professional peer group.

Depending on the goals you're pursuing, you might have a fabulous array of resources in your life right now among members of your peer group. You might not have drawn on these precious human resources yet, though.

The Untapped Power of Those You Know

Long ago, I attended a seminar during which the leader told us to draw a circle on a page. I did so. He then said to put a dot in the middle of the page. The dot represented me, and the circle around me represented everything I knew, everyone I knew, and all the influence and connections I had in this world. He then asked that we draw another circle and put another dot in the middle. That represented another person—presumably any one else in the room.

He then went on to say that every time you encounter another person, you potentially open yourself up to a world of opportunities, knowledge, contacts, and influence that you simply don't notice based on brief encounters.

For Sure

Funeral directors know that about 250 people will attend a funeral when the deceased is a person who lived in the same geographic area for most of his or her life. As society becomes more transient, and perhaps as people become even busier, that number is bound to drop. Nevertheless, this is a dramatic indicator of the power you tap when you affiliate yourself with another person—particularly, a like-minded individual.

People can surprise you! I have friends I've known for years, and I've only recently discovered some of their strengths and capabilities. I have one long-term friend who is fluent in a foreign language, and I had no idea until recently that this was so. Similarly, it's likely that none of my friends know that I won an art award at the age of 12 in a city-wide contest.

Ask and Ye Shall Probably Receive

As you contemplate the goals you've laid out for yourself and the people you regularly affiliate with, doesn't it make a ton of sense to start asking them questions? The dialog would run along these lines:

> "I'm trying to accomplish XYZ..."
> "Do you have any experience in this area?"
> "Have you ever worked with...?"
> "What would you suggest?"
> "Have you ever taken a course on...?"
> "Who do you know who might be able to help me...?"
> "If you were in my shoes..."
> "Is this something you're good at?"
> "Can you point me in the right direction?"

Seek and Ye Shall Likely Find

At age 28, I started intentionally affiliating with others. I was a full-time management consultant working in Washington, D.C., and I started joining professional groups and saving the business cards of fellow consultants working in other firms. When I became an author, I began seeking out other authors. With the aid of computer database software, I logged in the names, addresses, and contact information of 400 other authors.

As I began speaking to groups around the country, I also sought out other speakers, and today I have more than 600 speakers in my database—all of whom I've been affiliated with in one way or another over the last dozen years or so. Likewise, in other areas of my life, I have sought out people who do the same kinds of things I've been doing.

In all this time, I have encountered only a few individuals who were reluctant to become an informal peer of mine, and naturally, I didn't pursue such a relationship. In fact, I hardly remember who these people are anymore. Almost all of the rest understood, on some level, the importance of our affiliation even if we had no particular pursuits when we initiated the relationship.

Viable and Ongoing

Today I draw strength and support from the vast number of consultants, authors, speakers, and others who I know and have kept up with over the years. They also benefit from their relationship with me. When I have a question, need the name of a contact person or

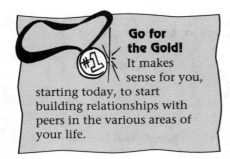

Go for the Gold! It makes sense for you, starting today, to start building relationships with peers in the various areas of your life.

a lead, am facing a road block, or am trying to identify a resource, undoubtedly one or more of my affiliates or peers can give me the answer.

Right now, write down three basic areas in which it would make sense for you to get to know more of your peers. The areas of your life in which you might want to look could include hobbies, religion, sports, or, heck, even work:

1. _____

2. _____

3. _____

Cyberpals

Using e-mail, you can pose a question to 8, 10, 15, or 1,500 people if you're so inclined (although I don't recommend it). I routinely ask a question of perhaps 10 or 12 fellow authors or speakers via e-mail. Sometimes, I'll send an e-mail message to one person and "cc" (send copies to) another 8 or 10 people.

I only submit queries to those people who I think have a reasonable chance of being able to provide an answer. Otherwise, it's likely that my query will look like junk e-mail (known as *spamming*) and will reduce the tendency of people to be responsive in the future. Sometimes I send the same question to individuals in personalized e-mails. This increases the probability that each person who receives my e-mail will send me a reply.

If you have e-mail, you've undoubtedly already used some form of this process to your advantage. Now consider upping your use of this powerful vehicle in pursuit of your most important goals. Carefully word your message to evoke the most useful responses.

Support Groups

Support groups are intentionally devised by someone. They often have ground rules or operating guidelines, whether written or unwritten. The group meets at the same time each week or each month, often in the same location. There may be a permanent group leader or moderator, or that function may be rotated. The relationships of the group members to one another during the meetings is largely governed by behaviors and habits that develop as a result of the ongoing experiences of the group.

Friends of Bill Smith

One of the most enduring and successful support groups in the world was originated by Bill Smith in the 1930s. Smith was an alcoholic who determined that by affiliating with others, he could help himself, and at the same time, all the members could help each other. This idea led to the founding of *Alcoholics Anonymous* (AA), and today there are AA chapters throughout the world. It is widely hailed as one of the most successful programs of its kind.

When you attend a conference or are on a cruise ship, and you see an activity called "Friends of Bill Smith," that means it's an Alcoholics Anonymous meeting. There's no need to be ashamed to attend such meetings. Your identity and whatever you say stay within the group. Moreover, the support and love the members give one another is heartwarming.

Focused on the Positive

The goal of members of Alcoholics Anonymous is not to give up alcohol. Do you remember the anecdote about Milwaukee Braves pitcher Warren Spahn in Chapter 19, "Visualization Techniques?" You don't want to set goals based on *avoiding* certain things. You want to set your goals using positive images. Therefore, the aim of members of AA is to remain sober, to be productive citizens, and to be responsible for their actions.

Because of its success, the AA motto has been emulated by other groups worldwide, including Overeaters Anonymous, Narcotics Anonymous, and even Messies Anonymous. To find out about AA and to see whether there is a chapter near you, look in your Yellow Pages under Alcoholism Information and Treatment Centers.

Anyone for Group Therapy?

Group therapy is another type of support group that consists of peers who meet on a regular basis to help themselves and one another. Such groups generally meet in the office of someone who has had training in psychology—a *psychiatrist, psychotherapist,* or *psychologist.*

Most groups meet once a week at a regular time, although that is not mandatory. The number of members can range from a handful to a dozen or more. Each person is usually facing the same general issue, such as coping with loss, dealing with commitment, or being more assertive.

Generally, about five to eight members is best; this way, each person has the opportunity to participate, and the group has enough people to maintain a dialogue. The group members pledge to one another that

> **Word Power**
> A *psychiatrist* is a medical doctor whose specialty is dealing with the human mind. A psychiatrist usually has an M.D., four years of residency training, and is trained to diagnose and treat mental disorders. Psychiatrists use various forms of therapy and may prescribe medication as needed to diagnose, treat, and prevent various disorders.

they will not share the proceedings of the meetings with anyone outside the group, and that they won't discuss any other individual's challenges with anyone else at any time—with the exception of the group leader in private sessions.

Word Power
A *psychotherapist* is anyone, trained or not, who treats mental and emotional disorders to encourage personality growth and behavior modification. No special license is required.

Word Power
A *psychologist* is someone who studies how the mind influences human behavior. A clinical psychologist usually has a Ph.D., as well as one to four years of post-doctoral training.

Get Some Satisfaction

Group members often report that they gain a great deal of satisfaction and even comfort by participating in discussions with their group. Many would not give it up if you paid them to do so. Although individual group members certainly may have an array of goals they want to achieve, the common denominator among the group members is centered around achieving goals to be more effective in everyday life, establishing more rewarding relationships, dealing more capably with loss, and so on.

Members of the group begin to share a common bond with one another even if they don't encounter one another outside the group.

If you're interested in being part of such a group and believe that this will help you achieve a goal you've set for yourself, open the Yellow Pages to Psychology or Psychotherapist and call a few numbers. Undoubtedly, you'll learn who handles groups in your area, whether a group is forming, and whether it may be right for you.

A Gathering of Men (or Women)

You don't have to be a part of group therapy to affiliate with others in a formal setting in pursuit of your goals. Most towns have men's and women's groups that meet regularly and are listed in your local paper.

Often, individuals who are separated, divorced, or widowed find strength and solace in meeting with others of the same sex who have had similar experiences. During such meetings, topics such as raising a child alone, coping with loss, dating, and meeting financial burdens are discussed.

Go for the Gold!
It's sometimes best if all the members attend the first meeting. The group then takes on a history of its own that is shared by each individual.

Other men's and women's groups in your community may exist as well. Some consist of people of the same faith, ethnicity, age group, and so on. My friend Bob in Chevy Chase, Maryland, belonged to a men's group for years that consisted of both married and single men who simply got together on a biweekly basis to discuss whatever individual members wanted to bring up at meetings. Bob stayed with the group for years because he got a source of input he did not receive in other areas of his life.

It Takes Two

Whether at work or away from it, teams—and more specifically, partners—have achieved some pretty remarkable things. Look at these famous teams, for example:

Lenin and Trotsky
(partners in social revolution)

Lennon and McCartney
(the Beatles legendary song writers)

Lerner and Loewe
(partners in developing show tunes)

Leopold and Loeb
(partners in crime)

Lois and Clark
(partners in journalism—in comic books)

Lewis and Clark
(partners in geographic exploration)

Go for the Gold! You don't have to be experiencing a crisis to join groups in your local community; you might just want to increase your affiliations.

Teams have been a part of the American scene as far back as history stretches. (Hmmm... Maybe it's wise to affiliate yourself with someone whose last name begins with *L*.)

If Not Friendship, at Least Respect

There's something special about collaborating with one other person that often can bring out the best in both of you. You don't even have to like each other. Richard Rodgers and Oscar Hammerstein II of Rodgers and Hammerstein frequently feuded with each other and allegedly did not talk with one another when they weren't working. Lennon and McCartney had their spats along the way to an otherwise brilliant partnership.

Even Gene Siskel and Roger Ebert (of Siskel and Ebert, the famed movie reviewers who offer a thumbs-up or thumbs-down rating for the features they review, and movie critics for rival papers—the *Chicago Tribune* and the *Chicago Sun-Times*) have argued on air for years. Sometimes, it looked like their partnership would not last. Or, perhaps the arguments are a contributing factor to their longevity.

As long as each partner respects the capabilities or contributions of the other, partnerships can go on and on, regardless of the type of relationship the individuals have otherwise.

Mellow Fellows

Some long-term partners maintain a minimum of strife—at least publicly. This includes contemporary pop music stars Steve Lawrence and Edie Gorme, basketball stars Michael Jordan and Scottie Pippen, Microsoft founders Bill Gates and Paul Allen, the political team of Bill Clinton and Al Gore, and leaping lions, even Las Vegas entertainers, illusionists Sigfried and Roy.

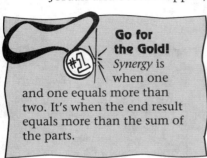

Go for the Gold!
Synergy is when one and one equals more than two. It's when the end result equals more than the sum of the parts.

If you're part of a partnership that has resulted in both of you accomplishing more than you would have on your own, go out and thank your lucky stars.

If you're part of a rocky relationship that somehow seems to yield wonderful results, go out and thank your lucky stars as well. You're benefiting from a type of *synergy* a typical person simply doesn't experience.

Mentors and Other Strangers

In terms of helping you achieve your goal, a mentor can be a godsend. A mentor is usually not your boss. Having a mentor outside your company or division is probably better in the long run, but it might cause a problem with your own boss, especially if he or she feels threatened by someone else giving you advice.

Here are some ways of meeting a mentor:

➤ Attend professional society meetings related to your field.

➤ Be part of an organization-wide task force.

➤ Maintain ties with someone from your last job.

Besides giving you advice on almost anything you can think of, a mentor also helps you broaden your horizons. He or she often will be pleased to introduce you to associates garnered over the years. When your mentor introduces you to important and interesting people, recognize that these are people it might have taken you years to meet on your own.

Some protégés develop accelerated expectations. The mentor makes it look so easy. You need to remember that it might have taken your mentor 25 years of experience and networking to do what he did.

You already may have mentors in your life that you're not acknowledging and not using for your optimum benefit. Wouldn't it make sense right now to identify those people in your life who have served or are currently serving as mentors, as well as those who can serve as mentors? Then, identify how to increase the potency of the relationship.

In Chapter 22, "The Tom Sawyer Effect: Formally Enlisting Others to Help You," I discuss at length more aggressive ways to enlist others in your cause. For now, it suffices to say that if you have no mentors in your life, it's time to find one. If you have one, great, but it's time to up the stakes.

Other Resources

You can find people all around you to affiliate with and thereby enhance your progress toward your goals. These affiliations do not need not be Machiavellian in nature; you don't have to get to know them simply because they are a means to an end. Instead, they can be dynamic relationships in which you become a resource for others as well.

Who Do You Know?

Word Power
Niccolo *Machiavelli* was an Italian political theorist. He believed that deceit and cunning were justified in order to achieve political power. These types of theories are described as *the means justifying the ends*.

In the days before software databases, there was an old saying that went, "The bigger your Rolodex, the more successful you'll be." In many ways, truer words were never spoken. Think of it this way: No matter what you're trying to achieve in life, whether it's to land a big contract for your company, to run a marathon in record time, to feed the starving children of the world, or to eradicate AIDS, your quest will best be served if you affiliate yourself with others.

In the insurance industry, when new agents are hired, the first thing the company asks the agents to do is list everybody they know who represents a potential customer. This list includes friends, relatives, former classmates, neighbors...you name it. This it the primary reason why I never wanted to be an insurance agent! Who wants to call on these people and try to sell them insurance!?

Even in an apparently solo pursuit, such as attempting to break a marathon record, affiliating with others pays off in ways you might not have experienced. Other runners can give you tips and insights that will accelerate your learning curve. Perhaps you'll find a running partner, and both of you will improve as a result of your affiliation. Perhaps you'll encounter others who simply become part of your cheering section, urging you on during those last hundred yards, inspiring you to turn in your best performance.

The List of Your Life

The corollary for you holds great meaning. What if you were to list everyone you know and then re-examine that list for possible affiliations? You and someone else can help one another accelerate toward individual and shared goals.

Your assignment is clear!

The Least You Need to Know

➤ Affiliating with like-minded others opens up a world of possibilities and helps accelerate your goal progress.

➤ It helps if those you affiliate with are seeking the same thing as you, at the same time, and with the same intensity. If they are located nearby, all the better.

➤ Community support groups listed in the Calendar section of your local newspaper can help you reach your goals.

➤ Small teams and one-on-one partnerships can help propel you to heights you simply can't achieve on your own.

➤ *Synergy* is when one and one equals more than two. Partnerships and affiliations help you achieve synergy.

Chapter 21

Steering Clear of Barriers

In This Chapter

➤ Being under-resourced

➤ Trapped in a nonsupportive environment

➤ Losing sight of your goals

➤ Engaging in resource-consuming ritual behavior

Congratulations—you've reached the final chapter on reinforcing your progress toward your goals. In this chapter, you'll look at all-too-frequent scenarios in which you may find yourself when achieving your goal or goals is in jeopardy. You won't want to miss it!

Proceeding Without the Right Resources

In pursuit of challenging but reachable goals, working without the proper resources can result in the goal being unreachable. As you saw in Chapter 15, "A Question of Time," it's possible to plot daily or even hourly what you'll accomplish and when, where you'll find the resources you require, and the entire sequence of activities in support of your goal.

What—Me, Worry?

If you set goals well, it would seem that operating with less-than-sufficient resources is a situation that doesn't come up often, so why worry about it?

The answer is that the best-laid plans of mice and men often go awry; sometimes, all the planning in the world can't take into account unforeseen barriers to your progress. You know this on many levels. In short, things change.

In the pursuit of any one of your goals, you set things in motion. The potential for two or more of these elements to rub up against each other is all but guaranteed. Hence, over time, all goals—but particularly maintenance goals—need continual monitoring. Perhaps you can refine your systems to the point where the monitoring is at greater intervals and requires less time and effort. You can't get off scot-free, however.

For Sure

You might be somewhat familiar from your days in science class with the notion of *perpetual motion*. Throughout history, inventors have attempted to devise a machine that represents perpetual motion—you initiate a process, and it continues on its own indefinitely. Except for activity at the atomic and subatomic level, what stops 99.999 percent of apparatus designed to operate indefinitely is friction. Parts rubbing or scraping against each other result in worn-out elements.

The Best-Laid Plans...

Consider the following challenges:

➤ You're in charge of digging a tunnel through a mountain as part of a state's highway system. Halfway through, you encounter more rock than the seismic engineers predicted you'd find. This is going to throw the project off by at least two weeks and put you at least $350,000 over budget.

➤ You are the directing manager for the local symphony orchestra. Two days before the big concert, the whole woodwind section comes down with the flu—apparently, they passed it to one another. The concert hall has been rented out, the tickets have been printed and distributed, and the show must go on.

➤ You're in charge of producing a technical manual for a big client in 11 days. Your computer system crashes and will put you behind at least a day and a half.

These situations and about two-and-a-half million others you could probably cite occur so frequently in the pursuit of our goals that we might as well not be surprised.

A 1995 Gallup poll surveying Americans on what they cite as the obstacles they fear will prevent them from reaching their goals revealed the following:

Uh-Oh!
Murphy is alive and well and living some place in your neighborhood.

CAUTION!

Obstacles	Very Worried
Catastrophic illness in family	41%
Environmental problems	39%
Cost of education	34%
War	34%
Rising taxes	33%
Stock-market collapse	28%
Pension cuts	27%
Inflation	26%
Recession	20%
Loss of job	19%
Poor investment decisions	19%
Cuts in employee benefits	19%
Inability to sell house	16%
Substance abuse in family	12%
Personal-debt problems	10%
Divorce	10%
Natural disasters	8%

Minimizing the Shortfalls

Although it's impractical to have contingency plans for every aspect of every project in pursuit of every goal you want to reach, you can use some common-denominator behaviors and strategies to minimize the chance of having less resources than required to achieve your goal.

Maintaining a What-If Orientation

In his book *Moving Mountains*, General William G. Pagonis notes that, during the Persian Gulf War, the U.S. forces maintained a constant state of readiness. "We began and ended every day by asking, 'What do we do if Saddam attacks today?'" says the general. "I held large classes, open to anyone, but especially to our talented reserve forces, to discuss scenarios and potential solutions. I'd ask questions like, 'A ship docked at Ad Dammam this morning. It's ready to be unloaded, but the onboard crane breaks. What do you do?' Or, 'We suddenly find out we're receiving 15,000 troops today instead of the usual 5,000. How do we adjust to the increase?'"

The general constantly told his forces that everyone needed to do the usual Monday-morning quarterbacking on Saturday night—before problems arose. Such dry runs through potential problems proved extremely helpful when, for example, the Allied forces did receive 15,000 troops on one day.

"General Schwarzkopf and I were determined not to be hobbled by immobile fire bases like the ones in Vietnam," the author said. "Any supply network would have to be flexible, movable, and responsive to the troops."

Talent Scouting

You don't have opposing soldiers in your way, but your challenges can feel mighty heavy. In the business world, staff members get sick, some don't show up on time, and some quit with little notice. No matter how effective a manager or motivator you think you are, it's not likely that you can wield divine power over your rod or your staff (just joking about the rod).

I worked as a vice-president of marketing and a project manager of an eight-person staff for a management consulting firm in Northern Virginia—my last position working for others. I learned the hard way of the necessity to continually interview people. I ran ads in the *Washington Post* and other places even when my company and my team did not specifically require additional help.

I wanted to have a bevy of resumes on file so that, in case something happened and I needed to draw on the talent and skills of people in the local area, I would at least have a place to start. (This was before the Internet, newsgroups, and various ways of electronically posting employment opportunities and reading people's resumes.)

Uh-Oh!
Predictably, some of the people you interview when you're "just looking" for talent will be whisked away by other firms. Hence, the time you spend reading their resumes, phoning them for interviews, conducting interviews, and maintaining any kind of follow-up could be seen as all for naught.

Was it a chore to interview somebody every other week even when we weren't hiring? You bet. It took time and energy, and I always had to explain to the interviewee that we had nothing in particular open at the moment.

I ended up hiring two people at different times—both at critical junctures during a project I was managing. Both individuals proved to be instrumental in our teams' ability to meet project deadlines.

Could we have otherwise prevailed? With the tight job market that existed in the mid-1980s, perhaps we could have found talent quickly and easily. Nevertheless, my habit of continually interviewing provided at least some semblance of safety in terms of being able to maintain sufficient numbers of qualified staff.

Identifying Critical Suppliers and Vendors

Is there some piece of equipment in your office on which you rely heavily? What if your computer or some other vital electronic gadget fails instantly and completely? Do you have a backup in place? If not, have you identified suppliers and vendors who could readily repair or replace the vital parts or equipment? Could you be back up to speed within a day? Within an hour?

Get Prepared or Suffer

Based on the nature of your work, you already may have systems in place. If you work in public safety, public health, transportation, healthcare, and so on, your department, agency, or division may have learned the hard way over many years the vital importance of having backup systems in place.

If you work in the typical office or for yourself, you might not have taken the time and made the effort to establish a folder, a file, or a roster of key contact information in case you need to replace something in a hurry.

Buy a duplicate item if the initial item is that critical. I write all my books by first using a pocket dictator. Sandy Knudsen transcribes the tapes, other people edit the transcripts, and then, somewhere near the end of the process, I come in and do the final edits before sending the chapters off to my editor.

For me, my pocket dictator and transcribing unit are so critical that I have two of each of them and have occasionally thought about purchasing more. The pocket dictators I own are exact replicas of each other. Initially, I did not want to own two. I bought one and after a few weeks, it ran into problems. While it was being repaired (under warranty), and I faced the prospect of losing precious days on a book project, I capitulated to a friend's recommendation that I purchase a second unit.

The vendor assured me that what was wrong with my initial unit was an anomaly. He vigorously asserted that the model I had chosen was the best in the industry at its price level and for what I wanted to accomplish. Believe it or not, I bought the second unit from him!

After he fixed the first unit and shipped it back to me, and I saw that it worked wonderfully, I had a great sense of relief. For the first time in my career as an author, I had a built-in backup system. On the handful of days in the last five years when one unit wasn't working properly, I continued on without a hitch because I had a backup unit.

I still own and use both units. There has never been a time when both units were down at the same time. I'm pleased that I forked out some additional money back then, because it has been well worth all the assurance I've had since then. To make sure that both units remain fully functional, I alternate using one for several weeks and then the other.

Name That Item

What piece of equipment, tool, resource, or thingamajig is so important in your work or life in pursuit of your goals that perhaps you ought to have two, three, or more? And, if it's so important, why are you hesitant to shell out the relatively few dollars an extra one would cost? You've blown money on so many other things that were of little value comparatively speaking.

Here's your opportunity to reinforce your goal progress. You can steer clear of barriers such as being under-resourced and not having a backup system in place. Hey, it's your career and your goals.

Initiating Reciprocal Relationships

Suppose that you and your spouse have small children and are just getting started in your careers. You don't have much money, but you would like to go out on weekends occasionally. The thought of hiring a baby-sitter at $5 an hour and shelling out about $25 every time you want to go out for the night, on top of whatever you spend while you're out, leaves you cold.

If one of your family goals or social goals is to enjoy your spouse and your life, how are you going to get around this barrier?

Refine Your System

One solution is to have a reciprocal relationship with another couple who also has a small child. One Saturday evening, you look after their child, and the next, they look after yours. No money is exchanged. You get to go out at least half the time you want to.

In the course of a year, you could be out on 26 Saturdays, saving $650 in baby-sitting expenses, while enabling another couple to do the same.

You could refine your relationships so that you don't need to look at the clock every minute you're out. If you don't get back by 10:00, no big deal—it's understood that you'll be back by 11:00. Or, of course, you could call. Instead of alternating every other Saturday, perhaps you could alternate Sundays and Saturdays within the same week.

Any way you devise it, there are many alternatives for establishing reciprocal relationships to benefit both parties and to help you achieve your goals.

Who Else Can I Turn To?

What other types of reciprocal relationships can you devise that represent win/win relationships, enable you to avoid the trap of being under-resourced, and potentially enable you to gain a good, long-term friend? Here are some suggestions:

➤ Someone you know is taking a math course and needs help. You're strong in this area and weak in writing, where the other person can help you.

➤ You don't want to buy expensive yard equipment to handle a job that you only need to tackle once every couple of months. Your neighbor happens to have such equipment and is willing to loan it to you, because you have other equipment that he would like to borrow occasionally.

➤ At work, you're a whiz on the company's database system, and a coworker is a whiz on conducting research via the Internet. So, you serve as consultants to one another as the need arises.

Build in Some Slack

It isn't easy to deliver the following message in a society in which people often operate on the edge—the edge of their finances, the edge of their time, and the edge of their resources:

To avoid situations in which you have less resources than you need to proceed effectively, build some slack into the system.

When I lived in a high-rise condominium in Northern Virginia, the treasurer of our condominium association made a bold statement to the condo owners. He announced a huge surplus for the year. Instead of using it to decrease everyone's condominium fee for the coming fiscal year, he thought it would be best if we allowed the surplus to remain. He invested at attractive rates, and the fund served as a contingency in the event of some unforeseen expense.

Three years later, there was a major problem with the building's generator. All 560 condominium owners were spared having to shell out several hundred dollars each on the spot to fix the problem because of the wise treasurer of several years before.

Uh-Oh!
How often do you hear of people putting a little away in reserve these days for the proverbial rainy day? If anything, just the opposite is happening. Personal debt is at an all-time high. If reaching a particular goal is important to you, you'll try to minimize the potential for being caught shorthanded.

Go for the Gold! For whatever you're working toward, there often is a host of minor things you need to have in place—from pens and pencils to batteries and disks. Assemble these kinds of things in abundant supply early so that later, the lack thereof doesn't result in even a temporary setback.

Safety Nets in Place?

What are some of the safety nets you can put into place right now to reinforce progress toward goals? Here are some suggestions:

➤ Saving at a higher rate than you have in the past

➤ Budgeting a little more time for downtime, misdirection, and distractions

➤ Evaluating mid-course opportunities that present themselves

➤ Assembling extra, incidental supplies

When Your Environment Doesn't Support You

If you have professional goals, and it's clear that the environment in which you work does not support your goals, your path is clear. You need to move.

If you have professional goals and initially it appeared as though your environment was supportive, but things have changed, you are in a quandary. You can

➤ Move, relocate, or find a new job—but this is usually a major undertaking.

➤ Continue on, despite the unsupportive environment, doing the best you can.

➤ Work to change your environment and make it somewhat more supportive.

You may have engaged in goal setting not knowing that your environment would turn out to be unsupportive. Perhaps a powerful ally departed or had a change of heart. Perhaps a new management team took over and decided to overturn much of what you have been working toward.

If you're in a nonsupportive environment, identify the critical resources or elements that could help rectify the matter:

➤ Do you need more funds?

➤ Do you need a larger staff?

➤ Do you need more time?

➤ Do you need more equipment?

➤ Do you need more supplies?

➤ Do you need peer approval?

➤ Do you need staff approval?

➤ Do you need your boss's approval?

➤ Do you need top-management approval?

➤ Do you need industry approval?

➤ Do you need legislative approval?

➤ Do you need social approval?

What specifically would it take for your present unsupportive environment to become a supportive environment? Can you frame this in a concise paragraph? If so, you have at least clarified a basic issue.

To get the right kind of support, you need to go to the right party—someone who has the authority and power to make positive change happen. The basic problem is that it is not always easy to identify exactly who this person is.

The title of the person you need to influence differs from one organization to the next based on a host a factors, such as organization climate, centralized or decentralized management systems, budgeting authority, and factors too involved to discuss here. You'll know when you've found the right person and influenced him or her accordingly, because things will rapidly change for the better for you.

Uh-Oh!
Aim too high, and your request may get lost by the time it filters back down to your more immediate supervisors. Aim too low, and you may find someone with whom to commiserate, but it's unlikely you'll get the type of support and action you need to make an unsupportive environment workable or even palatable.

Sometimes, the prevailing political, business, or social environment in which you work is not conducive to what you want to accomplish. If you can't get the bigwigs on your side, you'll need to go some place else, presumably where the bigwigs are already on your side.

Losing Sight of Goals

In his book *Galileo At Work: His Scientific Biography*, author Stillman Drake paraphrases the master by writing, "…it often happens that we do not see what is quite near at hand and clear."

It is far easier to establish goals and then promptly lose sight of them than you might imagine. Have you seen the movie *The Bridge on the River Kwai*, the 1957 Academy Award winner for best picture? You may recall the character played by Alec Guinness (better known to younger folks as Obi Wan Kenobi in *Star Wars*).

Guinness is commanding officer of his fellow Allies—English and American prisoners of war interred by the Japanese. Guinness' character becomes inspired by building a bridge—a goal imposed on him by the Axis powers in control. He loses sight of his larger, more appropriate goal as a member of the Allied troops: resisting his captor's war efforts.

As an Allied task force moves in to sabotage the completion of the bridge (by placing dynamite under it), Guinness nearly foils the attempt. He had become attached to completing the bridge.

Then, in a dramatic moment of high irony, as he nearly exposes his compatriot saboteurs, he is hit by gunfire. In his last breath, he asks, "My God, what have I done?" In his death swoon, he falls on the detonator and sets off the explosion.

You don't have to rent a video to witness dramatic examples of people losing sight of goals. Examples abound. Consider the politician who ran for office to serve the people and ended up serving himself. Think about the weight trainer, who perhaps started on his quest with the idea of attaining peak fitness, but instead veered off toward the pursuit of achieving a striking appearance.

Rediscovering What You Lost

Elizabeth Jeffries, a Louisville, Kentucky-based trainer and consultant, suggests in *The Heart of Leadership* that a fundamental way of getting back in touch with your goals, particularly if it has been many years, is to engage in a simple exercise. Recall how you felt when you first assumed your present position:

Go for the Gold!
By recapturing the initial feelings you had when you first assumed your present position or role, you can more easily get in touch with what was important to you then and what you had established as important goals.

What was your energy level?

What were your aspirations?

What did you want to achieve?

What specific goals did you set for yourself back then that perhaps got lost along the way?

This exercise works well—whether the time frame has been weeks, months, or even years.

Revisit Your Goals

A funny thing about big, important goals: Sometimes, we fall into the trap of thinking that we know them so well, that they're so obvious, that we don't need to revisit our goal sheet—the place where we wrote them down or saved them on our computer.

Yet, the bigger and more obvious your goal, the more often you may need to revisit it. For that reason, I keep a wallet-size card in my wallet that lists my goals on the front and back. As often as I have read that list, there are times when, with utter amazement, I'll read that list and feel as if I'm visiting a long-lost friend. There are pockets of time during which I apparently ignore things I have identified as vital.

Is this because I secretly don't want to accomplish my goals? Is it because I'm not following the advice I'm dispensing in this book? Not at all. It's because, as human beings, we easily stray from the course and lose sight of what we established as important. We have to constantly be on guard.

What Else Can You Do?

In addition to the suggestions already presented throughout this book, here are some more to help keep your goals in sight:

➤ Post reminders to yourself all over creation, including in your calendar.

➤ Mail letters to yourself that serve as reinforcers.

➤ Have like-minded others (the topic of Chapter 20, "Affiliating with Others: Capitalizing on Those Around You") periodically call or mail reminders to you. If it helps, have them do it at regular intervals.

➤ Give yourself the time and space to sit back and periodically view the big picture. If you have to, schedule this activity on your calendar.

In the midst of the fray, it's easy to lose direction. As cited previously, use that plane seat, that trip up the mountain, or that sun deck at the top of your building for reflection.

When You Coast, You're Toast

It would be wonderful if you could take one or more of your goals and put them on "automatic pilot." You know—assemble the resources, staff, and whatever you need to devise a system; get it up and running; and then, like a well-oiled machine, only have to check in every so often.

Awake from that daydream and plant your feet solidly on terra firma. You'll need to stay in touch with the reality that, for most of your goals, even long-term maintenance-type goals, to coast is to run into a brick wall.

It's rare that factors in your internal or external environment stay completely the same. Are you among those who've been able to maintain their weight for many years past their college days? If so, you might have noticed that you're eating less now than you did just a few years ago. Why? As you age, your metabolism slows down.

To maintain the same weight as the years pass, you have to eat less or exercise more. If you simply coast at the same levels, as your metabolism slows, you'll gain weight.

So it is in other aspects of your life and with the goals you've set for yourself. To coast in an environment that slowly but inexorably keeps changing is nearly a guarantee that you'll venture off course.

What are the areas of life in which people have set important goals and then for one reason or another coasted in pursuit of them?

> **Uh-Oh!**
> Like the ship slightly off course at the outset of the trip, if you don't continually make course corrections, a small veer to the left or right will quickly result in a huge veer away from your intended direction.

➤ Marriage

➤ Raising children

➤ Planning for retirement

➤ Maintaining an ideal weight

➤ Maintaining fitness

➤ Achieving a balance between work and leisure

If you can give up the notion of coasting in pursuit of your goals, you'll avoid one of the barriers that stops too many others right in their lounge chairs.

Ritual Behavior That Eats Up Your Life

We all engage in rituals—some of them productive, most of them comforting, and many of them highly unproductive and unworthwhile. Do you have to wait 'til the top of the hour to get started on a task or activity?

Do you need to over-engage in controlling your environment before getting started? For example, do you sharpen your pencils twice, adjust the venetian blinds just so, get three phone calls out of the way, put away three files that you've had out for days, and engage in other such behavior before you begin to work toward your goal?

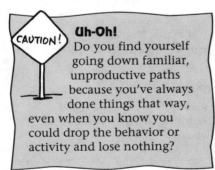

Uh-Oh!

CAUTION! Do you find yourself going down familiar, unproductive paths because you've always done things that way, even when you know you could drop the behavior or activity and lose nothing?

Perhaps it's time to reexamine these behaviors in light of the new you—who you are, where you're heading, and who you've chosen to be. Setting goals gives you the opportunity to continually move on from where you've been.

In the book *No Ordinary Genius: The Illustrated Richard Feynman*, edited by Christopher Sykes, we learn that when the renowned physicist and Nobel Prize winner faced a roadblock or a barrier, he was "unusually good at going back to being like a child, ignoring what everyone else thinks, and saying, 'Now, what have we got here?'"

Feynman apparently was so "unstuck"—the opposite of being steeped in ritual behavior—that when something didn't work, he simply looked at it another way and another way and another way until he devised an effective way to proceed.

On your path to achieving your goals, while steering clear of barriers, continually be on the lookout for another way to proceed. As one challenge after another arises, you'll find that this will come in handy.

The Least You Need to Know

➤ To steer clear of barriers, engage in what-if thinking—what if this goes wrong, or what if that doesn't happen?

➤ In pursuit of your goals, give yourself some slack to handle downtime, mix-ups, delays, and emerging opportunities.

➤ If you're trapped in a nonsupportive environment, move on, persuade the bigwigs to see it your way, or prepare to suffer.

➤ You can lose sight of your goals in a heartbeat, so build reminders and safeguards into your routine.

➤ In pursuit of your maintenance goals, if you coast, you're toast.

➤ If you're not getting the results you want, look at the situation another way, and another way, and another way.

Part 5

Going for the Gold: Advanced Strategies for Reaching Your Goals

In this, the last and most inspiring part of the book, I present five chapters that can help you accelerate your progress toward goals in ways you always wanted to learn about. Chapter 22, "The Tom Sawyer Effect: Formally Enlisting Others to Help You," focuses on how to formally enlist others in your various pursuits. In Chapter 23, "Reaching Two Goals at One Time," you'll focus on accomplishing more with less effort.

Chapter 24, "Upping the Ante," tells you how and when to make your goals even more challenging.

Chapter 25, "Lifetime Goal Setting," focuses on goals you might want to set for yourself from now until old age. Chapter 26, "Actions Speak the Loudest," presents a motivating, uplifting send-off that will take you from the last pages of the book right into goal-setting activity.

YEP. I SURE DO GET A LOT OF PRIDE OUT OF DOING THESE MONTHLY REPORTS...

The Tom Sawyer Effect: Formally Enlisting Others to Help You

In This Chapter

➤ Assembling a group of advisors

➤ Finding others who will empower you

➤ Career coaches and life coaches

➤ Resources all around you

In *The Adventures of Tom Sawyer*, by Mark Twain, Tom was faced with the large task of painting his Aunt Polly's fence. However, by inducing the other children in his neighborhood to see participating in the fence-painting campaign as a privilege, Tom was able to get the fence painted in no time with little manual labor on his part.

What if you could set up your world so that you were surrounded on all sides by people who were eager to offer you advice and support in pursuit of your goals? Does this sound too good to be true? If so, keep reading, because this is entirely possible and will take far less effort than you might imagine. In Chapter 20, "Affiliating with Others: Capitalizing on Those Around You," I discussed the power you can derive by affiliating with others and some basic techniques for harnessing the potential of partnering with like-minded others. In this chapter, you'll examine more formal procedures for getting people on your side to help you achieve accelerated progress toward your goals. I'll start with one of my all-time favorite strategies: the establishment of your own advisory board of directors.

Assembling Your Advisory Board

I have an advisory board of directors, and I suggest that you devise one as well. Your response might be, "Okay, Jeff, you're an author and a speaker. I can see why people might want to be a member of your advisory board. But I just work for XYZ Company stamping widgets. Who would want to be on my board?" There are lots of people who would like to be on your board!

If you poll most people you know, you'll find that they've never been asked to be on a board in their entire lives. They've heard about people on boards, but they've never been asked.

You can begin to assemble your board by looking for people in your immediate surroundings who can be members of your advisory board. These could include people in local associations, one or two people from work, someone from your church or community group, and perhaps a mentor.

Welcome to My Board

Allow me to describe my advisory board so that you will have some good ideas as to who you might choose to be on yours. I have two people from radio, a radio host, and a radio manager. I also have a couple of people from associations—both national and local. I have a lawyer or two, a magazine editor, a newspaper editor, a professor, a high school teacher, and three entrepreneurs.

I invite the whole group to dinner twice each year. I let everyone know in advance what career or business issues I'd like to tackle at the session.

First we have dinner—usually, some kind of smorgasbord or a buffet. Afterward, I pass out the agenda, which is a repeat of the questions I circulated before that evening. One by one, we go through the issues I want to tackle. I turn on my pocket dictator and let them have a free-for-all.

I record everything and later carefully transcribe each of those gems.

You might think, "Sure, people will come to my advisory board dinner once or twice, but will they come over and over again?" My board has met 14 times, and I almost have to laugh because I get requests from people I've never met who have said, "So and so is on your board and suggested that you might invite me to be on it as well."

The following is an example of my advisory dinner agenda items:

Jeff Davidson
Advisory Dinner

Topics of Interest:

_____

❏ Groups that want to hear my presentation

_____

_____

❏ Three other people I ought to know

_____

_____

❏ Names of people who have achieved balance in their lives—especially in unique ways

_____

_____

❏ New groups, networks, or groups to know

_____

_____

❏ Video producers

_____

_____

❏ How can I sell blocks of 100 or 1,000 books?

_____

_____

❏ New newsletters and publications

_____

_____

❏ How can I help you?

_____

_____

Folks Who Are on Your Side

Most of the time, at least in my experience, the advisory board is quite supportive. If there is some type of criticism or redirection, it's done in a gentle, constructive manner that you can easily take.

Over the years, my advisory board members have become good friends. I facilitate this by circulating a list at each meeting with everyone's name, address, phone number, and fax number. I invite them to bring their own literature, whether they're in business for themselves or work for corporations, so that they can become more familiar with each other.

By the third or fourth meeting, you'll find that the quality of the recommendations, as well as the leads, insights, tips, and strategies they present to you more than pay for the cost of the dinner.

Here's my latest invitation to the Advisory Board dinner.

It's time, John…

For the 14th session of the Jeff Davidson Advisory Board dinner. As you know, the purpose of the Advisory Board is to assist me, as an author who speaks professionally, to maintain a competitive edge through the shared experience, insights, and recommendations of successful professionals such as yourself.

The benefits to you will be to offer advice in an arena of high receptivity, to network with other members of the Advisory Board, and possibly to serve as a key reference for future books.

Participation on the Advisory Board of Directors consists only of attending two Advisory Board dinner meetings per year (dinner tab picked up by me) and having a good time. The meetings are held in October and March. Our 14th meeting is coming up!

The March meeting will be held on the 24th at my home, starting at 6:30 p.m. sharp, dinner at 6:50, and discussion from 7:30 to 8:20 (call if you need directions).

Please leave a message at (000) 000-0000 as to whether you'll be attending.

Yours truly,

Jeff Davidson

Attracting Empowering People into Your Life

I'm not sure exactly when it started—perhaps around the time my first book was published, *Marketing Your Consulting and Professional Services* (first edition, John Wiley & Sons, 1985). For whatever reason, I began going places and meeting people who filled particular niches in my life. If I was deficient in some area, I would meet someone who was strong in that area—not necessarily mentors, more like friends who simply helped me complete part of a puzzle.

When Authors Meet

I attended meetings held by various author groups around Washington, D.C. I met male and female authors, old and young, who wrote business, career, self-help, and how-to books, as well as fiction, poetry, and so on. I exchanged business cards with these people. I got to know them on a personal basis. We discussed the nuances of getting books published, developing chapters, strengthening your prose, and even using a thesaurus.

In some instances, we traded leads at publishing houses and magazines. Some authors even told me the names of their literary agents. In less than a year, I was fully immersed in the world of authorship and was already building a base of contacts I could call on for advice, counseling, and leads, or simply to share information I thought they would appreciate knowing.

When Speakers Meet

Around the same time, I joined the National Capitol Speakers Association, a branch of the National Speakers Association. Similar to my experience with authors, I began to meet speakers in abundance.

I realized that I was much more at home with speakers than with any other type of career professional. In fact, for the first time, I felt as if I had found my true peer group—people who are excited about things like I am; people who want to get up on stage and influence others. Once again, my file of contacts began to swell.

By the mid-1980s, I probably knew at least 100 authors and at least 200 speakers. By the late 1980s, it was probably 200 to 300 authors and 300 to 400 speakers. Today, it's more like 400 authors and 600 or 800 speakers.

If It Works, Keep Doing It!

Similarly, without any formal goals in mind, I made contact with publishers, lecture bureaus, book distributors, audio and video tape producers, and so on.

I seem to be on automatic pilot when it comes to attracting people who are the best at what they do and from whom I can learn and benefit considerably.

It is not logistically feasible to maintain an ongoing, active daily relationship with several hundred or 1,000 or more people. Within the various groups I cited earlier, however, three or four people in each group emerged as what I call *empowering people*. These were people I got to know well and with whom I came to have the type of relationship in which I could get on the phone and speak with them every day, although the frequency was more like once or twice a week.

As you guessed, you don't have to be an author/speaker to attract and assemble an array of empowering people in your life. You only have to vigorously pursue what interests you, and these people start showing up.

In case you're thinking that you have to be outgoing and extroverted to attract empowering people, guess again. I am entirely introverted. I have learned to be extroverted in social and business situations over the years, because it makes a lot of sense much of the time.

Let Them In

One of the keys to having empowering people in your life is to be open to it. This sounds simple enough, but many people never get past this stage. Think about someone in your own life who always

➤ Looks forward to hearing from you

➤ Listens to you closely

➤ Heeds your advice

➤ Is appreciative for having received it

Is this the kind of person you want to be around? Yes! Is this the kind of person to whom you want to freely dispense your wisdom? Yes! Well, that's the kind of person I am to my empowering people. They know that I want to hear from them and that I value what they tell me. I often act on what they say so rapidly that they're amazed at how quickly their advice took effect.

Empower Them as Well

Another key to attracting empowering people into your life is to have something of value to offer them as well—a concept championed by author Robert Ringer. He calls it *maintaining value-for-value relationships*.

Here are some ways in which you may be empowering those who empower you:

➤ The energy and enthusiasm you display in pursuit of your goals might be inspiring to them.

➤ Your goals in and of themselves might be of great interest to them.

➤ The questions you ask might draw answers out of them that they might not have articulated previously, and they value this.

➤ You expose them to elements of your world and your insights.

➤ Perhaps few others value them the way you do.

Empowerment Is Where You Find It

Okay, so where do you find empowering people in your life? Actually, the answer is everywhere. Here are some ideas:

➤ At your professional association meetings—for example, if you're an accountant, perhaps you meet somebody at the state chapter meeting of the American Institute of Certified Public Accountants

➤ At civic, social, and charitable association group meetings

➤ At adult education courses you take

➤ Through friends

➤ At conferences you attend, particularly if they're a presenter

➤ On airplanes, especially if you're seated in first class, because that's where the corporate brass and VIPs sit

➤ When you serve on the same task force, special committee, commission, or other elected or appointed group

➤ Online

Go for the Gold!
People who empower you also are empowered by you in some way. Otherwise, it's not likely that the relationship will continue for long. The way in which you empower them might not always be clear to you. Perhaps simply valuing what they say in a way that few others do fulfills a need that prompts them to keep the relationship going.

Go for the Gold!
Increasingly, people are developing relationships with others they meet in cyberspace via chat rooms, newsgroups, or by visiting each other's Web sites. Even if you never meet in person, there is significant potential for developing an empowering relationship in this manner.

Get Formal

Although the process of encountering empowering people is discussed in Chapter 20, I've suggested in this chapter that you formalize this process. I advise this formal approach for the simple reason that if you want to be a champion goal-setter and goal-achiever, you're going to need a serious plan for attracting a lot of empowering people into your life.

How Many Is Enough?

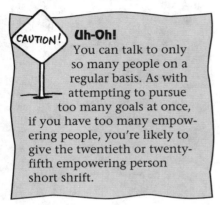

CAUTION! **Uh-Oh!**
You can talk to only so many people on a regular basis. As with attempting to pursue too many goals at once, if you have too many empowering people, you're likely to give the twentieth or twenty-fifth empowering person short shrift.

Set an initial goal of how many associates you want to have as empowering people. Perhaps it's 6 or 12 or 18. When I first sat down and noticed what I had created in my life, I saw that I had 18 empowering people. There's nothing magic about the number; less could have served me as well. More could also work, although you run the risk of encountering logistical problems.

For openers, suppose that your initial target is six empowering people. Chances are there are already six such people in your life or six people who have the potential to serve in this capacity. List at least three of those people right now:

1. _____
2. _____
3. _____

Staying Alive

With each of your empowering people, if the relationship is worth maintaining, you will need to expend some effort. What will you do to maintain the relationship?

With some people, you'll go to lunch occasionally. With some, you'll mail them items that support their interests or that indicate what you've been doing. You'll certainly call, fax, and e-mail each of them at least monthly—perhaps biweekly—and, with some, even weekly or more often. You will constantly be on the lookout for opportunities of interest to them.

You don't approach keeping in touch, however, as some kind of grinding, unrelenting task. Happily, this can come to you almost naturally. Because these six people are important in your life, you've posted the full contact information for each in your appointment book or calendar, which you carry with you all the time. These people are certainly in your e-mail address file. So, as you can see, maintaining these relationships can be somewhat natural and easy.

To facilitate my correspondence with my empowering people, I actually create a label page for each person (30 labels in all—three labels across and 10 down). Then, if I want to mail something to Bob, I simply go to a file folder of all my label pages, peel one off from Bob's page, and affix it to an envelope. If your PC and printer are so configured, perhaps you can print addresses right on your envelope. For me, labels work best.

This Too May Pass

As with members of your peer group, your relationships with empowering people from other groups—such as support-group members, mentors, and advisory-board members—may come to an end—hopefully, later rather than sooner. People move, change their direction in life, pass away, or simply lose interest in maintaining the relationship. It's a part of life.

Because the process of identifying and nurturing relationships with empowering people is a dynamic one, you're always bringing new people into the fold while encountering yet others you suspect will become empowering people in your life.

Uh-Oh!
You didn't think for a minute that the six people I want you to identify and have empowering relationships with would be the same six forever, did you?

CAUTION!

Networking Upward

As I began to experience spectacular benefits as a result of having a variety of empowering people in my life, I expanded my activities. I realized that there are people out there in the world, other authors and speakers in particular, who have blazed a trail far beyond what I have achieved.

If I seek them out, and they become empowering people in my life, then I'll benefit to an even greater degree. Other authors have had 10 times the books sales I've achieved. Some speakers are getting three times the fee I'm getting.

If such people are a regular part of my life, slowly and inexorably, if not rapidly and easily, I will move in the direction in which their wisdom leads. This turned out to be precisely the case. And it will happen for you in pursuit of your goals.

All About Career Coaches

Psychologist Harry A. Olson, Ph.D., in Reisterstown, Maryland, observes that most professional and Olympic athletes have personal coaches to help them cope with competition and play their game to their maximum potential. In fact, the better they become and the more elite their status, the more they need and rely on their coaches! Why? Because the higher they go, the more critical their moves become. The more important personal feedback becomes in avoiding mistakes. The bottom line: The coach gives them the competitive edge!

The concept of using a coach to enhance or improve some aspect of one's life or career is rapidly gaining widespread acceptance. Consider just these two examples:

➤ Corporate executives are using coaches to further their careers.

➤ Actors, singers, and those in the performing arts have long recognized the vital part coaches play in the development of their careers.

The Best Get Better

In my line of work, the notion of employing a speech coach has caught on like wildfire. Some of the most highly paid speakers in the business who have successfully delivered presentations more than 1,000 times routinely attend sessions with a coach. The coach analyzes and critiques every nuance to help the speaker be even better the next time out.

A Process, Not a Routine

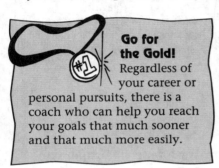

Go for the Gold! Regardless of your career or personal pursuits, there is a coach who can help you reach your goals that much sooner and that much more easily.

Deb Giffen, a success coach and vice president of Learn Inc., in Mount Laurel, New Jersey, has coached many high achievers from many different professions. "Coaching works because the fundamentals of success are the same from person to person, no matter what the person is trying to achieve," says Giffen. "Once you understand the elements of success, you can apply them to any field—which is why I can successfully coach people from fields that are quite different from my own personal background."

Hopefully, I have sufficiently whet your appetite, and you want to learn about what getting a coach can mean for you. Or perhaps you're interested in becoming a coach. You might want to check out these books on coaching:

➤ *Coach to Coach: Business Lessons from the Locker Room*, by John Robinson, 1995

➤ *Coaching: An Effective Behavioral Approach*, by Martin Lamsden, 1986

➤ *Coaching and Counseling in the Workplace*, by Donald Weiss, 1993

➤ *Coaching and Counseling: The McGraw-Hill One-Day Workshop*, by McGraw-Hill, 1995

➤ *Coaching for Commitment*, by Dennis Kinlaw, 1993

➤ *Coaching for Development*, by Marianne Minor, 1995

➤ *Coaching for Performance*, by John Whitmore, 1996

➤ *Coaching Mental Excellence*, by Ralph Verbacchia, 1995

➤ *Coaching, Mentoring & Assessing*, by Eric Parsloe, 1995

➤ *Coaching: Realizing the Potential*, by Kalinackus and King, 1994

Life Coaches

A life coach differs from a career coach in that you do not meet with the life coach to accelerate your efforts in pursuit of some particular goal. Instead, the life coach imparts wisdom to you that he or she has learned along the way. Such wisdom presumably will improve your life in general and may or may not specifically help you in pursuit of particular goals.

A Rose By Any Other Name

Life coaches come in a variety of names, such as *counselor*, *advisor*, and the generic term *coach*. Don't confuse this with seeing a psychiatrist, psychotherapist, or psychological counselor. If you feel the need for such assistance, by all means, seek out these professionals.

A life coach or counselor is not necessarily degreed, licensed, or certified. Instead, he or she provides much the same type of direction to you that a mentor or empowering person might provide, but the process is more formal. You meet with the life coach at regular intervals and pay a fee. You may be given exercises that you're supposed to complete between meetings.

Not as Known, but Just as Effective

Although the notion of using a life coach is not as widespread as employing a career coach, don't let that stop you from finding someone who can help you achieve your goals in all aspects of your life.

Here is some contact information for several coaching-related associations. You may be able to find a life coach from this list as well:

> **Academy of Executive Coaching**
> 1304 Desoto Avenue
> Tampa, FL 33606
> (813) 258-1180
>
> **Business Life Transitions**
> 2792 Main Way
> Los Alamitos, CA 90720
> (310) 598-8117
>
> **Coach University**
> 2484 Bering Drive
> Houston, TX 77057
> (800) 48COACH
>
> **Coaches Training Institute, The**
> 311 Richardson Drive Suite B
> Mill Valley, CA 94941
> (415) 274-7551
>
> **Hudson Institute of Santa Barbara**
> 3463 State Street, Suite 520
> Santa Barbara, CA 93105
> (805) 682-3883

International Coach Federation
2123 FM 1960 West, Suite 219
Houston, TX 77090
(888) 423-3131

International Coaching Society
4750 Vista Street
San Diego, CA 92116
(619) 282-5760

Professional and Personal Coaches Association
P.O. Box 2838
San Francisco, CA 94126
(415) 522-8789

Professional Coaches and Mentors Association
3020 Old Ranch Parkway, Suite 300
Seal Beach, CA 90740
(714) 220-9431

The Least You Need to Know

➤ You can set up your world to be surrounded on all sides by people who are eager to offer you advice and support.

➤ There are people in your life right now who would be honored if not thrilled to be on your advisory board.

➤ To have empowering people in your life, you must be open to them—look forward to hearing from them, listen to and heed their advice, and be appreciative. Have something of value to offer them as well.

➤ Top performers in all walks of life have coaches. Maybe you could benefit from one as well.

➤ Each day presents more opportunities for you to attract into your life powerful resources to help you reach your goals.

Chapter 23

Reaching Two Goals at One Time

In this chapter on advanced strategies for reaching your goals, I focus on how you can achieve leverage with your efforts. Wouldn't it be wonderful if you could engage in a single activity that helps you achieve more than one goal? Of course it would!

Combining Goals to Reach Them More Easily

Suppose there was a quick and easy way to undertake one task or activity in pursuit of two or more goals. Wouldn't that be an economical, time-saving, energy-saving way to proceed? You already do this all day long in little ways. Getting eight hours of sound sleep each night, for example, undoubtedly is helpful in the pursuit of various health or career-related goals. Similarly, caring for your teeth, getting regular dental checkups, and ensuring good oral hygiene supports both social- and health-related goals.

Okay, all this is obvious, but what if you want to actively seek ways of supporting two or more goals at the same time through a single activity, and the activity you should engage in to accomplish this mission is not so obvious?

Projecting Outward

Suppose that you're single, and one of your goals is to find a mate. You've determined that whatever you can do to be more attractive would be in your best interests. Suppose that another of your goals is to improve your interpersonal skills. What one basic activity could you engage in to accomplish both goals? Let me answer by telling you a story.

In a made-for-TV movie, Jane Seymour played the dual role of identical twins. One sister was confident, if somewhat shy, respectful, and forthright. The other sister maintained a facade of self-confidence betrayed by her sarcasm, lack of trust, impatience, and lack of respect for others.

I remember Seymour's portrayal of these two characters, because I found it remarkable that even though she was physically the same woman, when she portrayed the first twin, she was attractive and charming. When she portrayed the second twin, amazingly, she was not as attractive. She was still Jane Seymour underneath, but the character was someone I wouldn't want to know and certainly wouldn't want to be around.

Look Around for Confirmation

If you doubt that having greater self-confidence makes you more attractive to others, think about people in your office or among your circle of friends. Is there someone in that group who objectively might not be so aesthetically blessed but because of his or her self-confidence, and of course personality, projects outward and thus is attractive to others? I'll bet there is.

Go for the Gold!
If one of your goals in life is to be more attractive to others, instead of engaging in cosmetic manipulations, one of the most effective and least expensive ways is to be more self-confident.

Conversely, is there someone in your professional or social circle who most people would regard as good looking if they were to see a picture of this person? Yet, because of a lack of confidence and perhaps other factors, this individual is not regarded as attractive. We've all known someone like that.

Perhaps someone like that is sitting in your chair right now. If so, take heart: the key is self-confidence, and you can set a goal of having more self-confidence anytime you choose.

Method Actor

Kinesthetics don't lie. If you walk and talk with confidence; stand more erect; throw out your chest; take deep, measured breaths; and, in general, *appear* to be confident, guess what? You tend to *be* more confident.

A sense of confidence draws others to you. It doesn't guarantee enhanced interpersonal skills, but it certainly increases the probability that your repartee with others will improve. As others begin to find you more engaging and attractive as a person, you'll find that your interest in others increases as well. Hence, by focusing on improving your self-confidence, you will end up making progress on two or more goals you've set for yourself.

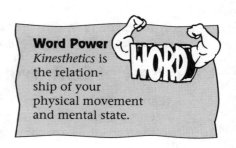

Word Power
Kinesthetics is the relationship of your physical movement and mental state.

Here's a diagram of what I've just explained.

Improve Interpersonal Skills

Be More Attractive | Increase self-confidence

Two Birds, One Stone

Suppose that you're single and want to meet the right partner for you. Apparently, this person hasn't shown up at the places you've been visiting, such as singles bars, dances, and so on. At the same time, you want to acquire some new skills so that you'll be more competent on the job and increase the probability of getting a promotion and a raise.

Name That Activity

For the vacation cruise, the brand-new convertible, and the Sunfish sailboat, can you name a single activity that potentially would enable you to reach both goals? I'll give you a couple of seconds to think it over... Buzzzzzzz!

Time's up! What is your answer?

If your answer is enrolling in some type of adult-education program, presumably in the evenings and particularly a class that happens to have a large number of individuals in the proper demographic category for you, you're our grand-prize winner! Schematically, this appears as the following.

Increase job skills

Meet someone to date | Enroll in adult-education classes

Years ago, when I lived in Falls Church, Virginia, I had goals of maintaining peak fitness and having a relationship with a woman I was attracted to. The activity I sought to accomplish both goals was to join a health club populated by large numbers of healthy, fit, young, attractive, career-minded women. I ended up meeting someone with whom I had a six-year relationship.

By now, you're getting the hang of this, and I can see that you're liking it. Let's look at one more example before broadening the concept.

The Best of Both Worlds

Suppose that one of your family-related goals is to spend more time with your teenage son or daughter. This hasn't been easy of late, because your schedules are rarely similar. At the same time, one of your personal interests is historical biographies.

You've read some of the popular tomes, such as *Truman* by David McCullough; Winston Churchill's autobiography; and *Abraham Lincoln* by Carl Sandburg. Your teenage son or daughter likes you, would like to spend more time with you, and happens to like videos. Guess what? You have a potential vehicle by which you'll reach multiple goals with one activity.

Once a week or so, pick up a historical biography on video or some other form of electronic media and schedule a time to watch it with your son or daughter. Stop the tape as necessary and discuss interesting points as they arise. Eat popcorn or have other snacks as you so choose.

After the program, you can spend time talking about the special challenges that person faced in his or her era. Fortunately, there's enough good programming today so that you can select a video that appeals to your teenage son or daughter and also happens to be a historical biography, which is your cup of tea.

Become more knowledgeable about world history

Spend more time with your teenage child

Schedule a fun video and discussion night

Creating a Goal Matrix

By expanding this concept a tiny bit, you can achieve some tremendous leverage with your time and efforts. Suppose that you construct a 4×4 matrix, such as the following.

	Goal A	Goal B	Goal C	Goal D
Goal A				
Goal B				
Goal C				
Goal D				

Now, across the top, write four of your most important goals.

Write the same four goals down the left side of the matrix. So, across the top, your labels might be Goal A, Goal B, Goal C, and Goal D. Down the left side, your labels would be Goal A, Goal B, Goal C, and Goal D. Now place an x in those cells where Goal A intersects itself, Goal B intersects itself, and so on. This would look like the following.

	Goal A	Goal B	Goal C	Goal D
Goal A	X			
Goal B		X		
Goal C			X	
Goal D				X

Exploring the Possibilities

Suppose that one of your goals is to safely and easily travel the world (it is certainly one of mine). Another is to keep advancing in your company. If worldwide travel is goal B and advancing in your company is goal C, what activity would support your efforts in both areas?

You guessed it—being transferred to your company's London office. Perhaps it would be for a six-month or one-year term.

During that time, on weekends, you could visit Scandinavia and mainland Europe. On longer weekends and holidays, you could take jaunts to Gibraltar, Corsica, or the Black Sea.

This kind of what-if thinking is exciting, if for no other reason than because it provides the impetus to look at your goals and your life in new ways. Each time you identify an activity that enables you to further your efforts in pursuit of two or more goals, you've reaped a personal bonanza!

> **Go for the Gold!**
> As you look at the goals you've set for yourself using a matrix, possibilities begin to open up that you otherwise might not have considered.

Let Me Count the Ways

Let's see how you might use the 4×4 matrix in multiple ways. Julie, age 33, is a single parent seeking to

A	Achieve greater financial independence
B	Finish her graduate degree
C	Have more of a social life
D	Maintain fitness

So, these items would go across the top of the 4×4 matrix and down the left-hand side.

	A	B	C	D
A	X	Only take classes I pay for! No more student loans!		
B	Get a degree that will enhance my career.	X	Take "fun" classes I can meet people in.	
C		Balance class, work, leisure time.	X	Do *active* things with others.
D		Include classes on nutrition and phys-ed.	Join a walking or hiking club.	X

Expanding on a Theme

Go for the Gold!
Although it's easy enough to draw a chart on an 8-½-by-11-inch piece of paper or to create a matrix on your computer, you might want to create a wall chart. Any office-supply store offers a washable or erasable board you can mount on your wall. With larger cells, you can view the chart while seated at your desk. With more room to write, more ideas might flow.

Yes, you can use a 5×5 matrix, a 6×6 matrix, and so on. I don't advise using larger than a 6×6 matrix, though, because things begin to get unwieldy. For openers, I suggest that you stay with a simple 4×4 matrix.

As you identify activities that support two or more goals and initiate them, you can create other matrices, inserting other goals across the top and down the left side to see what new combinations become evident.

Making Your Work Count Twice

This approach to achieving more than one goal via a single activity is so potent and so valuable that I've mentioned it in nearly everything I've written and every presentation I've made over the last several years. The concept is relatively simple, but the payoff is magnificent.

Without having to resort to a box, matrix, or chart of any type, quite simply, continually be on the lookout for any activity you engage in that can be used for other purposes. Bill Brooks, president of the Brooks Consulting Group and author of the book *You're Working Too Hard to Make the Sale*, advises people to always be on the lookout for the downstream potential of whatever they engage in today.

No Eye on the Future

Brooks observes that most businesses are only about 90 days away from bankruptcy. What does he mean by that? Unless a company conducts long-term and continuing business with loyal, repeat customers, it largely earns its money from the sales and business it does today.

To keep the cash flow positive, most businesses furiously fan the marketing flames to drum up sales now and keep the cash register or accounts-receivable ledger humming along. The sales staff needs to go out and drum up new business every day; if they don't, in a matter of weeks or certainly within 90 days, the company will generate no more revenue.

If the job you're doing and the effort you're making today simply earn you a paycheck at the end of the week, how are you gaining leverage from your time and talents?

> **Uh-Oh!** CAUTION!
> If you're keeping your head above water financially but not adding to your in-depth knowledge of how your industry operates, increasing your skill base, or making contacts that could be valuable in the future, you are only months if not days away from bankruptcy if something unfortunate were to suddenly happen to your job.

A Storehouse of Resources

When you actively look for ways to make your work count twice, you begin to build a storehouse of resources for the future, much like the squirrel who instinctively gathers acorns for the winter.

Every outline, every plan, and every strategy you've ever saved on paper or to disk has the potential for a continuing shelf life.

Presentations you've made—particularly that you audiotaped or videotaped—are veritable gold mines.

If you have served as an officer in any organization (see Chapter 20, "Affiliating with Others: Capitalizing on Those Around You"), the experience, the procedures, and the interpersonal contacts you made are all likely to have some future value.

> **Go for the Gold!** #1
> Potentially, every report, every memo, and every document you've ever written has enduring value if there are sections of it you can extract and use again, or if you can use them as models when tackling something new.

291

Other Ways of Serving Two Masters

As you consider your mental, physical, family, social, spiritual, career, and financial goals, continually look for ways to do something once but to have it pay off in two or more goal areas. A friend of mine was able to devise an envelope, for example, that he used in mailings for his business. This 1) increased the probability of reliable and timely delivery, and 2) was eye-catching and appealing to the recipient.

How did he do it? Using an attractive color scheme for his envelopes, he printed a message saying that his company loved the Post Office and that's why they entrusted the Post Office with their important mail. Postal workers loved this. In fact, a column about his envelopes was written up in the postal workers' national monthly newsletter.

The mailing recipients found it to be unique and eye-catching as well. Many people called my friend to tell him what a clever and innovative approach he had devised for sending his mail.

All Strategies Are Fleeting

Nothing lasts forever. Perhaps in time, others will imitate my friend's idea, or those who handle or receive such envelopes will become used to them, and eventually they will have less impact. If and when that happens, my friend undoubtedly will devise another strategy for accomplishing multiple goals with one effort.

Many filmmakers have long used the technique of producing movies that serve multiple goals. Whether or not you agree with his idea that capital punishment ought to be abolished, you have to acknowledge that Tim Robbins produced a critically and financially successful story in *Dead Man Walking*.

In a nutshell, the movie

➤ Made him a profit

➤ Explored the issue of capital punishment in a way few other movies had

➤ Enhanced his credentials as a director (he had already earned a solid reputation as an actor)

➤ Provided a vehicle for his partner, Susan Sarandon, to earn her first Oscar after receiving many previous nominations

Birds Do It, Authors Do It

Even Jeff, your trusted author, writes books with preconceived, intended multiple goals:

➤ To serve you the best way I know how

➤ To earn healthy royalties

➤ To be invited to speak all over the country and, in some cases, the world

➤ To benefit additionally as the books are converted to other media, such as cassettes, videos, or software

➤ To create a vehicle that enables me to be a frequent guest on television and radio talk shows, thus increasing my visibility and the demand for my services

Go for the Gold! The clearer you are about the multiple goals you seek to reach, the more likely you'll be to identify activities or strategies that support your quest.

Piggybacking Techniques

Undoubtedly, you have a lot of ideas now on how to further accelerate your progress toward reaching goals.

Anytime you have the opportunity to *piggyback* (to take care of one thing while you're taking care of another), go for it! The next time you're at a conference or convention and you're dressed to the nines, for example, here's a piggybacking idea you might not have considered:

Is there a photographer on site hired to capture scenes at the meeting?

If so, you can approach this person and perhaps engage him or her for a fee to take shots of you. Realistically, how many times in the course of a month or a year would you be able to get such high-quality, professionally produced photographs of yourself in such a setting? You could use such photos for your Internet Web site, brochures or literature for your business, your resume, or a variety of items.

Identifying Leveraging Opportunities

To devise piggybacking strategies, I use the following chart, which I devised with one of my coauthors and mentors, Richard A. Conner. I find it especially useful to begin filling out parts of this chart prior to attending an event. That way, I won't forget about potential piggybacking opportunities when I'm caught up in activities as they unfold.

Leveraging Chart

Activity _____ Date _____ Other _____

Contact _____ Phone _____ Fax _____ E-mail _____

Personal interests _____ Memberships _____

Preparation _____

_____

_____

_____

_____

Other visits _____

_____

_____

_____

Networking opportunities   Other opportunities

    1. _____   1. _____

    2. _____   2. _____

    3. _____   3. _____

Remarks _____

_____

_____

_____

_____

Copy the Chart and Use It!

What functions will you be attending in the next day, week, or month where you can achieve rapid progress in pursuit of your goals by taking advantage of piggybacking techniques? Why not take the time right now to write down three events or activities you'll be attending?

1. _____

2. _____

3. _____

Now, photocopy the leveraging chart three times—one for each of the opportunities you just listed. Jot down the potential opportunities as you envision them.

Later, you can add to what you've written. Whatever you come up with may represent excellent opportunities to further your goals by taking advantage of what you're already doing.

The Least You Need to Know

➤ Constantly be on the lookout for the type of activity that can support two or more of your goals.

➤ Use a 4×4 or larger goal matrix chart to identify an array of activities that may support multiple goals.

➤ Constantly be on the lookout for ways to make your work count twice—to both accomplish the task at hand and to gain future value.

➤ Be honest about the real reasons you embark on certain goals—often, you have a multiple agenda.

➤ Anytime you're out and about, think about the ways you can piggyback on what you're already doing.

Upping the Ante

Sometimes, on the way to setting and reaching your goals, you find out that you set your sights too low. As challenging as your goals might have seemed at the time, you eventually realize—even before you cross the finish line—that some of those goals apparently were well within your grasp all along. Your challenge becomes one of upping the ante: deciding to go for more because you've proven to yourself or feel in the very marrow of your bones that you're capable of achieving more.

Challenging Yourself

You're someone who has either constantly or will hereafter be setting challenging but reachable goals that are quantifiable and have specific timelines. You want to better your lot in life, whether it's along mental, physical, family, social, spiritual, career, or financial lines.

Because it's likely that you're reading this book at a faster pace than you're actually reaching challenging goals, you're probably reading this chapter prior to your actual need. Nevertheless, you recognize that sometimes you're fully capable of pursuing even more challenging goals than what you originally established.

You're not the first person to trip over this realization. Throughout history, and certainly in contemporary society, examples abound. In fact, some people apparently upped the ante in the face of loss!

In Good Company

Abraham Lincoln did all he could to win a seat in Congress. He lost far more elections than he ever won. In fact, in 1858, two years before he won the presidency of the United States, he lost a Senatorial bid in his own state. Obviously, he felt he was up for the challenge of running for an even higher office than the one he had just lost. History proved him to be correct.

Of those with a presidential quest, Ross Perot's biography reads like someone who continually realized that he needed more of a challenge. Before starting his computer systems company, EDS, which helped make him a billionaire, Perot was a salesman for IBM. As many of his biographies recount, he decided to start his own company around the third week of January 1962, when he had already reached his sales quota at IBM *for the entire year*.

So, you ask, when *do* you decide to make your goals more challenging? The answer isn't the same for everyone, but there are some common indicators.

If you did your gut-level best to set challenging but reachable goals that were quantifiable and within specific time frames, and you ended up reaching them in a fraction of the time you originally allocated, that's definitely a clue. I mean, it happens!

For Sure

When Magic Johnson got into the NBA in the 1979–1980 season, along with many other rookie superstars, he probably had a dream of making the NBA finals and winning a championship or two. Although Magic was the starting point guard for the team, during the championship series when Kareem Abdul-Jabbar had to miss the sixth game in Philadelphia due to injury, Magic filled in at center, scored 42 points, and turned out to be the series MVP! Thus, when the Lakers won the NBA championship in Magic's rookie season, one championship wasn't going to be enough.

As Your Power and Influence Begin to Develop

Ralph Nader took on the entire automobile industry in the early 1960s through the courts and with his best-selling book, *Unsafe At Any Speed*, which documented identifiable and known risks in popular-selling automobiles. Nader was rapidly hailed as a consumer advocate.

Early on, Nader learned that one well-developed case intelligently presented in the judicial system is more effective than 10,000 protesters clanging on the fences outside of General Motors.

He did not rest on his laurels, however; he initiated *public interest resource groups* (PIRGs) in every state, a national magazine called *Common Cause*, and much more. To this day, he remains a tireless advocate of environmental protection, safeguarding U.S. jobs and exposing corporate interests that may run contrary to the needs or wants of society. In many respects, Nader's entire career has been one of upping the ante to further the progress of causes that he sees a need to support.

When Every Fiber in Your Being Says Move On

Whether you reach chosen goals quickly or experience expanding power and influence, you still may choose to up the ante if a little voice inside you says, "I can do more." So, even in the absence of evidence in the pursuit of some long-term goal, sometimes you realize on a profound level that it's time to go for more.

Michael Dell, founder of Dell Computers, started his company out of his college dormitory room. Many times in his career, while still only in his 20s and early 30s, he expanded his company in the absence of what onlookers might call evidence. He upped the ante to the point where, by mid-1997, Dell Computers was creating custom systems for customers who ordered via the Internet to the tune of $2 million in sales per day.

In recent memory, have you reached goals that initially seemed highly challenging in relatively record time? Has your power and influence expanded as you've achieved some goals so that you can set even more challenging ones? Or, do you feel deeply that it simply makes sense for you to move on from where you are? If any one of these factors is present, that's significant; if two or three are present, follow your heart, not your head. Up your goals. Up the ante.

Go for the Gold!

There's always the danger of running into the barrier of biting off more than you can chew. If you've already racked up a number of significant achievements, though, and you have the self-confidence or have otherwise proven to yourself that you do indeed intend to finish what you set out to accomplish, I say, *full speed ahead!*

Small Risks, Important Exercises

As a prelude to upping the ante on big goals, what small gesture could you make that involves attempting more than you usually attempt? Maybe you can head up that fund drive for your church or community group, for example, even though you've never done anything like that before (more on this later).

A mysterious and wonderful thing happens when you engage in uncharted territory: Sometimes, you succeed! Even if you don't, you learn lessons along the way and add to the well of self-confidence you've been building.

I read about a mountain climber who said that, as a strategic maneuver, he sometimes began scaling the wall of a cliff where he knew he could not retreat. His only option was making it to the top, succeeding all the way (and then, presumably, finding a reliable way down on the other side).

I'm not asking you to scale cliffs—far from it. Here are some suggestions for upping the ante—going for more than your initial goal:

➤ If your goal is more income, ask for a raise even if it's months before the time when raises are usually given.

➤ If your goal is to be a leader, speak up at a meeting where you've never before spoken up.

➤ If your goal is to act more boldly, wear something that is normally a little wild or extravagant for you.

➤ If your goal is to manage a winning team, throw down a challenge to the members of your team or your staff at the next meeting.

The Incremental Approach

Throughout this book, I've discussed the wisdom of maintaining a balance in pursuit of your goals, maintaining relative simplicity, and taking an incremental approach even though results don't always show up that neatly. You can apply an incremental approach of sorts even when vastly upgrading your current goals.

Media mogul Rupert Murdoch, who has brought us such highbrow programming (I'm joking) as appears on his Fox Network, had the humblest of origins. He started out as a broadcaster for a local station in Australia, eventually got into management, then ownership, and from there, to ownership of multiple stations. He then branched into publishing, including magazines, newspapers, and even books.

Heading a growing conglomerate, he acquired businesses in the United Kingdom and the United States and opened up new territories in Southeast Asia. He is a pioneer in employing new variations in satellite broadcasting, and he even purchased the Los Angeles

Dodgers so that he could exploit their popularity in Japan, Korea, and Southeast Asia. Murdoch's approach was to solidify his base every step of the way before venturing out and acquiring more.

As he developed the management know-how and assembled highly effective teams, Murdoch's progress and growth seemed extraordinary to onlookers. Yet all along, his incremental approach to building his worldwide media empire has been readily observable.

Step This Way

How could an incremental approach work for you? Suppose that you're a nurse. In time, you become a crackerjack nurse. Then, perhaps, you become a trainer of other nurses. Then, you spend some time as a manager of nurses. One day, soon enough, you start your own nursing agency. You send in crack teams of nurses to healthcare facilities for a day or for several months, depending on the needs of your clients, all at a reasonable rate. Perhaps you then expand your operations beyond local boundaries to countywide or regional clientele. One day, you wake up and realize that you have built an empire that spans several states.

For Thine Is the Glory

Suppose that you're an active member of your church and have noticed that a number of paying members of the congregation have been slipping in recent years. You volunteer to be on a committee to revitalize operations. You devise a welcome-wagon type of approach to build church membership. You send packets and/or greet new people in your community, making them aware of your church and all it has to offer. You recruit some of the current congregation members to handle this function.

With that squared away, you also begin an initiative among the entire congregation, using the church's bimonthly newsletter to invite them to bring friends and relatives to the Sunday service. This proves to be fairly effective, so you issue a regular message in each issue.

Then, you appear on some local community shows discussing the affairs and activities of your church. One step at a time, in the course of maybe a year or so, you have begun to restore the strength and vitality of your church.

You build on your successes and recruit others to handle specific functions. After those individuals or teams are in place, you turn your attention to other membership-building activities.

You have taken a wholly incremental approach to reaching your goal, and it worked just fine.

Approaching Your Goals Sequentially

A *sequential* approach is somewhat like an incremental approach with one major difference. You have to proceed from A to B, from B to C, and from C to D. Each step *has to be taken* in chronological order, either because of built-in protocol or actual necessity.

In many industries, to obtain certification or a license, you have to pass a sequence of exams or complete a series of steps, such as in the accounting and real estate professions.

One Path to Certification

In 1981, I obtained a CMC designation—*Certified Management Consultant*. To qualify, I had to be in the consulting profession for five consecutive years full-time, including one year as a project manager.

Then, I had to request an application and pay an application fee; give one complete written description of my educational background, consulting experience, and professional activities; prepare five consulting engagement summaries, including one in detail; complete a test; have a one-hour interview with three members of the Institute of Management Consultants; and be approved for membership by two of them. Finally, upon acceptance, I submitted an initial membership fee and henceforth an annual membership fee.

To achieve my goal of becoming a certified management consultant, I had to complete all the requirements in sequence, as does every other candidate.

From Here to There

In your own life, when it comes to upping the ante (making your goals even more challenging), you might have to take a sequential approach, because that's the way the system is designed or because it's simply the most logical way to proceed.

If you want to be a full professor, you'll probably start off as a graduate teaching assistant, then perhaps move on to an instructor, then an assistant professor, then an associate professor, and finally a professor.

From there, you may become associate chair or chair of your department, and then someday, during your days of grace, emeritus professor, or even emeritus dean.

If your ambition is to run for higher office, you don't have to start at the local level, but that's the way many people have proceeded. They moved up through the ranks, paid their dues along the way, secured a political base, and then moved to the next level.

Follow My Lead

In those instances in which you've raised your sights and dramatically increased your goal level, and there's an established sequence to the process, your immediate goals are clear:

➤ Learn everything you can about the sequence. What are all the steps along the way? What are the positions, titles, and ranks you have to go through? What tests do you have to take? What are the skills you have to demonstrate?

➤ Talk to people who have moved up through the ranks. What better way to proceed along your path as efficiently as you can than to speak to people who already have blazed this trail? Speak to as many people as you can.

➤ Determine reasonable timelines for every step along your path. What are the norms, as well as the fastest and slowest times by which others have completed this process? Have people been able to leapfrog, and, if so, how and why? What are the advantages and disadvantages of proceeding through various steps faster or slower than the norm?

A World of Winners

The world is full of people who essentially followed a sequential approach on their way to achieving fabulous goals. Dr. Steven Covey is a prime example of someone who achieved one notable goal and then built on that achievement in reaching other goals:

Covey first conducted seminars for corporate leaders and eventually wrote the perennial best-seller, *The Seven Habits of Highly Successful People*. Since then, Covey has established a speaking, seminar, and publishing empire that employs hundreds of people and earns millions of dollars annually.

For Sure

Steven Covey has created his own publishing house, created and spun off his own literary agency, and developed proprietary products such as calendars, newsletters, software products, guide books, and so on. He also has written several more best-selling books and produced video programs and six audio tapes that are distributed worldwide. His influence now spans the far reaches of the globe, and *The Seven Habits of Highly Successful People* now is used in classrooms.

Step One, Step Two

Ray Kroc, who bought out the McDonald Brothers hamburger stand and then proceeded to open one franchise after another, represents another example of the sequential approach. The same can be said of Dave Thomas of Wendy's and Tom Monaghan of Domino's Pizza.

In fact, the business of establishing a successful franchise lends itself to the sequential approach. If you're interested in exploring how you can become a franchise owner and perhaps someday a multiple owner, get in touch with this organization:

> **International Franchise Association**
> 1350 New York Avenue, N.W. Suite 900
> Washington, D.C. 20005
> (202) 628-8000

In movie direction, the process often works in much the same way:

➤ Jodie Foster was first a child actor, then an accomplished adult actor, a winner of Academy Awards, a director, and then a director/producer.

  Others who established careers as actors first and then directors and/or producers include Woody Allen, Kevin Costner, Clint Eastwood, Mel Gibson, and Robert Redford. Not bad company, eh?

➤ Penny Marshall and Rob Reiner, once husband and wife, were successful television sitcom actors who have achieved superstar status as major motion picture directors, much like Ron Howard.

➤ In his mid-20s, Steven Spielberg directed the film *Sugarland Express*, starring Goldie Hawn. It received critical acclaim, although few people saw it. A year later, he directed *Jaws*; two years later, he directed the *Indiana Jones* trilogy. You already know about his stunning achievements, so I won't delve further into them.

Everybody starts somewhere, and the path to fame and fortune among directors largely proceeds from one film to the next.

Swallowing the Whole Hog

There's a Russian proverb that says that you can't cross a chasm in two leaps. Depending on what you're up against, sometimes the best way to proceed is to go for the whole shebang in one shot.

Suppose that a professional boxer who's had a fairly good record gets a big break. The powers that be, the promoters, decide that he gets a shot at the champ. This opportunity sometimes is out of sequence in the boxer's career, but it happens. If he loses badly, he might not get another chance. If he handles himself well, he might get a second chance, but no one can say when.

So, his goal becomes clear: Try to knock out the champ and to go whole hog for the grandest of goals in his weight category—to be the World Boxing Association champion. The boxer decides to up the ante and go for the gold now, this year, at a fight coming up in two or three months instead of later in his career.

He'll put all his energies into this effort. Never mind the career path—the time to shine is now.

The same thing happens when one athlete replaces another when the first goes down with an injury. The backup football quarterback who gets his big chance knows on many levels that he might not get another shot at being the starter. So, he's not content to merely fill in, to merely do a good job, to merely help his team win.

Instead, he wants to make a statement. He wants to show that he is major-league caliber —that he can run the team, from start to finish, win the game, and then go out on the field and do it again next Sunday.

The same phenomenon occurs when an interim coach is appointed to take the place of the ailing regular coach. Although everyone hopes for the best (with the possible exception of the interim coach), it is a possibility that the regular coach won't make it back. The interim coach, if he wants to be more than just a substitute, changes his procedures.

The interim coach begins working around the clock. He analyzes the team roster. He carefully looks at the team's strengths and weaknesses, as well as at which plays have worked in the past. He talks to the players one-on-one. He analyzes previous game films. In short, he pulls out the stops. He wants to ensure top management that whether or not the head coach comes back, he can do the job. And, if the head coach does come back, he wants to ensure that he will be the next coach when the time comes.

If his organization can't see it, perhaps another organization will take notice. The interim coach has upped the ante in terms of his goals.

Fake It 'Til You Make It

Mary K. Ash, who founded the multimillion-dollar empire bearing her name, used to tell her staff, "Fake it 'til you make it." Did she mean that you proceed with a facade, trying to con people into believing you have capabilities you don't? Not at all!

"Fake it 'til you make it" means that you act the part that you intend to assume. You engage in the behaviors, read the literature, interact with others, and conduct yourself in a manner so that you are already where you want to be.

Soon enough, this becomes your natural approach to life, and others around you can easily see that you deserve to have the job title, position, acclaim, or whatever other kudos come with your ability and achievement.

For Sure

Professor Stanley Davis, in his book *20/20*, coined the term *managing the beforehand*. Davis says that if you study world leaders who assumed their position via revolution, invariably you find that long before they actually held the reins of power, they already knew their supremacy would become a reality. Everything was in place, it was all but inevitable, and they had only to move into position.

The Ocean of No Return

What would you like to achieve right now that represents an upping of the ante, for which it makes sense for you to go whole hog—to fully immerse yourself in whatever it takes, to take the leap, and make a commitment from which you cannot return?

There's a wonderful scene in the movie *Mutiny on the Bounty*, whether you're watching the '30s version with Clark Gable and Charles Laughton, the '50s version with Marlon Brando and Trevor Howard, or the '80s version with Mel Gibson and Anthony Hopkins. Fletcher Christian, the hero of the tale, decides to burn the ship, *Bounty*, so that he and his men will become fully settled on Pitcairn Island with no possibility of departure.

That's burning your bridges, or in this case, quite literally, your boat.

The late Earl Nightingale once said that you can't get to second base if you won't take your foot off first. He also said that you can't get what you want if you remain "one of the timid feeders in the lagoon" who fears to venture out into the deep blue sea.

If you're psyched up at this point, here are some ideas for upping the ante and jumping into the fray:

➤ Get on the phone right now and make a call to the person you need to speak with to get your big goal in motion.

➤ Buy the plane ticket, train ticket, or boat ticket to go see the person or people you need to see.

➤ If your quest involves spending some money, take a look at your bank account and move the requisite funds into place. If you don't have the funds, start listing all the possible ways you can get them.

➤ Identify what needs to be dropped because it's no longer valid or perhaps is in the way. Then, without remorse, remove it from your life.

➤ If it works for you, announce your intentions to somebody else.

➤ Commit yourself on paper (see Chapters 14, "Committing to Paper" and 17, "Contracting with Yourself").

Deadly Sin or Divine Aspiration

Invariably, when you decide to up the ante, someone will come along and tell you not to do it.

"It can't be done."

"It shouldn't be done."

"You can't do it. You shouldn't do it"

"You're going to fail."

Don't be surprised if you hear these kinds of admonitions. The typical person does not embrace change, doesn't see the possibilities that you see, and can't envision a successful conclusion. Hence, you can't take a quick survey of others and expect to get any kind of meaningful input.

It is valuable if others who you trust and know you well point out specific hazards to your vaulted goals. If others are able to offer poignant, factual information that you need to know to have a realistic notion of what it will take to achieve your goal, then more power to them and to you.

> **Go for the Gold!**
> If you understand the impediments you face, you're far better off than if you proceed blindly. When you understand the pitfalls and still are committed to go full speed ahead, the choice is indeed yours, and it's a grand one.

Let's Get Unreasonable

I read once that nothing of lasting value is accomplished by reasonable men (and, of course, women, too). It is the unreasonable people among us, the discontent, the dreamers who nevertheless have their feet firmly planted on solid ground—the visionaries, if you will—who improve peoples' lives or, in rare instances, help to advance all of society.

Reasonable people can talk themselves out of anything, no matter how great the merit of the venture or cause. You probably could stand to be a bit more unreasonable when it comes to your goals.

The Least You Need to Know

➤ Up the ante when you reach a challenging goal quickly, your power and influence markedly increase, or every fiber of your being says to.

➤ A sequential approach to reaching even more challenging goals involves securing your bases at one level before moving on.

➤ If your goal is to be achieved through a sequential process, then learn all you can about the steps in the sequence.

➤ Sometimes you have to go whole hog, abandon ship, burn your bridges, and take your foot off first base to achieve your goals.

➤ Being unreasonable at times and not willing to settle can help you accomplish deeds of lasting value.

Chapter 25

Lifetime Goal Setting

In This Chapter

➤ 10-year plans

➤ Big people have big goals

➤ Tea for two

➤ Helping others

You could get hit by a truck and die tomorrow, but chances are you've got a lot of time left in your life. This chapter focuses on innovative goals you might decide to set from now until the end of your life. Does that sound like something worth reading? I thought you'd say yes.

Name That Decade

In Chapters 15, "A Question of Time," and 18, "All About Deadlines," I discussed using the power of deadlines, milestones, and other markers to aid you in goal achievement. One of the suggestions that merits further thought is the notion of choosing goals a decade at a time. This could be calendar-wise or based on your age. So, if you're 30, you could choose goals for all of your thirties, all of your forties, and so on. Because we're almost at the start of a new decade, let's proceed as if you have goals for the decade leading up to the year 2010.

A Decade Isn't So Long

In the old Soviet Union, economic and social progress was measured in five-year planning periods. Five-year programs also were initiated in the People's Republic of China and elsewhere around the globe. The experience of top government officials in such nations was that time passes quickly.

Go for the Gold! Certainly, 10 years is not too long an interval for planning your life. Indeed, if you reach the age of 70, 80, or 90, ten years will represent only 9 to 14 percent of your total life span.

In the United States, nearly every president in the last 30 years has commented that the four-year presidential term, however interminably long it might have seemed when he was embroiled in controversy, seemed to have flown by in retrospect. Likewise, if you went to college, you know that while you're studying and taking exams, it seems as though graduation is a long way off. Then, one day—poof—you graduate! Now, looking back, it seems as though that four-year period went by in a breeze.

Ten Years After

I learned the hard way how quickly 10 years can pass when I bought some property in Northern Virginia in 1981. I signed up for a 30-year mortgage thinking that I did not want to pay a higher monthly fee and own the property sooner, because I would undoubtedly sell it in a couple of years, and the length of the loan wouldn't be that crucial in retrospect.

Now, more than 15 years later, I would have owned this property outright had I taken a 15-year mortgage. Sure, I would have had a higher expense on each mortgage and would have had to rough it out, but look at what the result could have been—owning the property free and clear, collecting a nice, high rent, and setting myself up for long-term prosperity.

Instead, if I do not sell the property, I have years and years to go before it will ever be truly mine.

Maintaining a Long-Term Perspective

In your own life, you might be able to reflect on something you did 10 or more years ago when, with a twist and a turn, things could have been much more to your advantage today if you had applied a long-term perspective to the issue.

When assessing what you want to do in the coming decades, consider some of these factors:

➤ How old will you be by the end of the decade?

➤ How old will your children be?

➤ What long-term mortgages or loans will be or can be paid off by that time?

➤ Where will you live?

➤ Will you still be in the same profession?

➤ Will you engage in the same leisure-time activities?

To be sure, this is not a book on long-term or retirement planning. Nevertheless, if you can focus on at least a 10-year perspective, you'll be way ahead of the crowd and end up reaching more of your goals than you might have otherwise.

When, How, and with Whom?

Noted corporate trainer Bob Boylan asks his seminar attendees three basic questions:

➤ How will you live your life?

➤ Where will you live your life?

➤ With whom will you live?

You already might have the answers to these questions; if so, you're fortunate. What I'd like you to do right now is to use the following chart to sketch in some notes about what you're going to do over a 10-year period.

Year	Income	Savings	Vacations	Leisure	Friends	Other
1						
2						
3						
4						
5						
6						
7						
8						
9						
10						

Do I Have to Do This?

Uh-Oh!
As you learned earlier in the book, most people have a vague, half-baked notion about where they're heading in life. Perhaps that explains why so many people have to rely on Social Security checks when they reach the last decade or so of their lives.

Is this a difficult exercise for you? I wouldn't be surprised if it is. Why? Even if you're a fairly ambitious goal setter, chances are you haven't projected ahead for 10 years.

Still, if you can fill in even a few of the cells for now and perhaps a few more in a little while, you will begin to shape and design your life in a way that few others even attempt.

Now, if you're really ready to take the plunge, what are you willing to project between the period 2010 and 2020? Again, consider some predictable knowns, such as how old you'll be during that time, the age of your children, your likely income, where you'll be working, where you'll be living, and so on. Yes, it all may change by the time you get there, but the exercise nevertheless is highly worthwhile.

High Achievers Choose Lifetime Goals

Have you ever chosen lifetime goals and actually pursued them? Such people often devise a list of 50 or 100 or more things they want to do during their time on earth.

Lou Holtz, the former football coach at Notre Dame, is one such person. Early in his career, Holtz devised a roster of 107 goals he wanted to accomplish in his life. Some were ordinary, if personally challenging, such as to have all four of his children graduate from college. Some were a tad risky, such as learning how to sky dive. Some of Holtz's goals might make your list as well, such as meeting the president of the United States and being a guest at a White House dinner.

Go for the Gold!
For many people who choose lifetime goals, extensive travel—especially to specific destinations—frequently ends up making the list.

Putting Intrigue in Your Life

The notion of drawing up a list of 50 or 100 things you want to do before you die is most intriguing. After all, you can put down anything you want on your list, you don't have to show it to anyone, and you can make it as wild as you want.

Surprisingly, many people include goals that relate to improving their intellect, such as learning other languages, reading classical literature, and so on.

Direct from Your Author

Here is a subset from my personal list. Following that, I'll give you a variety of ideas you might want to draw on in composing your own goals.

Some of Jeff Davidson's 100 Lifetime Goals

➤ Visit all 50 states in the Union. (So far, I've been to 39.)

➤ Visit at least 10 countries each in South America, Europe, Africa, the Middle East, and Asia. (I've completed the mission in Europe and am making great headway in Asia.)

➤ Improve my leaping ability so that I once again can dunk in basketball. (The last time I did this was at age 26, and I'm not sure how I'll ever return to such heights, but nevertheless, it is a goal.)

➤ Have one of my books appear on the *New York Times* best-seller list and stay there for several months. (If you and 200 to 300 of your closest friends buy this book in large quantities and enough other readers do it, you'll help me make my goal.)

➤ Have 20/20 vision again without corrective lenses. (With all the improvements in laser keratotomy and corneal rings, this one's going to happen rather soon.)

➤ Own a vacation home in Montreux or Vevey, Switzerland.

➤ Become so wealthy that I give $1 million to worthwhile causes.

➤ Walk on the moon, Mars, or some other celestial body. (Who wants to remain earthbound?)

➤ Implement effective, widely approved programs for reducing human population. (At the current rate of growth, by the year 2600, we'll each have one square yard of space.)

➤ Routinely speak to audiences of between 10,000 to 20,000 people. (If you haven't heard me yet, you don't know what you're missing.)

➤ Attend an NCAA college basketball championship final-four weekend. (A couple hundred bucks to a scalper, and the tickets are all mine.)

➤ Throw out the first pitch at a World Series game. (Hmmm…let's see, should I throw my fast ball or my curve?)

➤ Obtain a Ph.D. in Sociology for the work I've already done in that field. (You may call me Dr. Davidson.)

➤ Just visualize the chapters of my books and have the words appear on my computer screen. (With the breakthroughs already en route as discussed earlier in this book, this goal will be realized quite soon.)

➤ Safely and easily travel to distant locations via teleportation. (Hey, if they can do it on *Star Trek*, why can't we? Beam me up, Scotty!)

Chew on These

As promised, here are some ideas to help you devise your own list. Aim for 50 goals initially, and then perhaps move on to 100 later. Be forewarned, however, that most people can get to about 20 or 25, but then they find that the going gets slow.

That's okay—as long as you begin to build the list, you're still traveling down a path that can result in wondrous developments in your life.

Things To Do During Your Lifetime

➤ Learn how to fly a plane.

➤ Speak Japanese, Russian, or Farsi fluently.

➤ Camp for two fabulous weeks in Yosemite National Park.

➤ Trace your ancestry back to the year 1600.

➤ Spend a week on tour with The Rolling Stones.

➤ White-water raft the Colorado river in the Grand Canyon.

➤ Be a contestant on the TV quiz show *Jeopardy*.

➤ Spend an entire summer touring the United States in a motor home.

➤ Read 50 of the classics.

➤ Be in the front row to hear Pavarotti sing.

➤ Take a five-mile walk along the Great Wall of China.

➤ Have seats on the 50-yard line at the Super Bowl.

➤ Take a balloon ride over the Oldevi Gorge in Africa.

➤ Learn how to interpret dreams.

➤ Teach a university course on the meaning of life.

➤ Shop on Rodeo Drive in Beverly Hills with reckless abandon.

➤ Run with the bulls at Pamplona.

➤ Pay for a needy student's college education.

➤ Attend Christmas Mass at the Vatican.

➤ Go ice fishing in the Yukon.

➤ Learn how to flamenco dance.

➤ Be madly in love with your spouse 20 years from now.

➤ Learn how to play the piano.

➤ Have your own TV or radio talk show.

➤ Establish a local shelter for battered spouses.

➤ Go deep-sea diving for buried treasure.

➤ Become an editor at Macmillan Publishing.

➤ Drive a race car in a NASCAR event.

➤ Play two-man volleyball on the beach in Venice, California.

➤ Watch the sunset on top of a mountain in Tucson, Arizona.

➤ Become a faith healer.

➤ Be able to successfully perform magic tricks.

➤ Be a stand-up comedian one night at the Improv.

➤ Learn a musical instrument at the Julliard School of Music.

➤ Rent a small cottage for the summer at Martha's Vineyard.

➤ Attend your high school class' sixtieth reunion.

➤ Explore the ancient ruins of Egypt with an archeologist.

➤ Have your poems published.

➤ Go on a two-month cruise around the world.

➤ Be selected as *Time* magazine's person of the year.

➤ Have a bit role in a major motion picture.

➤ Serve your district as a congressional representative.

➤ Maintain an urban street garden for the enjoyment of others.

➤ Learn how to meditate.

➤ Visit the president at Camp David.

➤ Join in a Renaissance festival as a costumed character.

➤ Have a hospital wing named after you.

➤ Serve as a big brother or big sister.

➤ Learn to recite the Gettysburg Address.

➤ Hunt wild game in the outreaches of Borneo.

➤ Attend a concert at the Opera House in Sydney, Australia.

➤ Be on a float during the Macy's Thanksgiving Day parade.

➤ Welcome in the new year with your loved one at Times Square.

➤ Be interviewed in a feature article for *Forbes* magazine.

➤ Reach your fiftieth wedding anniversary.

➤ Meet your great-grandchildren.

➤ Be a guest on *Good Morning America*.

➤ Have your recipe win a city-wide contest.

continues

continued

➤ Win the Nobel Peace Prize for humanity.

➤ House a homeless person until he gets back on his feet.

➤ Go a whole year without watching television.

➤ Volunteer to help someone learn how to read.

➤ Attend the opening ceremonies at the Summer Olympics.

➤ Write the lyrics to a hit record.

➤ Help your son or daughter buy his or her first home.

➤ Learn how to rollerblade.

➤ Learn how to sing like a professional.

Now It's Your Turn

As you can see, the list contains a mixture of the wild, the grandiose, and the relatively simple. Now it's your turn. In the following list, I'd like you to start off by devising your own roster of at least 10 things you want to do in this life:

1. _____

2. _____

3. _____

4. _____

5. _____

6. _____

7. _____

8. _____

9. _____

10. _____

Don't Be Surprised

Hereafter, when you encounter people who engage in one amazing activity or achieve one outstanding accomplishment after another, don't be surprised. Chances are, these people have devised such a list for themselves. They are champion goal setters and goal reachers. They intend for their lives to be exciting.

You've heard the old axiom "luck is when preparation meets opportunity." More importantly, you want to prepare yourself so that wondrous activities and events can unfold for you and you are more prepared to engage in the mysterious and unexpected opportunities that emerge. You won't be lacking in spontaneity, and you certainly won't be one of the people who sits around on the weekend figuring out what to do with his or her life.

There Are Limits

Often, I encounter written materials or lecturers who claim that "nothing is impossible." I cringe at such talk, because I know that it simply is not true. Many things are impossible based on the known laws of physics. For example,

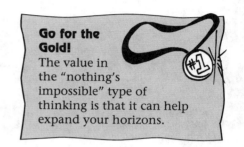

Go for the Gold!
The value in the "nothing's impossible" type of thinking is that it can help expand your horizons.

➤ You won't be vacationing on the sun very soon.

➤ Reversing the aging process, as in converting a 40-year-old back to age 10, seems well out of reach.

➤ The chances of traveling back in time and changing the course of history are tenuous at best.

What's Possible Is Astounding

Some things are impossible. Yet many things that appear to be out of the question to you right now are, in fact, quite possible. This is all the more reason to begin your 50- or 100-item list and to even add some items that seem totally out of the question based on what you now know or believe. Put them down anyway.

As time passes, you may begin to see reasons why these seemingly impossible goals are indeed within your grasp.

Goal Setting for Two

If you're in a partnership with someone, whether it's a business partnership, a friendship, or a marriage, one of the fastest and easiest ways to set mutually compatible goals is to first devise separate lists of what you want to accomplish, as I suggested in Chapter 7, "Goals for Family Life." You can include on these lists things you want to accomplish on your own and things you want to accomplish in partnership. Then, compare your lists and look for all the points of intersection.

Supporting Each Other's Separate Goals

For those items that you and your partner indicated you want to accomplish individually, look and see how amenable you are to supporting your partner's quest. After all, if he or she wants to do something that you can't stand, chances are you're not going to be very supportive.

If your partner has a variety of goals you can't support, chances are you may be headed for major friction. On the other hand, if your individual goals and your partner's individual goals contain a number of items that both of you feel comfortable with in terms of supporting one another, now you're cooking with gas heat.

Shared Partnership Goals

Next, look at the goals each of you selected in terms of what each wants to accomplish as part of the partnership. I'm hoping that you match up well here. If you don't, there's no need for alarm, necessarily; perhaps some of the things your partner listed represent good ideas to you and you'd be willing to add them to your list. Perhaps the reverse is true as well.

Goal Setting for Others

Throughout this book, I've discussed one of the myths people have about goal setting, which is that you personally have to set goals for yourself in order for them to be valid. This, of course, is not true. Many children have goals set for them by their parents. Many sales representatives have goals set for them by their sales managers. Cabinet-level officers have goals set for them by the president. Indeed, the people often tell the politicians what goals they want them to achieve.

Go for the Gold! When it comes to goals that you and your partner have, the more items that make both of your lists, particularly when it comes to the partnership itself, the more solid your future will be together. Your goals do not need to be a one-to-one match or mirror images of each other. The important thing is to discover the common elements of what both of you want to do or achieve.

In all these settings, the key component that determines whether goal-oriented behavior will take effect is whether the second party adopts the goal as his or her own. If so, a goal imposed on you by others can seem as though it has been yours all along.

In his book *Fear Strikes Out*, former Red Sox baseball player Jimmy Pearsal recounts how he suffered a mental breakdown in his rookie season. After long and engaging sessions with psychiatrists while Pearsal was institutionalized, he came to realize that it was his father's goal for him to become a big-league baseball player.

Pearsal's father was a fairly respectable sandlot player, and after he had a son, was dead bent on ensuring that the boy made it all the way to the major leagues. In this case, the father and son loved each other but didn't realize the ramifications of what was occurring. Through analysis, Pearsal learned that he had to make this goal his own to make it back on the field and to be able to stay there without breaking down again.

Fortunately for Pearsal, he had the fortitude and skill to undertake this effort. More importantly, he concluded that it was indeed his goal to be a major-league baseball player. He went on to play many more years with the Red Sox.

Fill My Shoes

Many children who attempt to live up to their parents' expectations—goals—meet with disastrous results. For every Tiger Woods, who was successfully swinging a golf club at age two, eagerly soaking up like a sponge everything his father taught him about the game and becoming the U.S. Masters champion by age 21, there are many, many more children who have a vastly different experience.

I knew a woman in college who was from a very wealthy family residing in Westport, Connecticut. Her mother had once dated Clark Gable! She and her brother and sister apparently had it all: wealth, intelligence, looks, social standing—you name it.

Her brother was "supposed" to be a big success, grow to be more than six feet tall, and have matinee-idol looks. Yet he attempted suicide on a couple of occasions.

An anomaly, you say? We'd have to know more about his psychological profile? Okay, then consider the legions of children of the wealthy, the powerful, and the celebrated, or the children of sports heroes who end up rejecting the game in which their mothers or fathers triumphed.

High Expectations, No; Encouragement, Yes!

To have high expectations foisted upon you at an early age is a curse. What does work? Encouragement.

For whatever reason, if you set goals for others, especially goals that may impact the course of someone's life, understand on a profound level the role that encouragement plays in helping the other party make these hopes his or her goals.

Equally important, observe the other person closely. What are his or her natural tendencies? What inborn traits, characteristics, skills, and capabilities does he or she exhibit? What does he or she enjoy doing?

As I've mentioned, my little girl, Valerie, has extraordinary capabilities when it comes to hitting a baseball.

I am not an overbearing father, however, and we are not out in the backyard every day practicing. Valerie and I play baseball whenever she says she wants to play and at no other time.

I think she can be a high school and college star. Perhaps even a softball Olympian. She has to want it, though. She's also interested in gymnastics and tumbling, ballet, soccer, and golf. I had no interest in any of these athletic pursuits, and other than playing high school soccer, never engaged in any of them. I encourage Valerie, however, to pursue these interests to wherever they may take her and for whatever enjoyment she derives from them.

Perhaps I ought to channel more of her efforts into baseball, because she has proven to be so outstanding in that sport. Perhaps she'll thank me later if I spend long hours with her every night in the backyard pitching ball after ball to her. It's hard to know exactly what is right for another person, even when you're her dad.

The Least You Need to Know

➤ The basic questions everyone encounters are what will you do with your life, where, and with whom?

➤ There's power and promise in charting out what you intend to accomplish in the next decade.

➤ Draw up your list of 50 or 100 far-reaching things you want to do in this life. What emerges may surprise you.

➤ When setting goals with a partner, first produce lists independently, and then find the common denominators.

➤ To be influential in setting goals for others, nurture their inherent capabilities and then encourage them, encourage them, encourage them.

Chapter 26

Actions Speak the Loudest

In This Chapter

➤ Why there's no time like the present

➤ All about commitment

➤ Making gain a refrain

➤ A fitting send-off

Like the worn-out old expression says, "Today is the first day of the rest of your life." Try substituting that cliché with this bit of wisdom: Today is the first day you can get started on goals that you have for now and the rest of your life. Doesn't that make things a little more compelling? In this chapter, you'll achieve a smooth transition from putting down this book to taking action.

Let me ask you a philosophical question. Can you store up happiness? Can you pluck moments of happiness from your life—put them in a bottle or in the freezer—and withdraw them sometime in the future when you want to be happy?

No, no, a thousand times no!

To be happy is to be happy now, in the present. When the future arrives, you will either be happy or you won't; you'll know on that day. Many of the goals you want to reach are best set now.

I know you have a lot of things to do and that you fully intend to get started on some goals next week or next month. Consider the goals that make the most sense to initiate at this moment, though.

Go for the Gold!
The official start time for many of your goals is now. It's now, because the behavior in which you need to engage isn't going to change 180 degrees at the stroke of midnight.

The Mañana Trap

Suppose that you want to lose the proverbial 10 pounds, and you tried many times in the past. "Let's see, I'll eat a big bag of chips today and some ice cream and some heavily fatted meats because, after all, I'm starting my diet tomorrow."

You laugh, and yet that is the mindset of so many people facing weight-related goals or other goals. They behave in ways that are detrimental to the accomplishment of their goal, because after all, they haven't "officially" started.

The Mindset of a Goal Achiever

On your mark, get ready, get set—GO! Sticking to your diet, moderating your calorie intake, eating healthy foods, taking vitamins, and regularly exercising above and beyond your lists, charts, and timelines require a proper mindset.

Suppose that I told you I have $1,500 in a savings account, and my goal is to get that account up to $10,000 within six months. I am going to start tomorrow, though. So, for today, I can spend everything in the account. After all, I have a full six months to get the account to $10,000.

What would you think if this was the way I proceeded in pursuit of this goal? Foolhardy, you say? Why deplete the balance you already have?

Good question. In fact, it's the same question you might ask someone who is going to go on a diet "tomorrow." Why add to your burden by stuffing yourself with calories today? You're only making your burden that much more difficult.

If you're serious about reaching any of your short-term goals (those you want to accomplish in a year or less), and similarly are as focused on some of your longer-term goals, there's no way of getting around this: You need to begin to engage in goal-supporting behaviors and activities in the present.

Talk Is Cheap

Actions do indeed speak louder than words. What do you tell your inner being when you stuff yourself with calories or deplete your savings account, all because you're going to "get started tomorrow," when such actions are contrary to your long-term pursuits? I'm not asking you to abstain from consuming calories today.

Indeed, you may choose to eat a few chips, a spoonful or two of ice cream, and half the portion of fatty meat you had intended to devour. By the same token, perhaps there's a critical purchase I need to make with some of the funds in the account I chose to grow to $10,000 within six months.

There are powerful gestures you can make that will deliver a message to every fiber of your being that you intend to pursue this goal with vigor. If your goal is to reduce your weight by 10 pounds (and remember that the most appropriate wording is to have a more trim, healthy appearance), go to your refrigerator right now, take out the ice cream, and pour it down the sink. Throw out the box of chocolate-chip cookies or, better yet, if the pack is unopened, drop it off at a shelter for the homeless.

> **Uh-Oh!** CAUTION!
> Do you have the fortitude to put down this book right now, go to the kitchen, and throw out the rest of the ice cream? This is not a test. This is your life. Either get up and do it right now, or think about someone you could give this book to who'll actually read and follow my advice.

If you intend to quit smoking and have clear, clean, healthy lungs, round up all the cigarettes in your household and throw them out. Don't bother donating them to anyone.

You know what? I think I'll deposit another $250 in savings.

To What Are You Committed?

After all is said and done, much more is said than ever done. Are you committed to the goals you have set for yourself? Do you intend to reach them? Stripping your kitchen of fat or sugar-laden foods or chucking all your cigarettes on the spot demonstrates commitment, although these are relatively small measures in the grand scheme of things. Yet these kinds of actions are as powerful a gesture as any when added to another and yet another and another.

While you're in the groove, what other action can you take right now around the house to signify your commitment to the goals you've set for yourself?

➤ Have too many hours with the TV proved to be a bane to your existence? Do you have the mental and emotional strength right now to pull the TV plug out of the wall, grab a pair of scissors, and snip the end so that you can't plug it back in?

➤ Is there a pile of stuff stacking up that you're never going to deal with? Can you muster the fortitude to simply chuck it all en masse?

➤ Are there clothes in your closet that you never want to wear again, because they represent the old you and you need to make space for the new you? If so, there are plenty of charitable organizations that would appreciate the donation.

Commit and Prosper

It all comes down to whether you're committed to your goals.

Even more important than putting your goals on paper (see Chapter 15, "A Question of Time") is a commitment at the highest level of your cognitive capabilities. If you are committed, you'll take action consistent with reaching your goals, independent of whether you're formally starting today. If you discover—via your unwillingness to take action—that you're not committed to one or more of the goals you've set for yourself, park that goal for now. Do not make it a part of your activities. Why? If you've set some goals but actually have no intention of reaching them, you run the risk of impeding your progress on yet other goals.

You and I both know people who have well-crafted lists of goals they intend to pursue that seem to just linger on for an indefinite period. Recall my observations in Chapters 1, "What Is a Goal as Opposed to a Wish?" and 2, "New Year's Resolutions." It's fine to have dreams, but if you want to convert dreams to goals, you need to choose ones that are challenging but reachable, quantifiable, and have specific timelines.

Archive It and Move On

If one or more of your goals keeps making your list, but you haven't taken step 1, put it on the 50 or 100 things to do in your life roster that I told you about in Chapter 25, "Lifetime Goal Setting." Then, at least you won't forget it, and you won't feel guilty for not having taken any action on it. In either case, get it off your current goals list, because it doesn't belong there if you're not committed to it.

From Where You Were to Where You Want to Be

Despite your best intentions, sometimes the reason why you don't take action even when you've engaged in all the other steps of the goal-setting process is that you begin to rationalize with yourself. This occurs when you think, "Hey, things aren't really so bad," instead of taking action. Looks at these scenarios, for example:

➤ If you're obese, you convince yourself, at least temporarily, that you're happy at this weight.

➤ If you're utterly alone, you dwell on the moments here and there where being alone has its advantages.

➤ If you're 52 years old and you have no real savings, you rationalize that many other people are in the same boat or that you're about to get into your prime earning years.

Everyone is subject to rationalization at one time or another. However, if excessive rationalizing keeps you from taking the action that would enable you to go from where you are to where you want to be, perhaps it's time to reconstruct your self talk:

➤ "I'm overweight, I've been overweight for years, and I can't stand it. I choose to reach my target weight."

➤ "I'm alone, utterly and miserably alone, and I want very much to have a partner. I choose to join a singles club."

➤ "I have no savings—nothing to show for myself for all these years. I choose to save $10,000 by June 30."

In each of these situations, as well as any others you can imagine, the quickest road away from rationalizing is to take action:

➤ Sign up at a health club today and start going regularly.

➤ Pick up the phone and join an organization where you're likely to meet other singles you are attracted to, and start attending at the next meeting.

➤ Take $20 out of your wallet or whatever money you have hanging around, drive down to the bank, and make a deposit. Then, make another one next week and next week and the week after that.

A Paralyzing Rationalization: "I Get No Breaks"

There's an old expression that advises, "Don't talk about luck in the company of self-made people." People who set and reach goals appreciate any luck they receive along the way, but they generally chart their own course.

Often, you hear or read about this person or that one who says he or she never gets any breaks. Some people think the deck is totally stacked against them when it comes to opportunities. These kinds of claims always confound me. If you will, consider the following:

➤ If you choose to engage in academic excellence, who on this earth can stop you?

➤ If you set your sights on being a master in using word processing software to the point where you score the highest on any test administered to those in your job classification, who in particular can stand in your way?

➤ If you choose to be a master at any other vocation, who but yourself will be your obstacle?

Are you telling me that somebody is coming by your house at night or your office in the morning and pulling the plug just as you are about to crack the books and delve more deeply into your subject area? Are you saying that the library is not open in your town? Are you saying that you lack the funds to make the minimal investments needed to get started? Are you saying that there is no one else on a planet of six billion people who shares your goal and with whom you could team up?

1,500 Evenings at Work

Between the time I was 30 and 40, I worked an average of 150 evenings (three nights out of five weekday evenings) every week for 10 years from 6:30 p.m. to 10:00 p.m., in addition to working eight hours during the day. While others presumably were watching TV, having their favorite brew, or simply pursuing their unarticulated goals of doing nothing at all and then lamenting that there were no opportunities for them, I had goals and was hard at work.

I guess I must be unusual. To me, however, it's not a question of *have* or *have not*—it's a question of *will* or *will not*.

The Hardship of Better Living

As hard as it might be to proceed month after month, year after year, without getting what you want, are you willing to accept the hardship of making a better life for yourself? If not, please don't feel as though I'm picking on you. You are simply part of the broad masses of society who accept their lot in life and vie for the table scraps that might fall their way.

If you are willing to accept the challenge of making a better life and are willing to get into action, the outcome of your quest generally is up to you. If you make it all the way, no one will deny you your place when you step into the winner's circle.

Action Is Invigorating

Planning is important.

Plotting is important.

Visualizing is important.

Taking action is essential.

Taking action separates the men from the boys, the women from the girls, the actors from the reactors.

Paralysis of Analysis

Don't be caught in your tracks because of the all-too-easy tendency to slip into rationalization or to engage in paralysis by analysis. Spend some time carefully assessing the situation; spend more time taking action.

To Err Is Human

If you're afraid of making mistakes, here's an insight for you: You will make mistakes. That is not a reason to stand still, though. Ask world champion goal achievers, and they'll tell you the way to succeed in life is to fail often, learn from your setbacks, and move on.

These people don't mean to imply that you actively go out and seek to fail. Instead, you make many attempts to succeed and in doing so, you end up encountering failure—perhaps a little more often than you care to. There's an old adage that goes, "It is better to have loved and lost than never to have loved at all." Similarly, *It is better to have attempted something and failed than never to have attempted it.*

After You Finish This Book

If you have followed the advice and suggestions in this book so far, you've already mapped out your goals, quantified them, and given them specific timelines. If not, perhaps you have a clear idea of what you will do once you put pen to paper or fingers to keyboard.

Here's a provoking thought: What will you do to ensure that reading this book wasn't simply a fleeting—and I'm hoping enjoyable—activity that ends up having no long-term impact on your life? What will you do differently this time to ensure that you reach the goals you set for yourself?

The answer to this question differs from person to person. For you, it might involve the following:

➤ Sharing your plans with a significant other

➤ Rearranging your room, home, office, car, or other vital spaces

➤ Purchasing goal-enhancing tools, such as a planning calendar or software

➤ Arranging a meeting

➤ Making important phone calls

➤ Taking off for a day to rest

➤ Engaging in an extended meditation

➤ Admitting to yourself that you don't know what you're going to do but are committed to taking action that transcends what you've done before

> **Go for the Gold!**
> Give yourself permission to transcend your heretofore known self. Proceed as if now is the most important moment of your life, because it is.

One of my mentors told me that doing what you've always done will get you where it's always gotten you. MOVE ON! Clear away the old, familiar, convenient rationalizations you've used in the past and the other dodges, stalls, and hedges that have kept you in a state of perpetual inaction.

A Send-Off for a Champion Goal-Setter

As we draw to a close, I want to give you an extended affirmation of how your life can and will be:

➤ You'll awake each morning following a complete restful night of sleep. You'll be energetic and raring to go.

➤ You'll eat a wholesome breakfast at an unhurried pace. You'll converse pleasantly with others in your household.

➤ On work days, you'll arrive early, scope out what you want to do for the day, and maintain a clear focus.

➤ You'll effectively interact with others—in person, on the phone, and via fax and e-mail.

➤ Your short- and long-term goals, maintenance goals, and highly challenging goals will remain in your conscience throughout the day. You'll set up your environment so that you'll frequently encounter goal reminders.

➤ You'll proceed with tasks with balance and maintain relative simplicity.

➤ You'll engage in activities with an incremental approach, although you'll often achieve disproportional, favorable results.

➤ You'll keep a constant eye on your goal list and modify, revise, and update your goals as situations merit.

➤ You'll enroll others in your quest, recognizing the power that partners, team members, and like-minded individuals can give one another.

➤ You'll maintain a balance in the mental, physical, family, social, spiritual, career, and financial arenas of your life.

➤ You'll maintain a positive, even keel, even in the face of temporary setbacks. You'll learn from the good and the bad.

➤ Recognizing that most limits faced by an individual are self-imposed, you'll constantly seek to up the ante when it comes to establishing challenging goals. You'll even devise a list of 50 or 100 things you want to accomplish in your lifetime.

➤ You'll maintain an action orientation. You'll carefully examine situations, but you'll expend more of your energies taking action in pursuit of your goals, recognizing that taking action is the essence of those who continually set and reach their goals.

In closing, *may the most for which you strive be the least that you achieve.*

The Least You Need to Know

➤ If you're serious about the goals you've set for yourself, you'll act and behave in ways that support those goals, starting today.

➤ If you're not committed to reaching a goal, perhaps it's best to take it off your active goal list.

➤ Rationalization and over-analyzing keep people from getting started even when they have highly defined, well-set goals.

➤ After putting down this book, identify precisely what you're going to do to ensure that reading this book was more than an interesting or enjoyable exercise.

➤ You have within you what it takes to reach your goals.

Glossary

affirmation   A positively worded phrase that supports a goal.

antecedent   Something that always comes before the behavior it produces. The doorbell rings (an antecedent), which prompts you to open the door.

Gantt chart   A figure that shows progress in relation to time. It often is used for planning and tracking projects. The Gantt chart got its name from Henry Laurence Gantt, an American engineer.

germination   In biology, germination means sprouting. It also can mean development, growth, or maturation. None of these concepts suggests an even progression.

intermittent reinforcement   When you receive some type of reward just often enough to keep you doing whatever you've been doing.

introspection   The art of looking inward to better understand yourself and to capture your true feelings.

kinesthetics   The relationship of your physical movement and mental state.

litmus test   This term comes from a test conducted for chemical acidity or basicity by using litmus paper. In everyday use, you perform a *litmus test* by using a single indicator to prompt a decision. For example, you might evaluate your interaction with others to determine whether you are maintaining balance on the job.

Machiavelli   Niccolo Machiavelli was an Italian political theorist. He believed that deceit and cunning were justified in order to achieve political power. These types of theories are described as *the ends justifying the means*.

motivate   Originates from the Latin word *movēre*, which means *to move*. Today, it means to inspire or to move someone to action.

other-directed   Refers to individuals who are more concerned about what others think of them than what they think of themselves.

psychiatrist   A medical doctor whose specialty is dealing with the human mind. A psychiatrist usually has an M.D., four years of residency training, and is trained to diagnose and treat mental disorders. Psychiatrists use various forms of therapy and may prescribe medication as needed to diagnose, treat, and prevent various disorders.

psychologist   Someone who studies how the mind influences human behavior. A clinical psychologist usually has a Ph.D., as well as one to four years of post-doctoral training. Psychologists specialize in psychological research, testing, and therapy.

psychotherapist   Anyone, trained or not, who treats mental and emotional disorders to encourage personality growth and behavior modification. No special license is required. A psychotherapist can be a medical doctor or someone with a Ph.D.

quantifiable   Something that can be measured or counted.

self-fulfilling prophecy   A visualization where you've pretty much concluded what's going to happen and hence increase the probability of it occurring.

shaping   The process of reinforcing successive approximations or small steps in pursuit of a goal.

skunkworks   A term made popular in the book *In Search of Excellence*. Refers to a group of individuals purposely assembled to tackle a tough or challenging assignment.

status quo   Refers to things as they are—the existing condition or state of affairs. If things stay the same or nothing changes, one is said to be *maintaining the status quo*.

synergy   When one and one equals more than two. It's when the end result equals more than the sum of the parts.

Resources for Champion Goal-Setters

Further Reading

Alessandra, Dr. Tony, *Charisma*, New York, Warner, 1998.

Alessandra, Dr. Tony, *The Platinum Rule*, New York, Warner, 1996.

Bates, Jefferson, *Dictating With Precision*, Washington D.C., Acropolis, 1981.

Bennett, Jarrett, *Making the Money Last*, Dubuque, IA, Kendall Hunt, 1996.

Bolles, Richard, *What Color is Your Parachute?*, Berkeley, CA, Ten Speed, 1998.

Brooks, Bill, *You're Working Too Hard to Make the Sale*, Burr Ridge, IL, BusinessOne Irwin, 1995.

Burrus, Dan, *Technotrends*, New York, HarperCollins, 1994.

Canfield, Jack and Mark Victor Hanson, *Chicken Soup for the Soul*, Deerfield Beach, FL, Health Communications, 1993.

Caposy, John, *Why Climb the Corporate Ladder When You Can Take the Elevator?*, New York, Villard, 1994.

Carnegie, Dale, *How to Win Friends and Influence People*, New York, Pocket Books, 1994.

Cathcart, Jim, *Relationship Selling*, New York, Putnam, 1990.

Connor, Richard and Jeff Davidson, *Marketing Your Consulting & Professional Services*, New York, Wiley, 1997.

Conwell, Russell, *Acres of Diamonds*, New York, Jove, 1982.

Coren, Stanley, Ph.D., *Sleep Thieves*, New York, Free Press, 1996.

Cousins, Norman, Ph.D., *Anatomy of an Illness*, New York, Bantam, 1986.

Covey, Steven, Ph.D., *The Seven Habits of Highly Effective People*, New York, Simon & Schuster, 1988.

Daniels, Dr. Aubrey, *Bringing Out the Best in People*, New York, McGraw-Hill, 1994.

Davidson, Jeff, *Blow Your Own Horn: How to Get Noticed and Get Ahead*, New York, Berkley Books, 1991.

Davidson, Jeff, *Breathing Space: Living & Working at a Comfortable Pace in a Sped-up Society*, Eugene, OR, MasterMedia, 1998.

Davidson, Jeff, *The Complete Idiot's Guide to Assertiveness*, New York, Alpha Books, 1997.

Davidson, Jeff, *The Complete Idiot's Guide to Managing Stress*, New York, Alpha Books, 1997.

Davidson, Jeff, *The Complete Idiot's Guide to Managing Time*, New York, Alpha Books, 1995.

Dixon, Paul, *Toasts*, New York, Crown Books, 1991.

Drake, Stillman, *Galileo At Work: His Scientific Biography*, Dover Publications, 1995.

Dychtwald, Ken, Ph.D., *Age Wave*, Los Angeles, Tarcher, 1989.

Dyer, Dr. Wayne, *How to be a No Limit Person*, New York, Berkley, 1980.

Dyer, Dr. Wayne, *Pulling Your Own Strings*, New York, HarperCollins, 1991.

Farrell, Dr. Warren, *Why Men Are the Way They Are*, New York, McGraw-Hill, 1986.

Feynman, Richard, *No Ordinary Genius: The Illustrated Richard Feynman*, ed. by Christopher Sykes, New York, Norton, 1996.

Fritz, Robert, *The Path of Least Resistance*, New York, Fawcett-Columbine, 1989.

Gallagher, Winifred, *ID: How Heredity and Experience Make You Who You Are*, New York, Random House, 1996.

Gitomer, Jeffrey, *The Sales Bible*, New York, Morrow, 1994.

Goleman, Daniel, *Emotional Intelligence*, New York, Bantam Doubleday, 1995.

Hart, Michael H., *The One Hundred*, New York, Citadel Press, 1992.

Hesse, Hermann, *Siddhartha*, New York, Bantam, 1982.

Hill, Napolean, *Think and Grow Rich*, New York, Fawcett, 1975.

Hollender, Jeff, *How to Make the World a Better Place*, New York, W.W. Norton, 1995.

Horn, Sam, *Tung Fu: The Art of Verbal Self-Defense*, New York, St. Martin's, 1996.

Horney, Dr. Karen, *Fear and Anxiety*, New York, Norton, 1991.

Hubbard, Elbert, *A Message to Garcia*, Applewood Books, 1993.

Jeffries, Elizabeth, *The Heart of Leadership*, Dubuque, IA, Kendall-Hunt, 1996.

Kushner, Rabbi Harold S., *How Good Do We Have to Be?*, Boston, MA, Little-Brown, 1996.

Mackey, Harvey, *How to Swim With the Sharks Without Being Eaten Alive*, New York, Fawcett, 1996.

Maltz, Maxwell, *PsychoCybernetics*, New York, Pocket Books, 1983.

Negroponte, Nicholas, Ph.D., *Being Digital*, New York, Vintage, 1996.

Nightingale, Earl, *The Strangest Secret* (cassette), Niles, IL, Nightingale-Conant Corp., 1994.

O'Neil, John, *The Paradox of Success*, Los Angeles, Tarcher/Putnam, 1993.

Pagonis, General William G., *Moving Mountains*, Cambridge, MA, Harvard Business School Press, 1992.

Peale, Dr. Norman Vincent, *The Power of Positive Thinking*, New York, Fawcett, 1991.

Peters, Tom, Ph.D., *The Pursuit of Wow!*, New York, Vintage, 1994.

Pitino, Rick, *Success Is a Choice*, New York, Simon & Schuster, 1996.

Porter, Michael, Ph.D., *Competitive Advantage*, New York, Macmillan Publishing, 1985.

Porter, Michael, Ph.D., *The Competitive Advantage of Nations*, New York, Free Press, 1990.

Salsbury, Glenna, *The Art of the Fresh Start*, Deerfield Beach, FL, Health Communications, 1996.

Seligman, Dr. Martin, *Learned Optimism*, New York, Pocket Books, 1992.

Senge, Peter, *The Fifth Discipline*, New York, Doubleday, 1994.

Shaw, George Bernard, *Man and Superman*, New York, Viking, 1950.

Tannen, Dr. Deborah, *That's Not What I Meant!*, New York, Ballantine, 1994.

Tracy, Brian, *Maximum Success*, New York, Simon & Schuster, 1994.

Twain, Mark, *The Adventures of Tom Sawyer*, New York, Penguin Books, 1986.

von Oeck, Roger, Ph.D., *A Whack on the Side of the Head*, New York, Warner, 1990.

Waitely, Denis, *The Psychology of Winning*, New York, Simon & Schuster Audio Cassette, 1995.

Woolf, Bob, *Friendly Persuasion*, New York, Putnam, 1990.

Yoho, Dave, and Jeff Davidson, *How to Have a Good Year Every Year*, New York, Berkley Books, 1991.

Index